Jet Set Desolate

Future Fiction London

JET SET DESOLATE
By Andrea Lambert
Published 2009 by Future Fiction London
www.futurefiction.co.uk
ISBN 978-0-578-01625-2
Copyright ©2009 by Andrea Lambert
All world rights reserved
Cover design by Gilded Peony
Photos by Keith Aguiar and Heather Renee Russ
Author photo by Katie Jacobson

To Matias Viegener, my mentor, who was instrumental towards both my emotional and artistic development through this difficult time.

I would like to thank the faculty of the CalArts Critical Studies Program, for steering this novel towards completion, and telling me when to cut.

Special thanks to Stephen Barber, whose insight and kindness led to this book's publication.

Thanks to Alex Castle for cover art.
Thanks to Katie Jacobson for true love.
Thanks to my parents, because.

To my inspiration, Jaimie Sharpe, Jason Madary, Kara Murphy, Sasha Hutchison, Sara Medeiros and the mayhem of the Frisco Disco, I will remember you.

Jet Set Desolate

Future Fiction London

Prologue

In Los Angeles, I dream of falling through the interior of houses, passing through hacked out holes in walls and ceiling, the exposed insulation and wires and dark spaces. I attribute this to the fragmented spaces we lived in, then, the parties in back courtyards where you walked through the basement to get there, the weight of dancing feet creaking above in the whitewashed wood, the people sitting on concrete ledges drinking in the dark.

At the Dustbin, my old house in Portland, my roommates pulled open the second floor walls to find a former tenants possessions, left when he went into the Peace Corps. We went through them. Property didn't exist. Boundaries were permeable. A boy leaving my room in the morning, passing me a book about the Spanish civil war. A condom on the floor. Passing me a Crass/Slits mixtape.

"What do you mean, you haven't heard my band?" Popcorn with brewers yeast passed hand-to-hand with sticky fingers. A food-stamp party, where the guys got back from tour and pooled their Oregon Trail. For seven years, basement shows with the lights down low, someone always whispering to me that the revolution would come.

"Vote for George Dubya., it'll just come faster!"

Climbing down the dark shag carpet stairs to where three men slept in the basement, their practice space a DIY cube of drywall. I would sit in the dark while they passed a fifth of Old Crow. "You're nineteen? Alright!" But in the cold Portland winters, my space heater and daily showers competed with the amplifiers roaring out of the basement for how much electricity we could afford.

I have a recurrent dream of falling through the Dustbin from the shingle roof through the fragile, sharpie-scrawled drywall and mounds of empty beer cans, cigarette ash and spit raining down and falling with me.

Chapter 1
baby pigeon

2008

My name is Lena Cosentino, I'm 31, and I like being an alcoholic. Beats all the coke I used to do.

Today is Valentines Day. My boyfriend has shining eyes with long eyelashes, and likes to play poker with toy giraffes. We share an apartment in North Hollywood. I slice the plastic off the steaks and he turns them lightly into a pan of butter and garlic. I pour wine on top.

This is the same recipe I used to make with $1.50 wafer-thin sirloins, fried in that apartment in the Haight district where I spent the last months with Brady. But tonight, Nick and I watched *Valley of the Dolls* and I take my antidepressants. I cry during a scene where Neely O'Hara, the Broadway diva broken by pills, sings to her amnesiac friend in the psych ward.

A bottle of wine later, I put on my corset, and we discover that Depakote retards orgasm.

2004

On a July night, with the fan whining, I heard Spanish opera through the window. San Francisco's Tenderloin district sprawled outside my apartment building, full of crackheads and residence hotels, massage parlors and liquor stores that greeted the dawn with a line outside.

A bowl with three floating gardenias sat next to the wine, the bottle empty, the flowers delicious. There was something about this flower that always struck me, the waxen abundance of the white petals, the deep verdant leaves, the boutonnière cut like a full stop at the end of a sentence.

But for me there were only the sodden mattress alleys of the Tenderloin, the only neighborhood where I could afford to live alone. Emotional distance was needed to survive here. I had lived in San Francisco for four years, and after stepping over shit and bum-tents walking to work, living in neighborhoods that reeked of piss and Colt 45, I knew I just had to walk on by.

Following the dot-com bubble of 2000, when investor capitalists threw millions into internet start-ups, people were flooding into San Francisco for high-paying jobs and a part in the next big thing. The suits wanted to be the future. I just wanted a job.

Before I moved here, I perused Craigslist in the Reed College computer lab in 1999, searching for a place to move. I saw people offering their linen closets for $900 a month if you weren't home very much. After six months of searching, I was finally able to move into a loft with two other girls, as long as the landlord, a recently-divorced, fifty year old man, who had hand-picked us very carefully and asked for pictures, was allowed full rights of entry. At all times. He liked to come over at night.

We left pretty quick.

As I wended my way through the rentalsphere, I found that it took an entry-level office-job, good credit and the hand of god to rent a room in even a bad neighborhood. Only the old-money wealthy lived in places where there weren't bars on the windows and used condoms clogging the gutters.

San Francisco, a city of 7 by 7 miles, was an incredibly desirable place to live at a time when its economy was exploding with dreams of future profits. This meant that for those of us on the edges, trying, the young Mary Tyler Moors, Neely O'Haras, trying to get a niche in and live the life we'd always heard of, well, sacrifices had to be made. I lived in the Mission; we paid $775 each for an ant-infested basement where I was terrified to go outside at night. Then I moved to a nicer place in the Duboce Triangle with two lesbian separatists. My fondness for cock made this a problem, and I was kicked out.

Enjoying meat, dairy, alcohol, drugs, straight sex, gay sex, I found my hedonistic nature created a problem in my search for a home. Sometimes you just want to eat a steak, drink a vodka tonic, and get fucked. In many parts of the country, that's pretty much Friday night. However, in this increasingly complex ideological paradise, where everyone could do and be and profess their own beliefs, I found I better get my name on a lease if I wanted any sort of security.

So finally I did, when I was working at the Devechio and Associates accounting firm. Put on my best dress shirt, took the bus to the Tenderloin, and signed away $850 a month plus $1600 deposit for my own studio, where no one could make me a transient. It had been long enough.

But it was lonely. The drag queens and daguerreotypes stared down from above my bed, with no answers on their gray teeth. Bars and clubs were the entirety of my social life, I didn't know anyone who deigned to spend time in daylight. It just wasn't an option. I worked in a conservative industry, with people I had little in common with. No lunch dates there.

My city starter-boyfriend and I broke up the month I signed the lease. I was too seduced by the other faces, other options. The people we'd been having Easter brunch and absinthe parties with for two years ended up being his friends. So I started going out. Despite the strain of late nights and long hours in the office, the thrill of meeting new and beautiful people was seductive. The lure of possibility and chance, that feeling when I got into a cab and went careening off into the night, all of that kept me involved.

It would be nice to go out for a while.

I picked up the phone and dialed Audrey. Whether I was her wing-girl or she was mine, she always had coke and had excellent fashion tips. Including, telling me when I wore the same look *three* nights in a row (Juicy Couture jeans, black heels, a dangerously plunging neckline and eyebrows with a waxing due.) "My God, you really don't give a shit, do you?" I suppose I needed to be kept in line, she taught me about pedicures, the wash n' fold, and never going beyond heavy petting to keep your claim on every man in the room. I was sloppy on this mark. But she was the best friend I had.

"Hey, hon," I said. "Is anything going on tonight?

"I don't know," Audrey said. "I'm kind of into this guy Jesse that's been staying here, but just between us," and she moved to the bathroom, I heard echoes from tile. "I wouldn't mind hitting the Rosetta Bar. I hear that Wetto-Stiletto is spinning, and - you remember Tyler? Mmmm, I'd like me some of that."

Dust in the corners of my room fell through spider webs to form drooping cables on the Christmas lights.

I would really like to meet a guy. Boyfriend had been an open position in my life for about three years, the glow of a commitment was almost too distant to hope for. The candy store sex-lives of me and my cohorts ran on the factor that tonight is the night because we likely won't be interested once the coke's worn off. People didn't have boyfriends here, there were too many glossy beauties to play with. We would go out every night and go home with someone new. I was 27 and I didn't know anyone married except my parents.

"So, yeah," Audrey said, "Why don't you meet us there. I'll bring Jesse, and you call Brady, he'll know where the afterparty is, for sure."

Brady bent his head carefully, crouched on my chair. He was 33, a gentleman in his velvet jacket with blue roses embroidered on the lapels.

He listened to me.

But for now, it was time to find a cab.

I wrenched on a pair of thrift store heels and pulled on a white trenchcoat. In the street outside, I'd prefer if no one asked if I was "working."

The heart is alone in a small white box, beating faster and faster until it begins to bleed, and a wash of red dyes the robes of the chorus to sanguine cauliflower blush. The blush of the embryo. The blush of the unknown.

Falling through the Rosetta Bar dance floor, I stumbled into Limone. Dark with strobe, bare shoulders dashing into dusk, a rush from the turntables and I turned around. She grabbed my hand and raised it above her head, and we danced for a moment to some ephemeral disco. Brady, beside me, slithered through the bodies, grasping hands and reaching to touch my shoulder. The warmth of his hand. He passed me a drink with the other.

I tweaked my face into a "blurry yet sociable" smile. I needed glasses, but didn't want to see the sneers my paranoia supplied. It was better to float in the warm glow of a gin and tonic. I slid back into the crowd. It was a mess of diagonal bobs in mid-toss, artfully ripped blouses with wet noses, elbows jutting, breathless embraces and always the arch and thrust of the synths. I slithered between a shirtless boy in a blazer and carefully tipped fedora, and a sweaty guy dancing next to him, until I got to the DJ booth. Tyler from Wetto-Stiletto spun away, one hand clasping the headphones to his ear, the other on the record. I stumbled on someone's foot and fell halfway across Kris Danger, the sidekick DJ, as he danced against the wall.

"Lena in the house!" he yelled, lifting me up. Sweat fell on my face.

I rained ineffectual slaps on his shoulders, "No, no, no, shhhh…Quiet…"

"Come on, Lena-baby, come on, no one can hear me anyway, it's loud." He set me down. "So, what up, sugar? You still chasin' the tail?"

"The what… well, you know, there's just so many boys, I can't even decide."

"Alright! You got a bump for me?" He smiled, five feet of sweat in a shredded T-shirt, gold chains with a pendant spelling KRISSY-BABY in rhinestones. He led me to the back room.

In this tiny club on Sixth and Market, the most dangerous intersection in town, space was navigated by status, stimulants and sex. To dance near to the DJ booth was a step up. To be invited behind the turntables was another. To get into the back storeroom, to stay after last call and do lines with the bartenders and owner…*I had always been brutally nerdy*. This was my moment. The soft heat of the bodies around me, mine sensitized to opportunity.

Kris Danger easily slid open the lock on the back room, and we stood among the cardboard flats of Grey Goose and Makers Mark while I put a key-bump to his nose.

"Oh, yeah, doll. You got it."

"No problem, ma cheri."

I took a hit myself, and the racing adrenalin slammed my nerves. This was an easy ritual of greeting by now, like a cup of coffee on the beginning of a long night. I looked down at the key, the white dust caught on the inscriptions of catholic saints. I licked it. Another thrum of pleasure.

"So wait, wait, what did you do before? I mean, I see you every night and I don't know you." I asked.

"Oh – you know. I used to work in investment banking. It was crazy. It was fucking harsh, but they kept promoting me, you know, it's like, the charisma, bada-bing. And I liked the Armani suits. Face it, I like clothes. But finally I couldn't deal, and Tyler and I were starting to DJ around, and I figured, fuck it. I started working at the Diesel store in Union Square and found I could sell this shit no problem, it was so much more fun, and, yeah, so now I'm here every Saturday, and we do gigs here and there, and yeah, it's the shit. I love it."

"Awesome."

"Can I have another? Pretty lady?"

"Oh, sure."

Someone pounded on the door. Black dust fell across the lintel.

"Goddamn coke-whores!" Kris said.

"It's me, Brady, relax. I've got party favors."

Kris slid the door open to admit Brady, Audrey, and a man I assumed was Jesse. Sunglasses at night. Pinched white cheekbones. Wiry muscles tensed through a black dress shirt, rolled up at the elbows to show purple veins. Ratty black hair slid diagonally into a rocker shag. I couldn't see his eyes. But I could smell him.

We stood there awkwardly for a moment.

Audrey flicked her long eyelashes. "Hey, boys. Lena." She was from Atlanta, so masterful at coquetry that watching her piss in a driveway yielded raves from the men around. Her eyelids, streaked with red and yellow, pranced over a mouth alternately sneering, sniffing, or jeering with laughter. She darted over to Kris.

"Baby," he said, "You won the Hipster of the Year last month, where were you?"

"Oh, what? I was in Europe. We barely saw the light of day."

"You missed your Imitation of 'Imitation of Christ' T-shirt."

"I don't wear knock-offs, darling."

I looked at her arm candy. While Brady passed bumps around, we got acquainted.

"Hey, where're you from?" I said.

"Vegas! My mom did room service for Circus Circus. Back in the day she met all kinds of Frank Sinatra-y badasses, coming to their door all sexy with a plate of steaks."

"That's cool." I said impassively. "What are you up to here?"

He smirked, creasing his stubble. "Well, since I got into town, I've just been crashing with Audrey here. She's alright...hot body, but her face is too fat, not quite my scene. Then I've been boosting."

"You mean stealing?"

"Refunding, baby."

"Aha."

"Yeah, got me some great Gucci slacks and resold them to Saks, they love a good story about buying them for your girlfriend and whatnot. I've got it down."

I darted a glance at Audrey. She was whispering into Kris's ear, her breasts falling soft around his shoulder. I could feel the bitter drain of the coke in the back of my throat. Brady looked at me, brown eyes, pinprick iris. I could feel him urging me away.

"And play *Camel Toe*, next time, darling!" Audrey said, pulling away from the DJ and reaching for us. "Babies, let's go back to my place and partake, I really am not feeling this anymore. These people, really, yuppies and thugs. We should start going out on Tuesdays. Saturdays are so gauche."

Swaying in front of her, I sang, "Working nine to five, what a way to make a living." Weekdays my alarm went off at six am. Audrey was a receptionist at a hair salon.

"Suck it up. Your dealer delivers, you have no excuse not to be out here with me. It's a job." She pouted, her rosebud mouth a Fragonard.

We picked carefully across the glass shards from the shattered French doors, peering through the Audrey's room. Her flat was in an old Victorian in the Haight district, with black gouges in the hardwood floors and bay windows opening on to a tiny courtyard of neglected vines.

"Oh, Lordy Lordy!" Audrey flicked a switch, and the small chandelier came on, blue light fragmenting across the floor. She took off her stolen Marc Jacobs overcoat and threw it on the floor

Jesse raised a coy eyebrow under sunglasses. Plucking a Nico CD from the stack, he tapped the bag on it to form a pile of white powder. Swiping the ends of both lines over to the side with a library card, he made them into a third. Making a slight bow, he passed the rolled dollar to me. I shivered as the chemical exploded through my body, tingling like cellophane in strobe. I leaned back on my knees.

Audrey pulled forth a Scrabble board, giggling, "Come on guys, board game time!"

Jesse sighed and smoothed a rough finger over the dust, rubbing it on his gums.

"I'll sit this one out, thanks."

"Okay, Lena, you and me, let's do it," Audrey said, spreading out the board. She tossed me some letters and we faced off on the hardwood. "You first."

"ZED," I intoned. "26."

"That's not a word."

"Yes it is, it's British for 'Z'."

"What are you, some sorority sister?" asked Jesse.

"That's not Greek, The Greek 'Z' is omega."

"Whatever, okay, my word is 'ME'," Audrey said, laying down the tile. "That's two."

"QED," I said, laying them out on the D. "33."

"That is so not a word."

"Yes it is, it's a logical conclusion. And then ME again, crosswise, so 35."

"Okay, no more scrabble, fuck this, I'm not going to play with you, cheater!" Audrey ran both hands across the board, spraying the tiles in random piles.

Jesse laughed, "Come over here, Lena, I think you just earned yourself another line." He dotted down a small daub and began to grind it up. Audrey shoved the board under a mass of gauzy wardrobe and sulked down to take hers. I smirked and watched the man's delicate fingers as they offered the bill, the lacing of scars I didn't want to see. I moved closer, smelling the nicotine, the drugs' metallic gasoline, his body's smell of cloves.

I began to consider my maneuvers.

His eyes kept slipping to mine in a way I knew too well, while Audrey jabbered on about something forgettable. When she was high she liked to talk about her job as the receptionist at Architects and Heroes, "truly the most elite salon, I might be able to get you in as a hair model if you buy me a bag."

I liked this sort of reckless hooligan, Jesse. His foxy-uselessness of long hands and shoulders, slinky under a leather jacket and black jeans. He mixed the Iggy with the Ramones, or other 1970s New York proto-punk clichés as they ran madcap around my mind. I had spent half my 20s in punk, and the lusciousness of the sultry unemployable made me wet. He probably had some tasty sewing-needle prison tattoos on that lanky body, and the scabies to match. Still, a man who could make me a ramen omelet and didn't think bondage was for latex pervs would be an admirable catch right now. His eyes were hammered to mine when Audrey stopped mid-sentence.

"Am I missing something?" she said.

"No. Everything's cool," I answered.

"Well then, I think I'm getting pretty useless. Why don't you two go take a nice long walk and fuck in a doorway somewhere, because I'm tired of not being listened to!" She rose and pointed us to the shattered door, the whole apartment leaning apocalyptic from too much Audrey on too many drunken nights.

I curled inwards. Our friendship relied upon a tacit complicity of our own petty bitchiness and similar vices. Unsaid dynamics were common when we hung out, but she rarely called me on my shit, nor me on hers. I had a good dealer. He delivered. I knew she'd call me in a couple days when she'd found another disposable boy to flatter her gutter-pissing routine with her cocaine still fresh on his nostrils.

Jesse casually pulled up his coat. He tossed a pair of keys to the floor, tucked the tiny ziplock in his pants, and grabbed my shoulder.

"Come on, Baby Pigeon, I bet you've got a nice place to show me."

Baby Pigeon? Sure…

I followed him out the door and down the long stair case to the street   The moon was still pockmarked.

The black lacquer gate closed behind us as we swerved into the elevator cage at the Alhambra building. Built in the 1920s, the place was a rickety palace of minarets and pigeon shit, the elevator spinning its gold tracery over mesh-studded concrete. Jesse stared at the red panels and mirrors spanning the pointed height, as they lurched upwards from the flash of ignition. I clicked my lips together, satisfied. I always took my toys up through the cage first.

Chapter 2
fierce filaments

    We stopped with a clunk at the third floor, and the gates sprung open. I led him down the stained grey carpet to #302.

    Jesse took in the velvet-lined oil paintings, the plastic grapes, the single wineglass that suddenly embarrassed me.

    "Nice, nice," he said, "You live here by yourself?"

    "Yeah," I answered, darting into the kitchen for the gin. I always had it on hand, in case I brought someone home, or couldn't sleep. My fridge contained tonic water, Tapatia hot sauce, half a carton of egg rolls and one lime. I sliced it.

    "Doesn't it get lonely?" He took the drink from me gently.

    "Yeah, it does."

    "You'd have more fun with roommates…"

    "Then I couldn't have guys over or cook."

    "What the hell?"

    "Lesbian separatists. My ex-roommate thought my super-femmy boyfriend – seriously, he shopped in the girls section of Target – was going to rape them at this dinner party. Seriously, we were just sitting there eating risotto when she comes by in her sweatpants, and freaked out."

    "I see. Was she hot?"

    "No, she was an overweight PhD student who had Dr. Diva written in leather and studs on her door and an obsession with Buffy the Vampire Slayer."

    "That's hot."

    "Anyway." I picked up my lime and bit it.

    Jesse gestured towards the entryway, "What's up with the missing light bulb?"

    "Oh, it burned out and I can't reach that far up. I asked someone to help me, and he broke the fixture, he was drunk, I don't know."

    He clicked his teeth, "You need a man around to take care of things, Lena."

    I laughed. "I'm okay, really."

    "I find that hard to believe. Don't you want someone, really, that will be here and take care of you?" He took a long swig of his drink.

    "I don't know, I don't feel that I really…deserve that? I mean, what have I done that I should deserve that? Love only exists in movies and Iowa. Not here."

    "That other boyfriend?"

    "He liked Audrey more."

    He shook his head, pursued his lips. "But how about this, are your parents together?" he asked.

    "Yeah, for thirty years. They're weirdly happy. They sit down every night and have salmon and wine and Dad does the dishes. I have no idea how that is possible."

    "Your pops cleans?"

"Mom's a seventies feminist, she works in a lab, and she told him, 'look, I appreciate you following your dreams, but post 9-11 is the worst time to start an airline , and I'd appreciate it if you helped out at home a little.' He got it. But, even then, after growing up watching both of them work all the time, I was in always in day care, and Mom would make these backbreaking dinners every night, I decided I didn't want any dependents."

"Huh."

"How about you?"

"I grew up in a trailer with my mom and my little brother, and then I totally lost track of them when I joined the Navy."

"The Navy, wow. Why?" I asked.

"I got kicked out of high school for beating up this teacher so bad he almost died. Then my moms figured the Navy would be a good place for me."

"Wow."

He took a last gulp from his drink. "But no, come on, you do need other people. We all do. What about Audrey?"

"Audrey," I said, "I don't know, me and Audrey are weird. We don't really communicate. We just go out and get trashed. She likes to get fucked up, so do I, we share our resources, but we don't really have a deep connection beyond that."

"That's kind of sad."

"Oh come on, tell me who you've had a deep connection with," I asked. "Like that happens?"

"You wouldn't know them, my friend Amos, and maybe Ralph. But you don't know them, they're junkies, they're not in this crowd."

"Hmmm…I try to stay away from needles. Coke is elegant, pot just makes me think TV is inappropriately droll, and acid is for babies. So heroin, huh? How's that treating you?"

He looked up at me through cracked sunglasses. 'You really want to know?"

"Yes, I do."

"I steal, like I said. I make my living from stealing and reselling things. I've been homeless for two years and I've always had a place to sleep between girls and hotel rooms bought from selling stolen shit."

"That's delightful. I'm a receptionist. At an accounting firm near the TransAmerica Pyramid."

"Oh, sexy office lady." He smirked.

"Oh god." I got this a lot.

"Oh come on, I think you know what I mean…Saucy secretary, do a little dictation, bend over the desk to pick up a pencil. Didn't you see that movie?"

I laughed, bending my head closer to his. "Okay, okay, I think I know where we're going, here." That movie was very sexy.

"Well then," he prefaced, "if you don't want to kiss me I will certainly understand, although I think you're the most beautiful girl I've ever seen and obviously too classy to go for a thief like me."

"Only the déclassé say classy. And besides, I might. I think the Robin Hood thing is pretty cute, too."

"Yeah?"

"So c'mere," I said. Jesse had gotten up from the plastic chair and was dawdling towards me with an insolent smile. He was still wearing the sunglasses.

He slid an arm around my waist and I lifted my head to meet him. Pulling me down, we fell against the bed. I tumbled into him as we kissed, rubbing my naked feet against his legs. It was only when he began to rip at my shirt, slipping worn hands to my breasts when I really felt it, the thrill of a hand that could hold me, hard, until I broke.

1. The curve of the small of the back.
2. Two hickeys on my inner arm.
3. One long scratch along his spine.
4. Spit.
5. Nipples tugged.
6. Foil wrapper ripped with teeth.
7. Gasp.
8. Rubber limp on tissue; pink latex tied in knot.

Walking the ten blocks up Sansome Blvd. to my work, I saw the protesters as soon as I got off the bus. The air was different, the static complicity broken. I remembered the flyer at the bar the night before.

SHUT THE CITY DOWN!
SHOW BUSH THE IRAQI BLOODSHED CANNOT GO ON!
FUCK ABU GHRAIB!
CALL IN SICK TO WORK OR SCHOOL, AND HIT THE STREETS!

Humming, "Ain't no power like the power of the people and the power of the people don't stop." I wished I could. There was no way. I had used all my sick days, and was starting in on my paid time off. I couldn't get fired now. I really couldn't get arrested. Not anymore.

April 30, 2004. Today. Prison abuse, in the headlines, naked men in hoods, welted, bullet wounds on buttocks. Pictures behind glass.

Chanting, yells, bangs, at the next intersection a kid in a Crass shirt flipped a SF Weekly kiosk and lit the pages on fire. He stared at me through the smoke.

"What the fuck, corporate bitch! Scab! Sell-out! People are dying and you just want your Starbucks!"

A hot flush of humiliation that the dress shirt and blazer did nothing to hide. I had to survive. I needed this job. I was too old to care about the dress codes of activism. But I did feel like an ass.

That night I heard a thud in the hall, and my door flew open.

"Look, Baby Pigeon, I got us some steaks!" Jesse yelled, barreling in. I looked up from the floor where I was daubing lip-gloss, and nodded. My rows of eye shadow and powder lay silent by the streaky mirror, the iron grill heater sending arrows of warmth through the room.

"What is this, a sauna?" Jesse said.

"Oh, I can't get the damn thing to turn down." I cocked my head and looked at him. "All the heat in the building's centrally controlled from some place in Oakland. There is nothing I can do."

"You're just a cute little lizard, sucking up that heat."

"I love it."

He tore off his leather jacket and tossed it on the bed. The sheets were tumbled with black tights and cracker crumbs. I had gotten very into hors-d'oeuvres: the only grocery store was ten blocks away uphill, and I had no car, so I got most of my food from the liquor store downstairs and the corner bodega. This meant crackers, cheese, a basil leaf and a dash of olive oil was not just a tasty snack, it was about all I ate. If I was going out and needed energy, I would have a can of mixed nuts and a couple of those "Club" brand canned Long Islands.

"How did you get that food, anyway?" Entrees were an exciting concept.

"Stole it from Whole Foods," he beamed. "Stick a prime rib under your shirt and they never even notice. Besides, I've got a friend in the bakery section and he hooks me up with lemon bars while I wait."

"Cool."

"Should I cook it up for us?"

He crossed briskly to the kitchen and descended into succulence. A savory breeze wafted through the sooty air. Soon, the medium rare blood was dripping down the middle of my plate. The tender fat melting warm, the bone gnawed well in the end.

The next day, I felt well-fed and happy as I opened the door to Devechio and Associates, my place of employment. Martin Devechio, the obese Senior Accountant, and little brother of the VP, was standing directly inside. He had once approached me in my receptionist's booth and made a joke about magic mushrooms. This seemed apropos. They were Democrats.

I rarely had contact with Martin, other then wandering into his office to find a file and observing that he had thirty icons in a complete disarray – i.e. no grid, no order – on his computer desktop. I took that as a sign of bad character. In addition, the files I wanted were splayed across the Berber carpet.

In the hall this morning, Martin's wife Judith, was standing next to him joking with another secretary. Judith, the Executive Assistant, was fighting her late thirties by bravely applying concealer under her eyes and dying her hair russet, while Sally was smug-as-a-button with her upcoming marriage, draping grey cardigans around her globular form. I assumed the CEO was in his office, doing something important.

I shuffled in and tried to set myself up unobtrusively at my desk. They appeared to be in the middle of laughing over some mad, thrilling joke, likely something about Survivor. I set down my purse and turned on my computer, hearing the whiz of electricity and wondering if there was any coffee in the break room. Making it was usually my job.

Martin raised a hand, looming in the white-carpeted, window-walled suite. Judith and Sally paused for a moment.

"Oh Lena, with that haircut, you look like you could run away and become a model! Look at that!"

There was a long silence where I reassessed my career goals with the company. I folded my hands together and lowered my head.

"Well!" Judith turned to her husband, angrily. "It's just a haircut. She does not look like a model. Where did you get that done, Supercuts?"

I considered pursuing a job as a Peachy Puff Cigarette Girl. As an Assistant Scat Picker-Upper. Perhaps my dealer could set me up with some clients.

"Yeah, come-on? Supercuts?"

"Um," I said. "Architects and Heroes. I was a hair model. I'll go make some coffee now." I got up and crept down the hall, holding both fists in front of me tightly like I was pushing an imaginary stroller.

When I got home from work that day, Jesse had stacked all this cardboard, magazines and computer paper over the edges of the pink velvet curtains.

"What the hell, Jesse?" I said.

"For the spy-cameras." He stared up at me, lying on my bed in my leopard print panties. "Me Tarzan."

"You have got to be kidding."

"No, really, these people set up spy-cameras in apartments like this and record people having sex. They've probably recorded us a bunch of times, and then, you know those old Filipino women down at Powell Street BART?"

"They sell earrings. Pretty feather earrings."

"No, they also sell the VHS tapes under the table, and they're secret tapes of people having sex. Really. So I'm protecting us."

"Okay. That's great, really. Do you have anything left of what you took?" I looked back at my desk, where a cigarette was burning on the edge of the white lacquer, leaving a black line.

"There should be a little left in that bag over there. I saved some for you."
I hit it.

He wound an arm around me, pulling me closer, and I nibbled at his collarbone. Arm to arm, cock hardening, he squeezed my breasts and said, "Ah, these palm nicely. Not quite turned-up titties, though."

"You take your turned-up-titties and shove it." I said, grabbing his cock and milking it.

"You're pretty though, you are. You ever model?"

"A little. Mostly trashy DIY stuff. Dresses made of caution tape, bottle-cap bikinis, you know."

"That's hella punk. Did you know I'm trying to get into FIDM?"

"You? Damn, I didn't know you were so inclined."

He got up, leaning back on his haunches. "It's like this. I've been boosting for so long, and I've been picking up these fucking amazing clothes, but sometimes, I'm like, shit, I could make something cooler than this, all this shit-talk about street cred, Jesse-Cat is about as street-level as it gets. Then if I could charge what these Vuitton bitches do, or even be all outlaw Basquiat turns artstar so those ponces would be paying to shoot up with me."

"Not bad. Merchandising nichey time. You should totally do it."

"Yeah, wanna be my Kate Moss?"

I dived for his cock.

Humidity hung around the bed, as the heat swarmed through the windows. We stirred in the bed, his arm draped protectively over my shoulders, my knees clasped loosely to my chest. The sheets were dark blue and dusted with lint, streaky with unknowable substances. It was August, now, and winsome waxed flowers lurked carefully in bowls next to gobs of rolling tobacco and cigarette papers. Jesse had decided it was cheaper that way, and delighted in rolling them over and over again, lining them up on the computer desk he had since colonized, filling my hard drive with Stooges songs and porn. I was careful, watchful. The warmth of his arm on my shoulder was delightful, but I had misgivings.

I sat upright for a moment; eyes starkly open, staring at the curves of the pink velvet curtains and empty glasses. Empty coffee mugs for two, dishes scarred and cracked from my previously pristine set. A halo of heat and cigarette ash hovered over me and I nudged Jesse.

He muttered low in his throat and said, "Baby Pigeon?"

"Jesse, I had this dream, this really really weird dream. I dreamt I was at this afterparty with these people I kind of knew, and I took what I guess was acid and had this really weird trip where I was putting on black lace gloves and wailing, this inhuman wailing, and I couldn't stop or pull myself out of it."

"You know you've got to stop going out, those people aren't good for you."

"You really think that?"

"No, they're not your real friends. I'm your real friend. Stick with me, stop going out to those fucked up things."

"But you go too!" I protested.

"Baby, I only go out, like, three or four nights a week, and of those weeknights, so it's more mellow."

"Yeah, and so I can't go, because I have to work."

"It's not my fault you work for those corporate wenches. Devechio and the bitch-ho."

"Eh. Well. Where does this apartment come from? Where does our food come from, what you don't steal."

"Okay, okay, true. We'll go out together this weekend." He perked up noticeably. Outside the moon was reflecting the window panes like icing in a wineglass, drunk by the silkiest stripper of them all. I snuggled up next to Jesse with a line of ache next to the one of love, curling my arms tightly in a ball and winding my mind slower into passing it all by.

Friday, as Audrey had deemed that an acceptable day to go out, Jesse and I met her at the Rosetta Bar.

"So, how's he shaping up?" Audrey asked me, her lips around a Cosmo.

"Not bad. He cooks for me, which is wonderful. I'd been getting home too late to bother with it."

"I noticed you'd gained some weight."

"He's noticed that too."

Billy Vegas, a rocker I had fucked once in a hotel room, came in with his jacket off, hair high and sweaty. He came up to me and squeezed my shoulder.

"Lena-baby, your crazy boyfriend just tried to kick my ass."

"Oh God. So sorry. Really." I said.

"Can't take him anywhere!" Audrey smirked.

Jesse rocketed through the crowd, sunglasses on, elbows spilling drinks as he passed.

"This is my woman!"

Audrey's eyes went wide, and mouth into a moue. She looked at me. Billy too.

I reached out to Jesse. "Honey, really, nothing happened, it was a long time ago."

"You sucked his dick! At the Phoenix!"

Audrey tittered. She never blew guys, she liked to claim. Gave one a reputation.

I smiled awkwardly and clenched my knuckles to my palms.

"I'm twenty-eight. If I was a virgin it would be weird."

"My girlfriend in Vietnam was a virgin."

Billy snorted.

"You know," I said, "There's this thing called sexual liberation, maybe you've heard if it?

"Slut!" He shot. Audrey could barely contain herself.

"Look, buddy, I have a lot of respect for your girlfriend, she's a total babe, but she's really chill and solid, too. You guys have a good thing going on. I'm not getting in the way. Can I buy you a beer or something?"

Jesse clapped him on the shoulder. "Okay, man, okay. Do you have a cigarette? In fact, do you have two? I might need one for later."

I watched them walk outside, the leather flap closing behind them.

The fake flowers, silk and brittle baby's breath filled my sight as I lay back on the therapist's couch and considered. To tell or not to tell. To remember or not to recall at all, to stare out the window at the cable cars coming up into Nob Hill. The therapist was a function of my San Francisco City Mental Health Program; for all that our lady of futility was lined with shards, our lady takes care of her own. They had hyperbolic social services. I thought of the city as a mother, the queen, draped in vomit, vodka, rainbow flags, and white tablecloths, Diesel handbags in Union Square and the lost line at the liquor store at dawn. Counting pennies always.

I am bipolar, and have been for thirteen years. I was diagnosed when I was eighteen, in 1995, a sophomore year begun by Zoloft and ended with Wellbutrin (an anti-depressant), Depakote (a mood regulator), and Risperdal (an anti-psychotic). These drugs cost $900 a month, and going without caused brutal withdrawals. When I was in college I had health insurance, and for a year after the nurse practitioner from the health center would provide me with them at her private practice. When I fell off of my parent's health insurance at twenty-one, I applied for Blue Cross and was told I had a preexisting condition that they could not cover. Then I applied for the Major Risk Program, which cost $300 a month, paid by mumsy as I was still barista-ing my way around Portland.

When they couldn't pay for my insurance any more I went on Medicaid. When I got my wisdom teeth pulled without a general anesthetic, the $200 not covered by my insurance, I saw my bloody teeth emerge from gums numbed by only be a local. When I got an abortion where the anesthetic (Ibupropin-800) was "forgotten," I decided it was time to get my punk rock fuck the man head out of my ass and sell out, i.e. move to San Francisco and seek out a corporate job that could allow me not to see my own blood on a regular basis
.

That I found. And so much more. I went to General Hospital to get my first month's allocation of meds and waited for six hours in a room full of the homeless, alternately catatonic and violent. The armed guards kept us in line, though, yes, they grappled to the tile that guy in front of me who seemed to be having some sort of psychotic attack, or seizure, or really anything else that happens when you don't get your meds. I was wide-eyed and twenty-three, and didn't think I had been that close to an AK-47 before.

When I made it up to the counter the guard didn't think I was being polite enough to the lady behind the bullet-proof glass, so he slammed me against the wall with his nightstick and said, "You wanna say that again?"

"I just said I've been waiting a long time."

"You're going to wait an awful lot longer with that kind of attitude."

But I got the two bottles for free.

Once I had had an intake, they set it up so I could get my meds at Walgreens, and gave me a series of therapists. The first two had been older Russian men who asked me how my periods were and stared oddly when I tried to talk about my sexual issues.

I had to deal with this sort of baggage somehow. And as I found, the upside of bipolar disorder, the intense creativity, dazzling mood, arrogance and recklessness was much like cocaine, on a good night. Very much so. The downside I knew very well, too, the depression that grounded me, useless and miserable. Drugs brought the mania back in a titillating, thrilling way, plus I got to spend time with other beautiful strangers who were freaking out similarly, at least until the bag ran out. Mania could be bought!

This was quite a discovery, as the pills and fifteen-minutes-a-month psychiatrist were not quite doing it for me. I had found that even after being a straight-A student, getting a useless English degree, floundering through the service industry, moving to the city, I still was only qualified to be office bunny and answer the phone. Sometimes I was allowed to order lunch. Being Generation X wasn't so great. It's a damn common story.

I wanted intensity, personal contact beyond the computer screen. I wanted a social milieu where the things I could offer were rewarded. Like a really good haircut. Work took all my time and gave me money to keep surviving, but no time to do anything creative. No one was interested in my paintings. Punk tried to reject the work-consume-work cycle, but I needed to bathe after awhile. So I started going out. With cocaine ever-present, I started doing it, and at this point so many arbitrary, nonsensical and cruel things were happening in my world that I really didn't care if it conflicted with my other pills. It made things seem exciting, and vital, and real.

The Iraq war was on, and I could do no activism. I didn't trust anything in the anti-drug propaganda, Sure there were burnouts, but I got high with executives, doctors, hairdressers! It seemed terribly pleasurable. It gave me something new to focus on.

With so many addictions to choose from – alcohol, fast food, gambling, video games, shopping, compulsive overeating, internet porn, kleptomania, coffee, pyromania, plastic surgery, tobacco, orgasms, work, self-cutting, the gym, steroids, laxatives, tattoos, diet pills, antidepressants, the internet, vandalism, critical theory, benzodiazopenes, and celebrity gossip, not mention things you snort and shoot, I felt I had made a choice I was comfortable with.

My third therapist was Bonnie, and she was comfortable with it too. She worked part-time in San Quenton and wore a striking assortment of reindeer sweaters, barely visible miniskirts and electric blue ankle boots that she pulled off magnificently. Things between us had deteriorated since she consistently canceled appointments, I suspected she had a bigger drug problem than me.

She said, "You know, Lena I don't care if you and Jesse go to the Power Exchange and you have ten guys on top of you and ten girls on top of him. It's about solving your problems. So, tell me one of your memories. Don't focus, don't overthink, just think of a moment in your past."

I closed my eyes.

1998

The gold angel wings of my Halloween costume shifted over a copper-painted dress cut shorter than needs be and pressed with plastic jewels. My eyes were circled with red, a Lucite diamond between my brows, red lipstick and a brush of bronzer.

My friend Limone swiped the last pieces of glitter off my shoulders and said. "Yeah, I think he's cute." The party swirled around us.

"I'm not sure yet. I think so. The digeridoo's a bit of a turn off."

"Just close your eyes and pretend it's a bass."

"No, Crusties have scabies, sometimes. My friend got it from this guy that was hopping trains, and it took her weeks to get rid of it. She had to put all of her clothes in plastic trash bags for two weeks, except for what shit she could wash in the poison. She coated herself in this poison."

"Medicine."

"Medicine?"

"Poison."

The condom lay on the conference table of room 208A. Reed College. I pulled myself up on one arm, from where my crumpled gold wings had split and were gouging into my shoulder. I exhaled with a rush of tears and felt the false eyelash peel and droop from one lid. From the floor, between two chairs, the burn from the thin institutional rug gouging navy blue into my thighs, I pulled my skirt down and tried to ease into presentable. The Crusty had called me a wingnut and left, the train's whistle calling him to a new city. I never saw him again.

I walked up Woodstock Blvd. clutching the stretched elastic strap of the wings and striding with a desperate fervor. Quietly, I let myself bleed into the drizzling night.

I stared at Bonnie's electric-blue ankle-boots. Her foot was twitching up and down, with boredom or disbelief I couldn't tell. Maybe I had told this story before. A cable car tolled, claxon-loud, outside.

It was evening when I got to the Geary Liquor and Deli. Grizzled men laid down dimes for half-pints of brandy, and elderly Vietnamese women gathered children and vegetables carefully. I piled onions together in my arms and slung them into a basket. Adding a packet of cashews and some milk, I ambled towards the cash register.

"So how is the pretty girl today?" said the cashier, smiling as he loaded my purchases into plastic bags. I came in here everyday, and we had become companionable. There was something about the liquor store guy, as I had found in all the cities I'd lived in. Something about the man that never sneers when you buy two pints of whiskey, the neighborhood's faux-therapist who you see more than your real therapist. He keeps up on your love life and your pains, and you check in with him every evening before the nights debauch, and then he lends you boxes to move with when the year is over. In this sketchy neighborhood, Djarra watched over me as I caught my cabs, as I bought half-pints of vodka to fit purse-sized and champagne and orange juice Sunday morning.

"Oh, Djarra, I'm fine, I'm just...tired," I sank one elbow onto the battered wood countertop, letting my eyes slide over the mosque icon and God Bless America decal on the cash register. An American flag the size of a Ford hung over shelves full of Peppermint Schnapps.

He handed me the bags. "You work hard out there, long day?"

I sighed, "Oh God." After the bus ride to the financial district, it was still a ten block walk each morning and night, in the high-heeled boots corporate-wear demanded, then eight hours of receptionistery and tax-forms. I could feel each jab of my ingrown toenail in the pointed shoes, each ache in my calves and a headachey-scratch from where I had pulled off a contact curbside. Rubbing my eye at the bus stop, who knows who had touched that bus seat, the little plastic disc had to go.

Djarra raised a finger, shaking it back and forth. "Oh, one thing, your boyfriend, he charged cigarettes. Parliaments."

"Oh...right. I'll have to talk to him about that. But okay, sure." Fumbling in my wallet, I pulled out a five and handed it to him. "Thanks."

He nodded kindly, and turned to restock.

My fingers tensed around the plastic bag. Blinking and blurred past racks of Elle and Horny Goat Weed, I focused on getting back to my place. Jesse needed a severe bitch-slap, at this point. But I just didn't want to be that kind of person, and more that that, I was afraid of starting a fight I couldn't win. I often chose my boyfriends based on their similarity to my body mass, i.e., who would win the fight if it came down to it.

I climbed the stairs to the ornate Moroccan façade of the Alhambra. The dome of the lobby was cool dusk over waxy palms in brass. I slid in and began to rehearse my spiel.

Swatting open the door, I advanced hell-bent through the hall.

"Jesse!"

"You're home, yay!" He leapt into the entryway, spit flying. Dust bunnies folded with tobacco specks on the floor.

"Um, yay..." I said. "You charged cigarettes, not good."

"Oh come on, you're home late, what were you doing? Turning tricks? Huh?"

"I saw my therapist. Everyone in the Greater Bay Area is in therapy."

"What the hell, you don't need that shit. Why do you take all those pills, anyway, that's Grade A mind control. We should just crush them up and snort them and have some fun with it."

"No, Jesse, I see my therapist because I have life issues. I have goal issues. I have trouble achieving. I have something known as a mental illness."

"Yeah, I've noticed that. It's called being an uptight bitch. Why don't you take off your power-bitch outfit and suck me off for a change?"

I put both hands on the side of my face. "Okay, okay, calm. Bonnie said to center myself." I pulled a bottle of wine out of the bag and set it on the kitchen counter. Ignoring Jesse, I fumbled about in my purse for the bottle opener, and began to open it.

"Drunko, something happened that you might want to know about...You know the shower?"

"Ye-es?" My voice petered out.

"Well, I should say the bath, but, yeah, I was trying to take a bath, and you know the stopper?"

"Yes. Those don't come with new apartments, and I am ghetto-tarded and never bought one. Just happens there isn't a Bed Bath and Beyond in the TL, and I'd rather spend the $2.99 on crack."

"Well I couldn't find it, so I used the stopper from a bottle of perfume, this wooden thing, and it got stuck in there and now I can't get it out!"

"Oh god, I can't even get my mind around that. Well, you're just going to have to get it out. And now."

He stomped and flailed, long arms hitting the walls. "I tried, honey, I tried. But we can't call anybody, because they'll see how messy the apartment looks and they'll kick us out."

"Somehow I don't think eviction due to filth can really happen. I mean, I really doubt it. But I don't want to call Ed after that last noise complaint, either, he's pretty pissed at us as it is...but, I mean, you're suggesting we don't bathe?"

"No, no, check this out, I found this way where, like, you empty it, right, with a bucket, and put the water in the toilet, and then when it gets far enough down you can take another shower, and then empty it again." He pled with upraised hands.

Jesse was exploring hitherto unfounded depths of squalor, and here I was to witness it. Floored, I strode to the bathroom and stared, appalled, at the vaguely unwholesome depths of the bathtub, the cold, dirty water. Next would come the mold.

He came up behind me and rubbed my stomach, saying, "It's all right, baby, it's all right. It's more European not to shower, anyway. My Navy buddy Kenny, this old guy, he said the chicks in France were mega-hot, no matter what the smell. You're that kind of babe. Pigeon-clothed, smelling liked washed-up shit, you're still gorgeous."

His hands descended, began unbuttoning my slacks. "Love the way you wear the same pants to work every day. That's fucking punk. You're just a walking subversion I can't even get my mind around. I bet your pussy smells so good right now."

He pulled me down on the floor with him, and threw my panties into the bathtub. Nicotine tongue on my clit, licking expertly, thrumming me to orgasm as I held his head and counted the days since I'd shaved my twat.

The alarm sounded, brutal, and I lurched forwards in my bed. Suddenly it hit me that I had to serve coffee for Mr. Devechio's shareholders today, and needed to look sharp. Carbon-cut-out secretary in an Express size zero dress shirt, full make-up and smelling like rose milk. This would take a little work.

"Oh, right, yes," I muttered. I slipped naked from the sheets and padded on sticky feet to the bathroom. The yellow walls of the bathroom were luminous and pale against the stark black floor and broken shower curtain pole. Another Jesse addition. I leaned over and stopped, noting the briny water filling the tub.

"Jesse!" It was 7:30 am, and my voice was harsh and loud against the dawn quiet.

"Mwa, wha-Baby Pigeon, what?" he said.

"I have a meeting today. I must bathe. Can you empty this for me?"

"You do it."

"It's not my problem. I never have to do it. You said you'd always do it since you broke it. Besides, it's nasty." I folded my hands. It's true, growing up, we had usually had a cleaning lady, if not a maid, but in my own apartment I didn't mind cleaning my own mess. Key factor, own apartment. Own mess. This was completely his past-all-human-understanding fuck-up, and I didn't want any of it to screw up my job. The executive assistant had made it excruciatingly clear to me that I had to look immaculate and conduct myself with the utmost decorum and not interrupt the meeting for any reason even if the Devechio's Greyhound, who was in chemotherapy, had a complication.

Jesse folded his arms over his head and sunk back into the covers. "I don't really feel like it, I'm tired, it's, what is it, 7:30 in the am, can't you let a man sleep?"

"I can't fucking believe you!" I stomped.

"Shut up, bitch. Let me sleep!"

"But you have to do it," I said. "You just have to. I'm really going to get shit for this, we had sex last night, I smell like trouser-trout, I can't go in like this."

"You smell like one of those three whores I got in Bangkok, but I'm not sure which one. Probably the one on the bottom."

"Look, asshole, I don't care how much pussy you got in the Navy, like oh, boy, I'm this white trash jackass with twenty-dolla, golly-shucks, that'll get me a whole barrel-a-twelve-year-olds! Hot damn!"

"Mmmph." Jesse rolled over in the bed and curled up, insensible.

The tub was grotesque. I tightened my eyebrows, clenched my teeth, and reached for the bucket. It shouldn't be long.

But as I scooped and poured, sloshed and dipped, the lapping of the chill water against my wrists reminded me of the filth my beautiful apartment had slunk into. For all that Jesse still felt like my partner in mayhem, it was dawning on me that the initial hiss of lust ignored the mold between the stubble, the terrible stench coming off of his teeth.

Jesse and I sat at Tommy's, a Mexican restaurant in the Sunset district. Audrey was with us, calm for the moment, drumming her rose-pink nails on the red tablecloth as the waiter set down another round of margaritas. I looked back at the bar, where the bartenders were squeezing lime after lime into a vat for mixer. On the rocks with salt, pure lime juice and Cuervo. I listened to the squelch of the waiters' shoes as they ran back and forth on the rubber mats that lined the inside track of the bar. I could hear the faint slapping sounds and the hoarse cries for uno mas. The voices were loud in the dim orange cave of the room.

Jesse took a sip of his drink, sucked down the juice from the lime on the rim, and slammed it down on the table.

"Oh yeah. Baby, you never told me about this place."

"It's really mine to tell," said Audrey.

I looked into my hands.

"Listen, Baby Pigeon, will you go outside with me for a second? I wanna smoke."

I rose, and wove between tables to follow him to the door. Outside, it was gloomy and grey, a horde of pigeons gathered on the dark green awning above us. They leaned into the rough concrete bricks of the building, the single story with its low, barred windows and the delicious scent hanging heavy by the door.

He lit a cigarette and ashed on the only clean part of the pavement. I closed my eyes. He took my hands.

"Listen, I've been thinking, do you…do you want to get married?"

I scraped my palms against the pebble-stubble of the bricks and stared into his black sunglasses. He dropped the Camel.

"Listen, baby, I found this ring in a, um, pawnshop, and I think, like, that's what you do, right?" He fumbled in the pocket of his black jeans, his long, pale fingers scraping at the rip at his hip. Pulling out an antique diamond ring on a thin band, he held it out to me on two fingers. "Do you wanna?"

I gasped. Part of me reached out for it: the security, knowing someone was mine and mine alone...not dying alone, as my Grandma Begninia had warned me.

"It's so hard to ride in the back seat," she told me, "it's hard not to have a man to go to dinner with. I want you to find someone."

To not live alone, night after night, with the take-out egg rolls and cold sheets. I wanted that warmth. I wanted someone to call 911 when I OD'd, not find my corpse a week later covered in rats and turquoise molds. Even if Jesse was the cause of death. Even if he bought the smack and shot me up. Even if I had to drive him to the ER time and time again for "heart trouble" best defined as speedballs. Even if all our love came spliced with madness, his companionship was better than the five years of loneliness I had felt.

Every girl loves a train wreck The slinky glamour he shook in his bones wrapped around me, beside me, within me. The two of us. That was all I had ever wanted in love, no picket fence, just me and a hopelessly bit steel hip lad in an apartment, together, in the city, hard and eccentric and really tight for each other.

He took off the sunglasses, and I saw the sincerity there.

Turning upwards to the sky, I said, "Yes, okay, yes, I will." He grabbed me around the waist, and, as he twirled me in a circle on the dirty concrete, a swath of pigeons took flight in a wash across the sky.

Chapter 3
the chair, our chair

I digested my bagel, getting up from the table at the Querelle. Bracketed between an always-shuttered Indonesian restaurant and an always-open Massage Plus, two card tables teetered on the sidewalk.

I caught up with Jesse, and we strode along Geary Street. Dividing the risky south side of the Tenderloin from the gradually more gentrified lower-to-upper Nob Hill that culminated in Grace Cathedral and the St. Mark's Hotel, Geary Street was my street, the street of my apartment, the street along which daily I rode the 38 bus to work. Today, some day in April, 2004, the street had a treacle-ochre glow along the high icicles of the apartment buildings, the bay windows facing in the narrow street running straight along Golden Gate Park to the ocean in the west, and along perilous descents through the financial district to the Embarcadero on the east.

We walked on. As we crested the hill, I saw a mid-century modern pedicure chair sitting outside a storefront with a couple of inlaid tables. A man with a shaved head and a yellow flannel shirt was wiping down the window in long, lanky strokes. As we passed him, I yelped, "My God, I love it!"

"Just looks like a chair to me," Jesse said.

"Only $120," said the man.

"Oh. Well, I guess not."

We continued. As the Tenderloin began to ease into Union Square, the boarded-up storefronts giving way to magazine kiosks and a kosher deli, a tall man with bleached-blond hair and gold teeth waved down Jesse and we stopped.

"Oh my God, Amos, fuck, it's been months!" Jesse slapped his hand against his thigh. "Where have you been?"

"Practicing. 24 Karat Gold is going really well, we're playing the Hemlock this Friday. You should come."

"Isn't that guy with the glass eye in your band?" Jesse asked

"Oh yeah, yeah. But, check this out. I got these teeth made for us for when we play, it's great." Amos snapped the gold tooth-facings from his teeth and gestured with them. They caught the light like vertigo castanets. The moving, spinning light flooded across the narrow Saturday street.

"Oh, well check this out. I'm engaged. Show him the ring, Lena."

I smiled shyly and held forth my hand.

"No shit, really?"

"Really. This chick's got a job."

I glanced at him. Goodbyes said, we turned around and began to hike back along the sidewalk towards the Alhambra. As we passed the antique store again, I saw that a sign reading "Sale $60" in black sharpie had been propped up on the base of the chair.

"The base separates from the chair. You two could carry that, easy," said the man, emerging from the store. Frayed green curtains hid the door. It was dark inside. He was still holding the dirty cloth, and there was a swath of dark furniture polish along his forearm. I looked down, and a dove was fighting with the sparrows for access to the pan of water left between gloves and an obsidian model of a horse's head.

"How about $30?" I said.

"$40."

"$25?"

"$30." His head twitched.

"It's got all these stains at the base, look, and it's so dirty, all outside and stuff," I said.

"That shit'll wash off, easy."

"The paint won't." said Jesse.

"Yeah, and with these tears along the footrest, look, they look like pencil marks," I said.. "How about $15."

"Oh, come now. $30?"

"$20, and that's all I can do."

"Okay, fine. As long as you can carry it away now today, that thing's been in my store for months."

"Alright!" I grabbed his hand. Half an hour later, I had the sloping quadrant draped across my shoulders, and Jesse was lugging the base, complaining. We stopped at the door of my building, and I fumbled for the key. Edging in, we thumped the parts down inside the elevator, and I gasped as I pressed "three."

"Why do you get these crazy ideas, Jesus." he said.

"I think it's beautiful."

And it was beautiful, when it was settled in the bay window, the three panes bent octagonal in the lazy afternoon sun. I lay back in the chair, my hands in my lap, and glanced over to where Jesse was downloading his fortieth Ramones song.

The vinyl smooth beneath my back. Our first purchase as a couple. MSN called this "nesting," I called it security. The luxurious weight of the seat, tapered to hold my legs.

1999

Working the counter at Star's Antiques, two Japanese men in beautiful suits came in. We specialized in mid-century modern furniture, the 1950s will to the future. I would wipe the vinyl with a damp cloth day after day, as nothing ever sold.

"Your arms, are those, tattoos?" The first man asked. I wore a short-sleeved summer dress, capping pink bunnies, Loteria cards, pulp lesbians in negliges, the usual mid-nineties flash. Me and you and everyone we know.

The two were excited. The taller man rolled up his sleeves, showing intricate work. The other, his jacket set in the counter, revealed a back piece continuing down his thighs.

They bought out the store. Arranged for overseas shipping. Shook my hand. I wasn't used to anyone shaking my hand.

In my room, that night, my boyfriend said, "You know those were Yakuza, don't you?"

"Well, they have excellent taste."

Our room was dark, the downstairs neighbor pounding the walls and shrieking something high-pitched and incoherent. This happened everyday. Eviction, especially for the section-8 mental, could take years in San Francisco. We'd rather not stir shit.

Jesse cut some coke into pinkie-length streaks. I pulled myself up from the bed and swept up the first, watching my eyes drift by in the mirror that held them. A low electronic beat hummed from the speakers. I felt the rising shimmer of elation spring through my body, electroshock to the clit.

"Mmmmm…" I shivered.

"You feel it that good? Damn, I don't really feel anything; I think from Vegas."

"Too many sequins? Too many tits? Come on…" I laughed, ripping strips in my kimono.

"Oh no, honey, I was dealing mad shit. Now I've got this crazy tolerance, I do a line and it's, like, yeah, I want another, but I don't get super high. Or super horny, like you seem to be."

"Hmmm, well, then," I purred, looking out the window at the skull-like brick. There was nothing outside but a wall marked with glimpses into other apartments, a hand here or a bath there, a bottle thrown or children crying with red begonias in a window-box. Inside, though, it was warm and I had my Jesse-pants, and a gram.

"Hey booty-bump? he said.

"What, bees knees?"

"Have you ever wanted to have a threesome?"

"Been there. With Limone."

"Really?" His voice took a sharp turn onto a freeway I'd never seen.

"I probably shouldn't get into it…fun, yeah. Has to be spontaneous, but it can be a good time."

He moved closer, cuddling up to me, whispered, "And who would you want it to be with, mmm?"

"My neighbor, Brady. He's hot. I don't think you've met him."

His hand slammed 150 volts of Navy training across my face. I reeled back, into the pillows, grabbing at the pain, feeling my numb nose. He glared down at me.

"Don't say anything like that about another man again or I swear…"

"Fuck, I'm sorry, I didn't think, you know how the shit makes you too honest, I mean..."

His scarred hands rammed me against the wall, the clunk of my forehead followed by a broom aria from the lady downstairs. After nights of coke-fueled sex slapstick, often followed by the suggestion that I go get myself a cab and don't wake the girlfriend on the way out, here I just went limp. He would get tired. The next slap came harder.

"He's gay, baby, gay, don't..." I put my face into the blankets.

"Gay don't mean shit. A hot ass is a hot ass." Spank.

"Honey-muffin."

He lowered his hand and tried to cup my cheek. I stayed still, holding the numbness within me. He shook my shoulders, bored. Slowly, I waited until he got up to cut a line.

I got up and went into the kitchenette, tears in a holding pattern. The porcelain lucky cat we'd bought together stared up as I collapsed into a chair, listening to the fierce clip of the razor blade on the mirror.

2003

My building's Moroccan gates slipped closed, and I strode head-down through the sprawled men, cups outstretched for dimes, up to the corner where a crowd had gathered. Outside of the HA-RA Lounge, a young girl was lying, bleeding from the forehead. A man in a white shirt was holding a paper towel to her head and muttering, rocking her back and forth to the curious-impassive stares. She was absolutely still.

I thought of Brady.

I stabbed both hands into my pockets and turned back. Tip-tapped past piss-stained doorways, Asian markets, kiosks hawking bright cable car chocolate molds, to a woman kneeling on the curb, sticking a needle into her purple-veined thigh.

In the lobby, under red arches, I ran into him.

"Hey, there's someone dead out there."

"Well, if that's what's happening, then, honey, I don't need to see it. Come on, let's have a drink."

"That's sweetie to you. Okay." I followed Brady into the elevator, a brass cage edged with marbled mirrors, and watched the grated concrete slide past under the bars. "Are you sure we shouldn't...?"

"Shouldn't what? Lena, look, you know how it is, the last thing you need in your life is getting involved with a stranger's drama...do you really want the police to know your phone number? Know who to bust when their quotas' low? You're looking a bit gaunt and bloody-nosed, yourself"

"Hmmm...."

"Well, what if she shorted her dealer, or her pimp's wanting more? Darling, no. We did not see that little bloodstain. Let other people deal with it who are better equipped."

"Um…"

"When you get that midnight knock, you'll know I'm right."

"I guess."

"You sweet little thing." The bell shrilled and we clattered through the hall to #608. The elevator slithered down. There were sirens outside.

A poster from Evita hung in the small room, next to an array of ruffled shirts. Brady poured a long drone of champagne into glasses, topped them with a flourish of orange juice, and sighed as he passed one over. I tasted the acid under the fruit before the sip went down. I curled up trying not to watch the long sweep of a seam down his leg, his large hands quartering a lime and dropping a piece into my glass.

I looked down and my hands were still shaking.

A long siren wail belled through the window.

Brady sat down next to me, crossed his pointed boots at the ankle, and folded an arm across my shoulder. "Its okay, Lena, remember, horrible things happen everyday, and we'll never know why they don't happen to us. And then someday the thing you fear will happen."

" You're so comforting. I heart nihilism."

"Lena. It's all I can do, sometimes."

I leaned my head back into his shoulder, knowing I shouldn't hope. His hand came around and stroked my collarbone, effervescence of the cheap champagne, the pinpricks. I reached for the condensation on my glass, letting him run his hand along my bare arm, trying not to dive onto him and pluck his nips. It was hard not to try.

The fan swished above ten years of Madonna records and postcards from Buenos Aires. A thin wail came through the window. I dug my nails into his chest and rolled into a kiss.

Our tongues met with the desperation of two lonely people finding a body to deprecate. His soft hands plunged along my back, cupping my ass, probing, while I discovered how queer to straight grooming differed. No twink, here. Nibbling his chest, kissing down his stomach, he smelled deliciously like Old Spice and crème de tres naranjas. He lay back, moaning. I cupped his balls, and went in for the kill.

Sucking his long brown cock, playing his shaved balls, I tried. After six or seven limp gulps, I looked up at him with a cocked eyebrow and his flaccid dick between my lips.

"I can't do it, Lena."

I winced. I didn't know where my shirt was.

"I can't give you what you want as a man." He wiped a soft fragment of hair behind an ear, sheepish. I sat up, leaving him naked and bobbling on his own.

"I know, I know. They throw around that turn-a-gay-man-straight phrase all the time, and maybe it is just media bullshit. I do, honestly, really like you, and you actually seem to be able to put up with me."

"No, I really like you, too. I just can't have sex with you. I wanted to try with you and see if I could, and my body said no"

"Captain Wang."

"Lena, please be real."

"I have to go." I turned my face away and began scrambling around for my clothes. Turned into a dim spider. I tried to fade flesh-tone into blond-wood into no, not-a-girl, not naked on his floor at all. Brady leaned back on his haunches, watching guiltily as I slunk into my shoes, leaned over to place a hand on his, and crept out the door.

I looked back, saw him place a hand palm down where my face had been, and saw him trace a finger along the woodgrain and shadow.

Arm up, hailing a cab, vicious-tense alone on Geary St., I chanted, "come-on-come-on, come-on." Like a dream a Checker cab veered out of nowhere and pulled up, flashing bright. I fell into the faux-leather grey, and it wasn't until we were careening down Van Ness that I started to cry. Diner neon and worn bars, warehouses and the screech of ambulances fell through the dark. I watched the colors stream past like a glaze, wiping tears off my face.

The taxi pulled up to a dark storefront. No sign. I clenched my teeth, paid the driver, and set foot on the asphalt.

I pushed through the leather curtains into the bass and synth-dicing. The Rosetta Bar. Spangles and shadows, pale shoulders under strobe. I slid in, lurking, I was dead already and hung on the wall like the gilt mirrors reflecting just more faces, more sharp hair and fluttering eyes.

A hand swiped my shoulder and I turned around, to Limone passing me a drink I didn't need and saying, "Lena, are you alright, you're pulling deer-in-the-headlights again." A glow-sticked cigarette girl leered at us, vulgar, waving her green neon roses. Limone grabbed me by the hand. and dragged me through red velour to slam us both on a couch. Smoke-machine drift hid the cigarette burns, but I could feel them as I picked nervously, the adrenaline, the spear of blood I saw as I passed the checker door into the street, Brady quartering a lime and dropping it like toxic Alka-Seltzer through a plume of champagne, fizzing and running over. A pool of dark water was inching from the bathroom door, along the chipped black-painted floor, beneath the rapid questions Limone was throwing at me. "No, it's not that, no, I'm not high, no, it's just too embarrassing, I shouldn't have tried..." And then I trailed off to the dim haze, watching the shoulders and hands of the sweaty, giddy, helpless people dancing. The tense beat lulled me, and I leaned back into the leather, running my hands through the dim animal pile of it.

"It's nothing," I said. It's nothing."

From my swivel chair at work, I could see the other secretaries bent over their desks. A bouquet of fresh lilies sat on the reception counter, for visitors to breathe as they waited. All around me it was as clean as Clorox wipes and invisible janitors could make it, the 34th floor of the TransAmerica Pyramid was air-conditioned cold with thick latch-less windows opening onto clouds. It was quiet, immaculate, my fingers twitching on the mouse browsing Craigslist, waiting for the phone to ring.

"Now Lena," said Judith, "I need the I-1098 for Mr. Allsted. Check Sally's inbox."

"Okay." I moved from my chair, walked down the hall, and began looking through the wire tray. Sally looked up from a bridesmaid site, and winced. She was getting married in a few months, and I had not been invited. I ignored it, focusing, until my hand caught somewhere beneath the forms. I shook it and it came loose. The tiny diamond glinted, the gold band chafing.

"What's going on over there? You really should ask before you look through that," Sally said.

"Oh, sorry, my ring got caught."

A pointed, "Oh."

I blushed, pulled out the form in triplicate, and set it on Judith's desk. Outside, the roar of anti-Carlyle-group protesters could barely be heard below the dank blank space of compressed air. The protests had been going on every weekend for months, and I had learned to walk a couple of blocks out of my way to avoid harassment. Judith and Sally would joke about them, especially if they saw employees from the firm in the elevator. I kept silent.

When I got home, pushing open the greasy door of #302, the room was quiet except for a soft gnawing noise.

"Jesse?' I said, inching down the hall, beneath the burnt-out lightbulb that he hadn't fixed. At the kitchen counter I saw him, his naked shoulder blades bent over shreds of cardboard.

He looked up guiltily. One hand was gripped knuckle-tight on a fork, the other held a huge, much-gnawed chunk of brown sugar.

"I was hungry. You really should keep more food around the house."

"You, really, should get a job."

"I can't, baby, I'm Robin Hood."

"Face deep in brown sugar. Do you want some parsley with that, or maybe a Caesar salad?"

"That would be nice. Chop chop."

"Really, I mean it, get a job. My credit card's maxed out."

He grabbed me by the shoulders, rubbing his bristly, sugary lips against my eyes. "You wanna get some, huh, you want some good hot fucking? You wanna show your daddy a good time, miss powerbitch? You wanna take off that powerbitch shit!"

"Mmmmm…." My wallet falling to the floor, I let him bend me over the kitchen table. Psychedelic, flowered, a 2 by 4 folding table for two, it let me pretend domesticity as I served take-out. *Mom, dad, I'm trying. I lack resources. My man's a cunt.*

But tonight he pulled up my pinstriped pencil skirt, said, "God, bitch, pantyhose, who are you trying to fool?"

"Sorry, babe, Judith said the tights were no go-"

"I don't give a fuck, you're supposed to be pleasing me, and 'nude', what is this, 'beige'? This shit is wack!"

"It's called correct office attire. I have a dress code. That's why I make the big bucks."

"Then get a car so we can ride to Donny's in style, taking the bus to your dealer is for scrubs." I glanced at the grey-blonde hair on his legs. The jagged scar that ran from his thigh to mid-calf, where no hair would grow.

"I take cabs, no one's going to pull over a cab. The minute you get in your own car with drugs you open yourself up for arrest. And the $20 you save on the cab, or car bullshit, is that much higher we can be. Check that, me."

"Bitch." He stuffed the pantyhose into my mouth and began wrapping it around my face so I couldn't see. I got wet, sudden and molten, my tits in the tight bra hot against the table. He wrestled my hands back and said, "Can't you invest in some bondage cuffs, this is your fetish, anyway."

"Mmmph."

"Shaddup. I know how you want it." He massaged my waist, flicking apart the buttons in my blouse. As his hand tugged angrily at my bra, his cock rubbing the ridge of my damp panties, I remembered how he showed me his last girlfriend's webpage last night. She was a burlesque dancer named Bunny Scarlettes. He'd met her when she gave him Ecstasy at the Catclub, with the condition that he stay with her all night. They'd fucked into the next four weeks, until one of her clients offered her cash to go to Bali.

I had scrolled down the pictures of her, in corsets and thongs, the price of a session. Did he google this to show he was a quality catch – he got chicks others had to pay for? I, a lower bastion on the glam charts, should pay him for his services. He fiddled with my clit, yelled, "You cum yet?"

"Mpht?"

"Cum, you frigid bitch."

This economy made sense to me. I spent my youth in Portland, where the high-status girlfriends for wanna-be rock stars were strippers. In the 1994, when I graduated from Reed College, all of my female friends were in the sex industry. Students especially, as Sallie-Mae began to call. There were very few entry-level white-collar jobs, like the Girl-Friday-paper-pusher and lipstick bits I pursued now in

2004. Called a sell-out back then by my gutter-punk friends, I tried offices, an oil paint factory (fired, too slow on the labels), coffeeshops, waitress, retail, all to find ramen a poor diet. My punk roommates found glory in it, said if I wasn't such a bourgeois daddy-lovin scum-sucker I should get a real job and shake that ass I was so proud off for some real cash, because working for the man was no way to live, and all of that edumacation was the man's mind control, and only filled me full of bullshit that my pussy was too good to shake.

Jesse shook it good. I couldn't breathe. Face down on the tile he poured a petit boteil of my auntie's truffle oil onto my ass and greased it up good. Shoved his cock in and rode me until I couldn't remember who shook what ass on what stage in the shimmer-shamble disco ball of it all tore down.

That's why I kept him around.

Grabbing $40 from the ATM, I turned around to see Jesse rapt in conversation with a homeless man. It was right by the Civic Center BART stop, where the Walgreens had a needle exchange and security guards. I was trying to meet up with my dealer Donny. We sat on his couch weekly, and Jesse would wax vicious and meander, while I pulled forth two twenties for the gram. Donny would take them with a glance which said he knew the score and was choosing not to speak, perhaps waiting until a more crucial time…or perhaps not at all.

In the interim, Jesse was hugging this guy. Draped with teeth on leather bands, his hair braided and tangled, shreds of burlap, I saw these guys all the time. They were ever-present in the city, especially where I lived. My rule was always, *don't engage. The way to escape harm is pass under the radar.* I covered myself up, wore hoodies, kept my head low and walked fast. It wasn't that I hated them, or what their abjection meant. I knew it could happen to anyone. I knew how close I could be.

I just thought the desperation I felt, then, if magnified to their level, could make one do anything. I didn't want to be the person who caught their eye to target. Even if the only catching was handing them a nickel.

Stuffing the money in my purse, I inched forwards.

"So here's my girl," beamed Jesse, "Come here, baby, okay, this is Pocket, he was my best friend in rehab, absolutely, we went through hell and back together."

Pocket stretched out a grimy hand, and I drew back. I was having enough trouble with runaway infections, my ingrown toenail was a gangrenous mess. Laying out the welcome mat and handing bacteria a lemonade was not a good idea.

"Jesse, I think we need to meet our guy, now, I think you better say goodbye." Pocket's hand hung empty. The city hall dome leered blue and gold in the mid-day sun. My palms ran with sweat.

"Come on, Lena, get real, what's our phone number again? I want to give him our phone number. We've got to hang out soon, yeah!"

I wrapped both hands around my purse and said, "Jesse, we need to go. Now."

"But what's our number? I have to give it to him, he's my friend. I don't ditch out on my friends. Here, I know, I'll give him your cell number."

"You absolutely will not! Now come on, we are leaving, you are not going to give this guy any of my numbers. Come on!" I grabbed him by the shoulder and pulled him away.

A silver Escalade pulled up to the curb and Donny waved from the window. The crystal-clean windows glistened.

"Bitch, don't be such a priss," Jesse said, as I bundled him up and forced him into the back seat. Air conditioning, surround sound, and Donny's tranquility enfolded us. My body dried. It was still only three o'clock.

"So you kids made it, I almost didn't see you over there," Donny said, pulling up to the light. His wide hands curved over the steering wheel as he bent in concentration, then took a right down Eighth Street.

"Oh my god, Jesse was trying to give my cell phone number to this homeless dude, it was so wrong," I whined, leaning over my armrest. We sped down Mission Street .and headed south.

"Bitch," Jesse muttered from the back seat.

"Oh shit. That's fucked, man, you can't do that. She don't know this guy, you know him how?"

"Rehab."

"There you go. That's not cool."

"See!" I said.

It was getting harder to maintain order. The way I kept my life making sense was by boundaries, making rules. Drugs are okay on weekends, sex is okay if you own it, force yourself to work no matter what.

In Wasteland, Limone and I lingered around a rack of white dresses. The barn-like store was strewn with vintage gowns, cowboy shirts, asymmetrical slashes, sunglasses, racks of denim and petticoats galore. At this point, however, I was out for something specific. A wedding dress.

"See, I don't know, some of the shit I've heard says I should wear something tea-length and off-white, because I'm not – obviously – a virgin."

"That's ridiculous," said Limone. "Who said that, your mom?" I had known Limone since college, and she was good for this sorts of thing.

"No, my grandma." I fingered the sleeve of a lavender shift.

"Are they happy about it?"

"I think so. They weren't so stoked about the trailer bit, and the fact that he has no contact with his mom, doesn't know where she is. They're really into family."

"Well, you know, Limone said. "Modern world. That is a little weird, though, that he has no clue. Estrangement is one thing, like if he came out or some abuse thing, but just – nothing? He's not even interested?"

"I know. What do you think of this one?"

"That low back is nice, and, yeah, it is off-white. Are you sure you don't want to get a little bit flashier, though?" She tilted her head to the side, the murmuring crowd around us sorting and sifting, finding and seeking.

"Subtle is as subtle does. Right. This one's kind of cute, a little more mod."

"Short."

"That's mod."

"I know, but I suppose your mom won't like that too much. By the way, what do you want us to wear?"

"Oh god, I hadn't though about that? Black dresses? Black and white are nice and graphic, dramatic. I can't really handle those seafoam puffy-paint things."

"Oh, thank god. Vera Wang is out of my budget."

"Really, I'm just trying to make this work." I set the dress back on the rack, and turned around, bringing both hands to fists at mouth-level. I looked up at the layers of lamé and tweed, the chandeliers above lit by green and red bulbs, the tufts of scarves falling down in waterfalls from hooks on the wall. Silently, I shut my eyes.

"I'm so glad we all got to get together," said my father. "I was beginning to wonder who Lena's pool-boy was, and now that you're engaged, well, it's something I better catch up on!" It was silent at the table, the flutter-trip of waiters at the perimeter, the mauve walls and gold-red smoke of the ceiling. I stared acutely at my fork.

"Oh Darling, I'm just so glad you aren't...well...alone anymore. Really, it was getting a little embarrassing," said my mother. She fluffed her silver-blond curls with cold hands. "Let's celebrate." She reached for the pinot grigio. "You know, I read in Wine Spectator that this was the one to try."

"Really?" said Jesse. "I go for the Old Crow, m'self." His coke-jowls creased along the cheekbones edge.

"Is that a merlot?" She bent her head.

"Yes, it is, mom."

"Oh, honey. You always did like those artists."

"Artists, yes, he's an artist." I said. "It's this new form called shop-dropping. You relocate objects. It's been featured at Swamp Electra."

"Oh, Janey's gallery. Do you ever hear from her?"

I picked up my fork and gouged it at the empty space between us. Smiling graciously, I said, "Yes."

On the corner of Duboce Street and Fillmore, Jesse took a swig from my flask and wiped his hand on his leather jacket. The dark street flooded around us, the curbs iced with broken glass. A long stretch of dark green ceiling extended behind a silvery storefront, a sign for Armenian food over the gold-mottled door. Streetlights stomped between doors and windows, casting delicate blisters of light.

Jesse gestured, "There, see that guy?" A spidery squiggle darted between two cars. "I bet he has some."

"Well, I'm not talking to him. I don't score from people I don't know." I said.

"Okay, you wait here." He loped off in long strides, his black jacket gradually blending into the street.

"You are such a dirty whore," ranted Jesse, sitting down on the bed. An Iggy Pop CD with a light sprinkling of speed lay on a chair amid tossings of bras and cigarette ash. Mid-morning light streamed through the window, illuminating the purple veins and track marks on his rolled-up sleeves. I didn't want him to shoot it, the last thing I wanted was for him to OD, but at that moment I was just jerking back in pure amphetamine terror. I leaned back on the bed and said, "Jesse, sweetie, come on, let's talk about tomorrow night. Audrey says Kris Danger is spinning."

"I don't care." He reached for the lightbulb on the chair.

"Honey, don't smoke it." I reached out a hand.

"Bitch, I'm going to smoke it if I want to, I think you should too, it's better. It don't tear up your nose like snorting it does." He flicked the lighter and glided it onto the bottom of the light bulb, higher and lower, together, sucking it through the glass tube he'd inserted in the bulb. It glowed with an iced silver splinter, an eye of a sacred cow fed only on cathode rays & tinsel.

"My nose is fine," I sulked. I hadn't had nose hair for a while, and a thin rip was starting in my septum.

He held the mouthful of smoke for a moment and exhaled. A veil. "That's not what I heard. Someone said you were getting nosebleeds in the bathroom. Real cute."

"Like you would know. You don't even talk to anyone I know anyway."

"Well, you don't talk to anyone at all."

"That's because you won't fucking let me talk to anyone, you won't let me go out, you won't let me – "

"That's just because you'll cheat on me, I know what you do when you get alone. You're a whore."

I remembered the long nights traipsing the edges of dance floors, those months before I met him when a short skirt and boots could contain a whole world of potential mornings. The abandon was part of the thrill, brunch or no.

"No, honey, really. I'm good. Really," she said, looking up at him. "Last time I just hung out with Audrey, anyway, and that was just calm, no big deal, we didn't even…"

"You did coke with her and tried to stay out all night, I remember that, you – "
He lunged at me, rocking me back on the bed with splayed hands and a gasp. I fell
backward on the red pillow with a silent exhale, a quiet faint with my face blue-
white, as his hands grasped my shoulders.

"Baby...," I yelped, prone on the bed, staring up at the sunglasses he never
took off: the grizzled cheeks, the hollow of his sunken cheekbones.

"You are nothing but a whore, I know about you and your shit."

"What...? I'm good, really, I mean," I said, trying not to internalize what I
wasn't sure was even true, or bad, or quite as bad as he said. At this point even my
own past before I met him was blurry.

"I know, don't try and play innocent with me, I know what you're up to," he
said.

"What? Working all day and coming home to you? Come on."

"You – you – you do bad things, I don't know what you do when you're at
work, how do I know you're really at work, maybe you don't have a job at all,
maybe you – "

"Jesse! I have a job. Really. I don't pay our rent with air."

"Whatever," he said. "You called in sick today. The whole thing could be a
front." He sat up and let me go.

I pulled myself to the head of the bed, curling my knees under myself,
huddling smaller, smaller, trying to be still. Pigeons cooed softly outside as a bottle
broke against the side of the building. A man outside yelled drunkenly, incoherently,
and the light was finally too bright to see.

Waking slowly, my eyelids fluttering against the afternoon light, I reached a
hand across the bed to Jesse. He was leaning back on his elbows, sunglasses on.
Sparrows chattered on the windowsill. He rolled over and turned to me, smoothing a
hand across my stomach.

"You look all thin again. You look like when I first met you. We should do this
shit more often."

"I'm not so sure about that." I leaned on one shoulder, my hair splayed into
spikes on one side.

"No, really, you were getting really fat. Every other girl I've dated has always
been a two, and you were a four. No man will ever want you if you're a four."

Oh, those Marie Callender's frozen dinners. Easy for him to steal, lately. And
so tasty. All that gravy packing on the pounds. I was usually proud of my body. *Look,
I may be a lunatic and a failure, but, hey, I have this crazy hourglass figure and a
nice ass.* It got me more validation than my degree had. I let it drop.

"Do you want a cup of coffee?"

"No, you know I don't drink that shit. What's wrong with you, haven't you
been paying attention?"

"I pay a lot of attention. Too much attention." I pulled the blankets up to my shoulders, staring at the lattice where the fabric had rubbed raw.

"Whatever." He got up, rolling through the dirty sheets, pulled his jeans on, and marched into the bathroom. I closed my eyes for a moment, then opened them briskly when I realized twenty minutes had passed. Poking my cold toes from the covers, I dropped onto the frozen, golden floor and crept across the hall. Past my painting of a trapeze artist with red velvet curtains, the gold tassels tangled and dirty. Past the dust bunnies ranged along the edges of the baseboard.

I set one hand on the bathroom door and said, "Baby?"

"What?"

"Are you okay?" I pressed the side of my face against the white wood.

"Look, fine, open the door if you want."

I did, and saw him limp against the clawfoot tub, the syringe on the toilet and the long line of my favorite red-striped scarf dashed with his blood. The glare through the window speckled his bare chest. He waved me away.

"Go out and get me a bagel, woman!"

I turned away. Walked to my computer and put on the Velvet Underground, just to taunt him. "Live your clichés, honeybunch," I whispered to myself. *I Found a Reason* came on, the guitar tumbling into the room in shy plinks, hanging in the sun that lit their lounge chair in bright oblong blocks.

Striding back to the bed, I sat down heavily. Pressing both hands into the mattress on either side, I thought about the wedding cake they we imagined, with white frosted cubes and fondant pigeons. I thought about the dress I had never bought, the dresses I had tried on at Ambiance, with their beadwork and iridescent sheen. I thought about the fact that I really looked terrible in white.

When I opened the office door the following Monday, Judith and Sally were going through the stacks of paper on my desk. I stopped behind the counter.

"Oh, look at this, this is unbelievable." Judith said. Sally laughed. I had taken to drawing comics on the computer paper, I was that bored. The one she held was about a one-night stand, I could see the outline of a leg thrown up. Next was a tiny book made out of yellow legal paper and stapled, containing a poem for Jesse, and purple highlighter kitty drawings. Next was a stack of address labels for the company with black streaks of copier ink across them.

"Oh, there you are! Well, I see you have an interest in arts and crafts. That's lovely. Knit at home. Are we not giving you enough work?"

"Um, sorry, so sorry. I won't do it again. Sometimes I run out of things to do."

"Well, then, ask one of us for a task. Tax season is approaching, and we are going to be needing 200% from you."

"Oh, and also," Sally said. "We organized your desk. You had a lot of past projects and loose ends lying around, and we tossed them."

"Thank you." I nodded.

On my lunch break, I pulled out my phone and began to dial the home number. MUNI rails sliced the sidewalk. Jesse needed to hear this.

He picked up right away.

"Hon, they found my comics! I'm so embarrassed." I pulled up in the sheltering steps of the Bank of America building, under columns cool with shade and stone.

"Well, fuck those cunts. Come home, right now. I swear to God, I've got, I've got…" There was a longer pause and a rustling sound. "I'm going to slit my wrists right here, if you don't come home. And I'm putting all of the mirrors and shit out with us, so they'll see your stash when they come to find me. Have a good time explaining that, girl." I stared at the crisp reflections of the carvings on the shale.

"What the hell? I have to go back to work, Jesse. I have to go back in ten minutes. Can this wait?"

"No, we have got to talk this out now."

The 38 Geary bus rumbled by, sending streams of exhaust into the air. "Jesse, this is really fucked up….but whatever. I'll be home. But don't do anything until I get there, I mean it."

"Late."

I snapped shut the phone and stared at the sun as it blazed over the rapid businessmen, cars and cabs and shadows of the bank's columns on the pavement. Setting one foot ahead of another, I trod down two blocks and began to slog up Battery Street to the office, piecing together what transparent excuse I could give. Wobbling on a Snapple lid, I shied back from the inevitable discomfort, the rupture in my professionalism I would have to cut. The truth was too impossible. I had passed a criminal and background check to get this job. I would say he was sick.

I burst through my door to see Jesse's hand on the bathtub. His greasy bangs emerged by the faucet, dribbling with soap stains and muck. I fell on my knees, both hands grasping the tub's edge, and said, "What the fuck are you doing?"

"What does it look like I'm doing, bitch? Having a bit of the old damp!" He lifted the razor blade we'd been using to cut lines. "Now take that back, or bye-bye!"

"Oh come on, you can't be serious." The blade was iridescent with white flecks and glare. Powder clung in a tight line along the edge, an edge I knew we both could barely keep from licking.

"Oh yes," he glared. "I don't fuck around. I was in the Navy. We don't fuck around."

His sunglasses lolled on the toilet as I stared down at his creased blue eyes. I rarely saw them. "I see. Well, sweetie, come on, I know there are some things you want to live for, think on it. Think, a twenty-bag of speed and a hot 18 year old, a nice bloody steak from Whole Foods, that next girlfriend you're going to have that's far thinner and has those "turned-up titties" and "teensy labia" that you talk about...come on, Jesse, you don't want to end it now. I'm not as good as you can get."

"You're shit."

"See, think like that and you'll be doing fine. You can move on." I gritted my teeth and pulled at his wet shoulders. He was naked under a daguerreotype of Louise Brooks.

"No! Fuck this, I'm going out," he said.

"Don't, I'm not worth it, really...come on, you're Jesse-cat, you're a prowler, a predator, you'll have foxy ladies and be Donny's right-hand man in no time."

"You're ridiculous."

"What do you expect me to do, sweetie, I'm trying to talk you out of killing yourself. Jesus." I pulled back the hula girl shower curtain. "We're just meant to live apart, I think. I need to be alone to think on what I've done. It wasn't right. I didn't give you enough. I was way too selfish." I knew I was lying, but at this point all that mattered was getting him out of the tub and away from the razor, away from the blood pulse beneath his wrists and the speed psychosis hovering in his eyes.

"That's right." His eyes snapped open. "You and your job, your friends, your partying. Get it straight. I should be what matters."

"I know, honey, I know. I work too much. I should've made you more of a priority. Believe me, you'll find a nice loyal girl who'll take care of you, maybe Bunny Scarlette's back in town, or Audrey has some time. Think on it. I'm too boring for you. I'm just a receptionist. Now, here." I eased my arm through the water with a silent splash, aiming for the blade.

He jerked up, ripping it through the water to hold it, grim, between us.

"Don't you!" he cried.

I leaned in further, pushing down his shoulder, and as he reeled, the hula ladies bearing silent witness as he yanked the razor by my wrist. Missed. I cringed back, slipping on the sodden tile. He lunged at out of the tub, and we grappled arm in arm for a moment until the razor flew free and skidded under the bathtub.

"Come on, sweetie, pumpkin, pie, come rest, come with me," I said, catching him and moving my hand down his back. He let me pull him into the bedroom, a skeleton against the curtains.

I laid him gently on the bed, and turned to the kitchen. Watching over my shoulder as he turned fetal, I opened a drawer and pulled out a handful of knives. My mother's set, a Christmas gift. I slid out of my shoes and padded to the door, leaving it open as I snuck out to the garbage chute. A ring of grime surrounded the rickety flap, opening out to a metal tube to the ground. Glancing around, I thrust the knives into the opening, wincing as they rattled down.

"Baby Pigeon?" said Jesse.

"Coming, coming," I said, locking the door behind me. I snuck back down the hall. He was crying, dripping on the blanket. Rattling through dusty shirts, I grabbed his stolen library books and glanced back at his body.

A cold gasp of indifference went flowing through me, as I touched the loneliness I knew lay ahead with the bright specter of the morning, greasy new heads on my pillow, a new life, full of whatever debauchery and joy I could discover in the wrought-iron scrolls and strobe-lit trolls of the city. As I threw black jeans and used works into a duffel bag, I knew that whatever last drops of bourbon would lay, vacant, in my glass, it would be worth the freedom to drink alone. I grabbed a last note he had written to me and stuffed it fiercely into the orange canvas, ripping finger-size holes as I willed myself to live past the ache, willed myself to wake up the next day and the next without that arm around me, that protection from the world's viciousness that beckoned me home. As I zipped the bag, watching the pigeons glower and shriek outside the window, the wind blew the ash away: the ashtray at my feet as clean as gardenias.

Chapter 4
but oh the night air

2008

"Nick, oh god, I have to download this one song, Poison, it's – "

"The band?" My boyfriend got up from his computer and walked over to mine.

"No, Bel Biv Devoe, it's early hip-hop, like, - "

"That's because hip-hop is gay."

"No, you noob, this is my jr. high dance song, like when you were eating Otter Pops."

"Use Soulseek."

"No, I hate Soulseek. It reminds me of Jesse.. I use Limewire."

"See, two out of three junkies agree, Soulseek is better than Limewire."

2005

I leaned over the man in my bed, Blake, and picked up the phone. It was 8:30 am and we were high, having stayed up all night talking about my romps and his rehab. Flights of sunlight flared across the hardwood floor as we lay there, naked, the sheets scrolling across our bodies. *He is a charmer*, I thought, taking in the somber eyes and, the wisps of russet hair over a high forehead. It was six months since I had kicked Jesse out, and the dance floor had yielded many a fine lay. He stared up at me and said, "I can't take responsibility for what happens, Lena, I mean, don't do this for me."

I stroked the side of his face. "I'm not doing this for you, Blake, I'm doing this because they're working me to death and I need a day off. I was going to do this anyways, you're just providing a nice little excuse for me."

I dialed.

"Hi Sally, this is Lena." My voice rose, questioning.

"Yes."

"I'm just calling in because I'm feeling really, really sick, and I'm going to be out today."

"Okay. I'll put the word out." She sounded oddly cheerful.

"Thank you." I set the phone down. The Jesus hologram above my bed blinked down. Blake curled up, wrapping himself around the pillow. I was probably fine, I decided, I had purchased a birthday card for the HR lady with my own money a couple of days ago, and felt that that should at least count for something.

We shared a long look, his nerves matched with my anxiety, reflected in dilated pupils. The sunlight warmed my shoulders.

"I'll be okay, hon, really. Come on, let's do another line and make out." I snaked a hand up to the Peaches CD on the bedside table. As the rhythmic taps of my library card began to break up the rocks, I drank in the metallic sweat of his body.

I snapped awake to my phone. The neon clock by the bed glowed 4:16, and for a moment I couldn't figure out what day it was. I pulled myself up on one elbow and realized, yes, it was Thursday, alright…shit. I reached up for my phone and snapped it open to hear Judith on the other end.

"Lena?"

"Yes, this is she."

"Okay, I've been trying to reach you all day, this is important; I'm calling to tell you that you are terminated from Devechio & Associates as of today." The brisk voice faded off as the ground dropped off from underneath me and all thought of appeal became impossible. Good Lord. He wasn't even all that cute. He was, in fact, gone. A slight indentation crushed the marshmallow bedsprings down. There were two cigarettes hanging diffidently from the ashtray.

I tried to answer. "Oh."

"Yes, we will be sending along your severance package and paperwork, and we would ask that you return your building pass and keys in the self-addressed envelope provided."

"Yes. Can I ask, but, what was it, what did I do?" A soft whimper of light wafted through my curtains, streaking the glossy wood. I prayed for a hefty severance check, maybe it was time for a NEA-sponsored sabbatical.

"Mrs. Devechio didn't really say anything. I don't really know, I'm sorry. Wait, are you going to be okay?" I was sniffling, as Judith fell into some semblance of humanity for a moment.

"I'll be fine. Thank you," I wavered.

"Are you sure?"

"No, really. Good luck, I guess."

"Good-bye," Judith said.

The phone fell out of my hand with such finality that I wondered that the windows didn't fall from their casings. The room was full of honey-infused sunlight, my pretty-boy was gone, I was alone, twenty-eight years old and unemployed, and for all the bravado I'd invoked I felt desperately lost for the moment. For perhaps a long moment. For perhaps many months of long moments, I couldn't know.

The thought of approaching thirty with no career and the Connect-four board of my orderly days now blown open to endless nights…this could be fun or terrifying. I would apply for unemployment and food stamps immediately, and downscale my vodka choice. Popov. The small bottle. I could always call my old temp agency, or start looking on Craigslist, but for the moment all I could think of were splats of water beetles crashing their way against the screens.

The firm was the financial teat that funded my indulgences, the miserable mode in which I pushed it all along. While the endless haze of internet browsing and free linguine was great, working sixty hours a week during tax season, with my ex snorting the profits, was not. Somewhere in those past years of safety pins and dumpster-diving, I had acquired a terrible work ethic.

Portland, 1996
In the basement,, watching a member of I Hate Computers doing an unplugged set, Mike strumming, "You hate your boss, she busts your balls, so you just consume and escape." Claps from the crowd, laughter from young mouths.

I was on the way to the liquor store a few hours later, and found a large, messenger-delivered envelope sitting in the lobby. I ripped it open. There was severance check for $4,449.91, a letter about 401K liquidation, a "how to" pamphlet on unemployment, and $1.24 in cash (the pennies slipped out onto the carpet, orange flecks on the blue). That must be for the birthday card.

I stared at the check, the blue paper wrinkling under my thumbs. This seemed impossible. I could live off this for months! Did this make sense? I suddenly felt guilty for failing them, in face of this final kindness.

I could buy a lot of coke for this.

I took off up the street for the Wells Fargo on Van Ness, intent on depositing this before I spilled a drink on it.

Back in my apartment, I opened the unemployment pamphlet. The approach seemed basic – apply for seven jobs each week, and enter their contact information into the spaces provided on the worksheet. Mail the worksheet in, and I would receive a check. The amount of the check depended on the amount I had been making previously. I did the calculations, and found that I would receive $354.00 a week. Not bad. I did the calculations again. That's $1,416.00 a month. Rent was $850. I would survive.

There is no moment like the present, and if you do enough drugs there becomes no moment that is not the present. The separately segmented hatches of memory, of days and moments passed away, just compresses and boxes out into that weird haze of where you left your car keys. There becomes this desire to not be ruled by it, and there becomes this desire to obtain more. Recreate. The science of leisure, of free time management. I was excited to start

Wavering in my room, I tossed from bed to the window, looked out the curving glass to the brick outside. The opposite denizen's apartments were cluttered and lit with warm light, echoing with the chatter of little parties. Glasses clinked with a shiver along my nerves. Should I or shouldn't I…. I leaned over to my computer, fiddled with the mouse, and put on a Brigitte Bardot album. There was a particular song on here…*Tu veux, où tu veux pas! Est-ce que c'est oui, où c'est non?"* A sprightly twinkle flowed through the room. I leaned back in the chair, picked up the phone, and scrolled to Donny's number. I did this every Friday, even without Jesse. More for me.

I dialed.

It trilled for a few moments, and then the message.

"Hey Donny, it's Lena. Give me a call, its 673-9920. Bye." I hung up and set the phone down. The glasses clinked loudly outside. I clenched my teeth, turned up the Bardot, and counted. It was usually twenty seconds.

Sure enough, after the twenty-sixth my phone began to sound. I snapped it open to hear: "Hey, what's goin' on?"

"Hey, I was just wondering if you could drop something by."

"Sure, what are you trying to achieve?"

"A forty."

"Alright, see you in half an hour."

"Awesome, thanks." I hung up, smiling. Meeting Donny was one of the few good things I had gotten out of my relationship with Jesse. None of this fumbling around with handfuls of cash slid under tables in the Burger King or whatnot…he just delivered.

I went to the dresser and pulled out a miniskirt and tights, grabbed a sequined butterfly blouse from a hanger, and picked up some pink heels. We were going to drop by the Rosetta later, and I was sure to pick up some ephemeral boy to while away the early morning fiend with. Staring down dawn, someone to talk to in those widening circles of more and now and always the now, the now!

I sat on the floor and put on lipgloss, my head throbbing. The phone rang.

"Hey, come meet me by that place," Donny said.

Swinging on a coat, I ran down the stairs to the lobby. The blue dome speckled with gilt stars bridged an octagon of columns, each bracketed with palms. I picked past the gates. Walking down the block, I saw a shadow in a blue Subaru. A wide grin. I grabbed the handle and pulled myself in.

"Hey, what are you up to tonight?" he said, giving me the bag. I carefully slid it in my clutch and clicked it shut.

"Oh, you know, there's this party, and this other party, I'm gonna check it out." Two twenties slid across the seat.

He tucked them in his pocket and nodded.

The building's star windows lit the stoop and a pile of take-out menus. I ran up the stairs and threw my purse on the bed, whisked up my Virgin Mary key, and pulled out the baggie. Full.

I plunged the key into the powder and took a deep sniff. A wave of pleasure rose through me, aching with electric thrill. This was what made it worthwhile, the sheer sensual joy of the vice, a habit so normalized by electroclash culture that a bag of coke was more an accessory than a sign of degeneracy. As long as I appeared proficient, I wasn't too worried about it. My goblet of vodka spilled a raspberry twinge through the air.

That night, there was an afterparty at the Adelaide loft. I stirred my gin and tonic, watching the bubbles rise and pop at the top of the glass. My hands were cold, a tremor due both from the meds and having finished the bag an hour ago. Four people got up and trooped out the door, and I watched them go blankly, knowing it was useless to follow. Whenever I had it I gave it away in a night, to whatever guy I had in my bed, or the million acquaintances I participated in this exchange rate with.

"Oh hi," said the bowl-cut boy sitting next to me, "You look upset."

"Oh, I'm fine, really, it's no big deal."

"Oh come on." He was smooth-skinned and olive, trimly cut into a black suit and tie.

"Well, okay, I lost my job today and I'm sort of trying to come to terms with it."

"Oh shit, what did you used to do?" His open brown eyes were so far from the preening I was used to.

"I worked at an accounting firm."

"You're an accountant?"

What a cute little thing.

"Oh god, no, I was a receptionist."

"Okay. But you got laid off – "

"Fired," I clicked my teeth.

"Oh shit."

"Yeah, so I'm just kind of figuring things out. It's a bit intense."

"Did you get unemployment?"

"I applied, and that's my ticket for the moment," I turned to him. "So here I am."

"Well...do you want some coke?" He smiled like a valentine.

"Sure." We got up and aimed for the door, weaving between heads and shoulders until the concrete expanse of the floor opened up. Clicking past the couches and piano, I realized the nail-nubs of my heels would remain bare for a long time to come...cobblers did not come cheap at volume. Whatever. I'd settle for a bump at this point, a pedicure was really pushing it.

"Here, Lena, let me get my friend," he said.

I realized I hadn't told him my name.

"You see, you see, there's something I have to..." He jogged back to the room, emerging a second later with a similar man wearing Lou Reed sunglasses.

I followed them bemusedly into the bathroom and leaned against the wall. I lifted one foot and spiked it against the pressboard wall, trying to look at least somewhat foxy.

"So you are?" I asked.

"Jay." He held forth a hand. Clean, warm, with trimmed nails. I shook it.

"Now, okay..." He took a piece of folded yellow paper from his pocket and proceeded to unroll it over the counter. It was roughly painted wood, likely erected when the loft was converted and most of these DIY adjustments were made. He grabbed a copy of SOMA magazine from the floor and began to carefully drop powder into a small pile.

I busied herself with his friend. "Hi, I'm Lena."

"Oh, I know." He nodded pertly. Acne flashed on freckles.

"Come on," I said, "This isn't the Matrix. You're not going to fetch me off to some mystical trans-Baudrillardian wonderworld, are you? Now, really."

"Here," said Jay, gesturing at me. I nodded and took the line, then looked around for an answer. After a sustained glare, he looked back up at me and said, "Oh? You had a question?"

"Come on."

"Right. Well, you know Jesse, right?" he said, jostling from one wall to another.

I stiffened. "Jesse. Yes, my ex. What – "

"Yeah," Jay said. "Jesse and Carl and I have been living in my van since you kicked him out of that place in the Tenderloin. I hear quite a bit about you."

"Great, I can only imagine." Wilt.

There was a soft rosy glow in his cheeks. "Yeah, We went past your apartment the other day, that old Moroccan-looking place, and rang the doorbell until the manager came out and kicked us out, and then we went down to Eddy and Hyde and scored some Oxycotins, and shot them in the back of the van."

"Fantastic. So should I expect to be assaulted? Needles in the mail? Should I take off for a couple weeks?"

"I don't know, I mean, he's pretty fucked up most of the time. He's got this amazing ability to tell which alleys downtown have outfits in them, and who's carrying, and what they'll front. Want another line?"

"Sure." I was beginning to wonder who was innocence and who was experience here. "I have to ask, how old are you?"

"Nineteen." He cocked his chin up, challenging. "Now I've heard from Jesse-cat that you were – ah – "

"A lady never tells," I laughed, "Okay, fine, twenty-eight."

"That's what I thought." Jay and Carl nodded at each other purposefully.

"But no, seriously, I have to know, like, how dangerous is he now, and what does he say about me?"

"Well, he goes back and forth," Jay said. "Sometimes its like, 'Oh, she's the most beautiful girl in the world,' and other times it's like, 'That fucking bitch, I'm gonna rip her tits out.'"

"Oh, that's lovely. Nothing like a psycho junkie. Party in his pants."

Jay put a firm hand on my shoulder. "It's okay, really, we can keep him busy."

"Oh yeah, like two skinny *minors* that I just met are going to fend off Jesse? I mean, he was in the Navy, he used to hit me, and once he almost bashed in my computer monitor with a hammer. He's dangerous."

They both seemed very calm. "I mean..." began Jay.

There was a heavy knocking on the door, and a man's voice. "Come on, I'm kicking all of you people out, I've got shit to do tomorrow."

"Okay, okay, we're out," Carl said, opening the door and shepherding us into the room. I was stranded in a verbal coma, aghast, as I fumbled down the steps with them and out onto the sidewalk.

Outside the sky was blue-white and a few pigeons were beginning to scrabble away at the dented concrete. An empty bus pulled up and pulled away, and a homeless woman wandered by, rattling a McDonald's cup from side to side. The Burger King next door was enclosed in folding gates, glimpses of flaccid plexi-lettuce visible through the black lattice. The orange sign of the descending BART station was dusted with soot. I looked around at the dirty swath of Market Street and realized suddenly what I wanted to do with my night.

I walked up to Jay's dark head, tapped him on the sleeve, and said, "Hey, do you want to get a cab?"

As Jay followed me in to my apartment, I watched his eyes widen at the painting of Jesse hung high.

"I thought you, like, didn't do anything."

"That's what Jesse calls it. This wasn't worthwhile to him. And, no, he didn't sit for it. I had another painting going of an old boyfriend, and he said that pissed him off, and I should change it to him. So I did."

"So you paint boyfriends."

"Basically. Sometimes girlfriends."

"Kinqué."

"Straighty."

He laid his lanky form across the pedicure chair, and picked at the vinyl.

"So, what's the kinkiest thing that you'd like to do?"

Half an hour later, I was tied to the bed with old stockings, and he was ramming his cock in and out of my drooling pussy. He stuck two fingers into my mouth and said, "Suck it, bitch, suck it, suck it like Jesse's cock."

Tasty. I could taste the nicotine on his fingers, and the sweetness of speed. Something candied, like fried plantains, squashing between his fingers in the hot afternoon.

I imagined Jesse, his come spurting forth in my mouth, his hands around my neck, palming my tits, wet.

A week later, I stared at the notice wheat-pasted to Taqueria Buenuel's doors,

THERE WERE FOUR MEN SHOT HERE DURING
THE WEEK OF MAY 9TH – 15TH
THERE WILL BE POLICE SURVEILLENCE
FOR AN APPROPRIATE PERIOD
PLEASE USE CAUTION IN THIS AREA

Watching the stationed cop car, I padded swiftly to the gate, trying for discretion in a black sweatshirt. I was just out on a friendly visit, I told myself, as the bell droned vacantly in the hall.

"Hello?"

"Hey, it's me." The door buzzed, and I climbed the stairs.

Donny was waiting. "Hey Le-na."

"Hey."

"You okay? You look a little skittish. Usually you're wasted." His face creased in a smile.

"Um, ha ha. No, what's up with the police, that really freaked me out." The guppies were clustered like barbed wire against the rugged gravel.

Donny moved heavily to the back room and settled down on his chair. "Lena, the police are here because people died, they are not here to fuck with you. Really."

"Okay. God, I hope so." Teeth tight.

"But, you have to know, if that was you that got shot out there, there would be the FBI out and everything. But since it was four black men, they send one cop car to the taqueria and that's it."

"Fuck."

"Yeah, so don't feel bad about being white, but just think about that." Donny nodded and turned to his Tupperware.

"Shit. Okay."

"Don't sweat it. So, you want a forty?" He began to scoop the powder from the plastic, setting the bag on a scale.

"Yeah. But yeah, there's something else, though."

"What?"

"I just heard Jesse's lurking around the TL, and I wanted to ask you that please if you see him, don't tell him that you know me, that you've seen me, god, that you see me at least once a week. I'm trying to stay as far away from him as possible."

He rolled his eyes. "Oh, that guy. Well, last time I saw him, I told him to never come around again. He'd been hanging out and asking me for fronts, acting all fucked up like he was on speed, it was no good. That was a while ago, though. But, yeah, if I see him, I don't know you." He handed me the bag.

"Thanks. I really appreciate it." I said, tucking it in my makeup pouch.

"We're cool." Donny nodded in farewell, and I padded out the door to the long hallway and the street, taking care to look away as I glided past the police headlights. I drifted carefully up Mission Street to 18th, past Vietnamese meat markets, vacant bar neon, and the final burst of paralytic traffic, as I lifted a hand, lightly, for a cab.

I jostled up against Audrey, bashed in by the cavalcade heading into the Rosetta. Thrown up against Brady, she smiled gleefully as he fell past me, spilling a drink on my shoulder. Loud electro jangled from the speakers, mixing into disco covers and driving techno.

Drink obtained, I followed Audrey back through the crowd to the bathroom. Pushing the door open slightly, we muddled into the crowd of tweakers and vultures and settled against the light green wall. Pale ivy twined down like a noose.

Pulling off my scarf, I said, "You know who gave me these hickeys, Audrey? A nineteen year old boy! Nineteen! I'm nine years older than him! That is so not cool."

"Nineteen, huh. You still got it, then, I guess," Audrey said, pinching her lips.

"They keep getting younger and younger, hon...Johnny, twenty-two, Blake, twenty-one, Bret, twenty, Jay, this kid, nineteen, that hot boy, Louis, that I hung out with at the Rosetta last night, the one who actually looked good with no shirt on....I can't do this anymore..."

"Come on, Lena, sure you're twenty-eight, but if the young men still want you then you've got to be doing something right."

"You're gratifying my ego, darling, but you remember when I didn't dye my hair for a couple months and you were actively pulling me aside at parties and saying hon, get the Revlon...it was salt and pepper, I'm serious."

"Lena!"

"What?" I looked up.

"Calm the fuck down. Here, take a Valium." Audrey said, passing me a blue pill.

"Okay." I took it with light fingers and gulped it down with water from the sink.

"Better?"

"Yeah?" I said. The ivy spiraled tighter near the mirror, which had been chipped off in two-line flakes. An emaciated boy with a red silk scarf was rocking back and forth from his perch on the countertop and clapping. His stubble and scruffy blond hair stuck out like translucent wires, belaying nights blurred into gritty vodka dawns. It was very loud yet very still. I leaned against the wall and let the full wave of the Valium take hold.

Later that night, I slumped on the black leather couch in the back of the Rosetta, breathing deeply and letting the flood of pharmaceuticals blend with the alcohol in my system. It was oddly peaceful back here, dancers packed in tight under the strobe, strictly trimmed heads almost closing in above me, yet my own private bubble down here in the dark. I couldn't shake the feeling of transgression. Certainly Blake had been youngish, but it hadn't seemed relevant. Jay, however, that troubled me, and for all that I had an unspoken pact to delve into my inner darkness this month, that did not involve pulling in innocent, fresh-faced, teenage…junkies? Oh Lord. Perhaps I should have taken two.

A body hurtled off of the dance floor and onto the cushion.

"Blake?" I straightened up. Rehab-boy with the somber eyes. Another ex-junkie to play patty-cake with. Could I collect the whole set?

He pulled his shoulders forwards to lean on his knees. "Oh hey, Audrey said you were somewhere around here. She seemed a little pissed."

"She's been like that a lot lately. I don't know, she's kind of a cold person. You know, when you have a friend and you wonder if she just needs a well-dressed doll to carry to bars, but isn't actually into an emotional attachment."

"That sucks."

"Well of course it does. But she gave me a Valium tonight, so at least I'm having a good time." A keyboard crescendo rose through the speakers.

"Lucky little you."

"I wish I had one to give you, but they were hers and I'm not about to ask." I pulled back, giving him a once-over. "So, what have you been up to since that horrible morning? As I recall you took off while I was sleeping, ahem?"

"Sorry about that. You were out cold and I had to go to a client's house for some web work."

I clucked my tongue against my teeth. "Well. I got fired."

"Oh shit!" A spangled heel flew up from the dancers.

"So not cute. I'm on unemployment for the moment, and actually I'm having a pretty great time being free and all that, but it's still kind of sketchy."

"I'm so sorry… What are you going to do?"

"You know what, all I really want to do *right now* is get a bottle and go sit somewhere quiet, it's impossible to carry on a good conversation in here."

"I can handle it. Do you want to come over? I live pretty near here. Actually, above here."

"How terribly convenient." I lurched up from the couch. Gripping the doorframe cautiously, I waited, watching Big Al twirl under the streetlight. The cigarette-spotted concrete shimmered with each patter of his sneakers, turning, turning, his grey t-shirt stretched tight, his arms pointed above his head, his goateed chin bent upwards to the moonlight. I watched as he came to a thunderous stop next to a man with horn-rimmed glasses, amid a smattering of applause.

I quickly took in the gist of Blake's new apartment, 15-foot walls furnished in all-IKEA from the candleholders to the couch. I tapped a heel on the spare concrete floor, pure dot-com pre-fab live-work. It reminded me of my old place.

> Crucial, the differences of meaning to the word loft.
>> 1.) The mythical large, no-walled space, must be in the glamorous industrial district of either New York, San Francisco, or Los Angeles.
>> 2.) The "Loftaminium" or post-modern condo, a real estate trend.
>> 3.) The loft-bed, a platform for sleeping erected to save space.

"I sleep up there," Blake said, pointing at a loft over the kitchenette.
 "What about your roommate?"
A head popped up from the couch.
"What the fuck, guys, I've got to work tomorrow."
I glanced at Blake.
"C'mon, man, meet Lena."
"Look, some people do work on Fridays. We don't all get to go the bar and shake-a-tail-feather."
"Can you move to the-"
"The fucking bunk-bed! Call it! It's a bunk-bed!"
"Should I...?" I mentally counted the bills in my purse. Cab fare home was about $5.
"Fucking fine, whatever." The guy got up and lumbered over to the ladder, slinging his way upwards.
When his foot disappeared, I whisked the paper bag off the pint of gin. "Do you have any ice?"
"Oh, sure." Blake toddled to the kitchenette and knelt down by the mini-fridge. I trailed after, surveying his shelves of cup-of-noodles and tortilla chips. "Hey, check this out," he said. "Star ice-cubes."
"Gotta love the IKEA" I laughed. "One-stop shopping."
He looked sheepish. "I know it's not the most ironically bohemian way to do things, but whatever, it's easy. Urban Outfitters is way spendy."
"It's true."
"Swedish minimalism isn't far from that fifties modern shit, I can pretend."
He passed me a drink.
I draped myself over the couch, imagining what that guy had been dreaming. I lowered my eyes and sipped the drink slowly, looking up at him through my eyelashes. Watching Blake as he settled, coltish, into the cushions, I felt alternate

waves of pleasure to have such a lovely to fuck, and a bit of fear for when the money ran out.

There was nothing that could be done about it now, though, the final step was irreversible, and indeed all I could do was embrace my headlong government-funded joyride for all of the sweat-tossed sheets and moments of euphoria it might yield. Perhaps somewhere here, somewhere amid all the stained staircases and bitter vodka dawns, the violet-soft skin and the thrill-skids of a cab at last call, somewhere here there would be something worth finding.

I dipped my brush in the burnt sienna and carefully began to add it to the blob of white paint. Taking a daub of yellow ochre, I eased it into the pile and dipped my worn brush in the turpentine. A quick rinse in the linseed oil, and I took a swipe of the taupe and began to fill in the face on my canvas.

Painting was something I did when I couldn't do anything else, when I felt stuck and despondent and a pathetic waste of flesh. It always brought me to a higher level, where I could do something meaningful and productive, and was no longer just a kitten between the sheets or a wizard at scoring drugs. At times I was so removed from myself that I didn't know how to come back, and this always grounded me, brought me into intimate contact with the exact shade of cadmium red light to be shaded in on the girl's left cheekbone. The details, they became exquisite when I really focused.

Blending rouged tones into the chin, neck, and jaw of the self-portrait, I sighed with relief. Marlene Dietrich trickled from the computer. I could smell the acrid fumes of the turpentine, feel the comforting slickness of the linseed oil on my fingers. Linseed oil was one of my favorite smells, a trigger dating back to my high school boyfriend and his art lessons in the poolhouse with Bob Dylan and black coffee. In college it began to go somewhere.

1996

I teetered on a ladder in the Paradox Café, hanging a piece. The opening was that night, the first of several that year. My hands gripped the black fur frame, a woman smoking a cigar roughed out in yellows and purples. A plastic gun was hot-glued to the left side.

Crouching on the floor, I could feel the muscles in my legs twinge and ache. I ignored them as best I could. With the newspaper spread out on the floor and the many tubes obsessively lined up, I was doing the best that I could. Staring at the plum curtains, I felt the scar on my nose and sighed. Although my tiny apartment was now swept and tidied, there was still an echo of Jesse, a certain crunch of loose tobacco that would shudder across the floor from time to time. I anxiously swept again, but the shoe-tap indentations on the wood could never, ever be smoothed.

1997

Sitting in my linguistics professor's office, I clenched my knees together under the vinyl mini-skirt and watched him as he touched the pill bottles, my pill bottles, edging the image of a white-haired woman in a leopard print halter top. They alternated with cigarettes. My roommates had tugged on the menthols, called them a "waste of tobacco," pulling some off. I had been up late the night before with hot glue-gun repairs.

"How much would you like for this?" he asked.

My eyes widened. I really couldn't imagine. "$100?" It seemed like a lot of money.

He looked up at me and smiled. "I'll write you a check."

I sliced in the outlines and shadows with a thin brush swathed in blue and burnt umber, tracing the nose and creases around the eye. These lines would be obscured soon enough, but it was important to put them in there, to at least draw in the definition so it did not blur into a morass of peach and brown.

"Oh, the fun part, the fun part," I muttered, wiping the tiny brush in a turpentine-drenched cloth and dipping it in the white. Cautiously dabbing in the eyes, I glanced up at my own briefly, and strained not to smear. Pulling out the burnt umber from a pile of browns, I squeezed a tiny blot onto the plate I was using as a palette, and loaded up the brush. As I knew that the miniature cityscape behind the figure was obsessive in every window and murky rooftop, I had to get it just right.

Biting my lip, all thoughts of Jesse and pills and aching, coked-out mornings behind me, I spiked the pupils in tiny dabs, following the brown with the iris. A tiny spec of white for reflection, and they stared back at me, awake. I always felt the eyes were when the painting became human, whether reproachful or benevolent, staring off the wall as silent witness.

The end of "Lola" dripped soothingly across the room, followed by silence. I got up to switch the CD, stretching my stiff legs and back. A series of clicks ricocheted through my spine. Stepping back, I took a long look at the painting. The hair still had to go in there, streaky black, but that would be easy with a little galkyd gel. The background was filling in slowly; the grim skyscrapers and endless buildings upon murals, upon windows, upon warehouses. My figure was hiding in a mass of masonry, the head and shoulders clear and the rest spilling behind me as I walked treacherously through the avenues.

Chapter 5
limone

I strode out the Rosetta door into the pockmarked thrill of Sixth Street. Gnarled men lurched by, waving watches to sell, a woman in flip-flops ran through the crowd that had gathered in a Marlboro haze to pose. Jay was standing in a cone of streetlight, his white shirt open to a brown chest he shaved daily. The prickles under my hand with the just-hatched softness of him. Brand new, too new, like a fresh Lego set still smelling of plastic bags and clean. His flatironed hair was crowned with a soldier's cap, his jeans flared just-so, his boots pointed and shined.

For a homeless boy he sure dressed well. Enough disco-dollies in the crowd allowed him showers. He dubbed his look "gutter mod."

Smiling slyly, I ambled up to him and waved a hand in front of his eyes.

He flipped his hair, "Oh hey, Do you want to go inside?"

"Sure." I turned. He followed idly. The warmth of bodies pressed us in, the glitch and clench of the beat tumbled from the speakers. I pushed myself voraciously through the shoulders and elbows, falling against the stucco wall, waving to someone I couldn't see.

Limone poured herself through the crowd in a satin blouse and collapsed against the wall. "Lena! I've been looking for you." Her lips were parted, her hair spiking off, her mauve concoction drooping off one shoulder.

"Oh sure, what do you need?" I said.

"I need to talk to you about something, but not here," Limone said. "Do you want to come over tomorrow? We could make drinks before the bar, do a little pre-partying." She curved her lips upwards in a smile.

"Oh, sure. Delightful," I said.

"Cool. You still have my number, right?"

"Yeah, yeah, it's in my phone."

Jay sidled up and leaned next to me, saying, "Jesse asked how you were today."

"Oh god. That's alarming. Did you know he used to want me to take down those kabuki drag queen photos in my room because he said they made his friends think he was gay? Living with his girlfriend and he's paranoid of being gay!" I waved a hand over my shoulder and laughed. "Like I would mind."

"Lame," Jay said. Audrey came fluttering by, all pouts and preening, and disappeared behind the DJ booth. She didn't look back.

A soft hand jolted Pabst over my shoulder as I answered. "Yeah, and then when I kicked him out I found all sorts of crazy porn on my computer. I mean, sure, we used to look at some of it together, he had this whole story going about how he used to be a storyboard artist and he needed to keep his skills up by drawing from the human form."

"Oh, ain't that convenient…"

"Tell me about it! Kind of like the uncle who lived in Oakland, where he had supposedly left his storyboarding portfolio, and then when we tried to call him or find him because I wanted the jackass to get a job, he couldn't remember his name or address."

"Huh. That whole repressed thing makes sense, though," Jay said. "I remember this one time he was down on the floor of the van shooting speed and jacking off, and I had just shot mine and was lying back when his hand shot out and grabbed my crotch."

"Aha!" I said. "What did you do?"

"I just pushed it away, and then he would deny it up and down later when I called him on it."

"How funny." I ran a finger along the wet edge of my glass, looking at Jay through my eyelashes. He set his drink down on a ledge and leaned into me, all awkward elbows. I smiled and snaked an arm around his waist.

"Did I tell you my favorite movie is *The Graduate*?" he said impishly.

"That's fabulous," I pulled him close. "Mine's *Cougar Club*. Shall we...ah...go to the little boy's room?"

Thankfully no one was in line, as we snuck in to a stench of urine and mirror-laced graffiti of every band known to man. I ran my hands down his sides, taking in each rumpled caress of Goodwill blazer, each dewy flush on his cheeks as he grabbed my chain belt and pulled me against the sink. I slid up the porcelain, jeans damp, and kissed him hard, resting my forearms on his shoulders and ignoring the roars of bass outside.

His skin was soft as un-popped bubble-wrap, but he was smaller, weaker, conquerable through my legs over his shoulders or nails scraped down his side. I could have him for my own if I tried, perhaps to halt the Jesse-hurt that was still spinning through me. I thrust my tongue into his ear and smiled as I felt his body tense and squirm. He was listening.

An old woman was hunched in the Chronicle kiosk, staring at me with solemn black eyes. I shifted, uncomfortable, as the woman tossed a paper into the air and it shredded into fluttering sheets that wafted into puddles and walls. The Tenderloin's Clairmont Hotel was shedding intermittent lights from a glaringly sterile cracked-out lobby. Huddled figures darted and shuffled in front. I strode across the pitted street, past the Thai restaurant that spoke gentrification with its cucumber salad. Finally, the neon of the New Century shone dashing glitter-flecks of pasties and darting thighs, lighting up the sidewalk for a few moments. I tried not to look, the thick-necked bouncers lurking in cheap suits, but the luminescence of the mirrors and girlie posters drew my eyes nevertheless. Stripping. It was a financial option I would prefer not to think about. But one I might come to.

Perhaps I could eat less, pare down the hors d'oeuvres to only four crackers a day. Or three. I had already found that I could feed myself on one can of refried beans a day, half at noon when I awoke, and half before going out. Cutting down my drug intake was not an option.

I drifted over the glass-scattered pavement to a squat block of apartments. I reached up and dialed #440, Limone's place.

There was an echo of fuzz like television snow, and her voice chimed, "Lena?"

"I'm here..."

"One sec." The buzzer rang and I pushed the gate open quickly. The second door was heavier and required all my weight as I fell into a dank room with antiseptic green walls. I strode through the lobby under the stale hum of the yellow lights, and climbed up a rattrap of staircases.

Limone opened the door with a snap. "Hey! Come on in."

We sat on her bed beneath a line of Edie Sedgwick postcards. On an altar by the bed, dried roses melded with three rusted keys and a statue of St. Jude. She handed me a glass of red wine. I relaxed instantly.

"So, dear, how's Architect's?" I asked.

"Oh, god, well, didn't you hear, Audrey got sacked..."

"Really? What did she do?" I could imagine a few things.

"Well, you know, it was one of those – not professional enough – things. Plus, she was really cunty to the owner about her new extensions, said they were, I believe the word was, 'stripperly.'"

"Oh damn."

"Lena, hey, I need to ask you," Limone said, tugging at my sleeve. "You know that guy you get your stuff from, could I have his number? I want to be able to get a bag for Saturday."

"Oh, sure, just don't tell a million people, he's trying to keep things kind of quiet. It's really no big deal, though." I reached into my red alligator clutch and pulled out my phone. "Okay, Donny, it's 732-8855."

She input the digits to her Nokia and set the phone down. Two fingers crept up into my lap, and swept across my stomach. "Could I ask..."

"But of course." I set the mug of wine down and curved into her body. With my other hand, I clicked the purse open and rummaged around to the secret pocket. I pulled out a fresh gram.

"Awesome."

"Do you have a surface?"

Grinning, she lay down on her back and slid open her shirt. Small, pert nipples, pierced. I lay down a line between them.

"You always were resourceful." I said.

"Girl scout motto."

Rolling a twenty tightly, I leaned down and sniffed the radiant powder. A chunk caught in my throat, and I leaned back, a hand on her warm stomach, to feel the frisson of pleasure.

"Oh God, I can't believe I've known you since college, and we, like – " I babbled.

She looked up at me, "My turn." I bent and licked the last specks from her chest.

My neckline was below-tits already.

Limone pulled the silver rayon apart, cut two lines on my collarbone with her debit card. She took them and kissed her way down to my stomach, pulling my top down as she went. I didn't mind, my hands were wild in her spiky black hair, along her narrow body, folding around her tiny perfect ass.

"Dolly, I have so got the toy for you…" she said.

"Did you go to Good Vibrations again…naughty bunny!"

"No, it's not the rabbit, it's this other thing. One sec."

She leaned over to a cardboard box under the bed, pulling out a blue vibrator and a tube of budget Walgreen's lube.

"Yums! Have you got the blow?" I said. Key to keep the momentum.

"Wait…wait…" Limone fumbled in the sheets. I sat up, adrenalin mounting, powder on my nose and nipples…

"Oh shit…we lost the drugs!!!" Limone yelped.

"Fuck!!!"

"Wait…" She pulled the baggie out of her hair.

"Oh, thank God." I stared into the mirror she had mounted at the head of the bed. Always prepared.

We slid soft to soft, my hands finding her hips, daring to part her lips and feel the hot wetness of her clit. I put the finger to her mouth and she sucked. She flicked the vibrator on and teased me with it, climbed behind me, half-strangling me, and licked my tongue as she plunged the blue toy into my pussy. I moaned, wet.

The vibrator tumbled out of her hand as she fell into the sheets. I gasped, drenched in pleasure, pulling my face up from the reflection in the mirror. White Christmas lights warred with the careful dawn light.

"Just like old times." Limone said. She pulled herself up on one elbow, black hair sticking out in all directions; pale skin looking as polished as first foundation.

"You're magnificent." I said from the bed.

She smiled and tucked the vibrator into the cardboard box with the blindfold and condoms. The soft sheets were pulling us down. She draped an arm around me and pulled me closer, so they we were nestled like two baby sparrows. The blind dawn seeped through the curtains as I closed my eyes.

"Here, pour me another glass of that," Brady said, holding out his holly-twined Christmas mug for another mimosa. We had been up drinking for hours, chasing cocaine with sips of André Brut, the cheapest champagne possible at Geary Liquor and Deli. Rapping the edge of the bag against the "Death Before Disco" CD, Brady carved up another couple of lines and held them out to me.

"But of course." I dipped and sniffed up the first, passing him back the CD with its cracked plastic over the strobe-light's flare. A slender line of white bisecting gold and blue. The coke was salt on plaster, I sucked it up and passed him back the surface, where he finished it off and set it back on his table. We were in Brady's apartment, a small, octagonal lair with a burgundy drape over the bed, and a silver gelatin portrait of a man from behind, bending over, his gaunt tailbone visible over a black drape and wasted legs.

"That's me," Brady said. "Yeah, this friend of mine wanted to take pictures of me, so I let him, and this is how it ended up."

"Wow. It's so…severe. Are any of them more…cheerful?"

"Cheerful? Yeah, right. Well, okay, I'll show them to you. They're actually pretty good." Ducking with pride, Brady pulled a large portfolio from his closet, wrenching it clear from layers of fake fur. Throwing it on the floor, he lifted the first page and showed a portrait of himself in a black velvet jacket and eyeliner, loitering past chain link fences and stained asphalt.

"Oh, that's awesome. I like that," I said, paging through the huge prints. Capturing his hollowed eyes and flair with the makeup brush, Brady had the dark glamour of a silent film star. The gleaming photography paper lit his face in celluloid. I paged further, until I came to the one of him from behind, kneeling. I closed the folio quickly.

We all had our moments. Our subconscious yawns to the inner ache. I felt them on my canvases too. Though I usually tried to hide. But from the camera one cannot hide, and I admired so thoroughly Brady's desire to put his most vulnerable moment on his wall. That was true honesty. That was intimacy with the inner self. I wished I could approach that, as I hid in submission and tried to lose myself in weakness. There was no grace in being weak. I opened my eyes again and stared at Brady's portrait. I admired that more deeply than I could say.

"Here, do you want to do some sleeping pills?" he said, brandishing a prescription bottle. I took it without a glance.

"Sure, how do you want to do these?"

"Well, we could snort them. I like that better, because then it just hits you really fucking quick."

"Sure. I'm still on sabbatical"

He laughed.

Shaking out a pill and holding it with his library card, Brady reached for the lighter on the coffee table and began to smack the card with increasing ferocity. White powder spilled. Brady lifted his card and began to spread it out, laying out two lines and holding one out to me. I took it, and settled into the bed next to him.

"Nice, nice, very nice. So…dreamy…"

"But of course. I mean, come on, this is serious shit. Not Nyquil. It's one of my prescriptions."

"What's it for?"

"I'll tell you later. It's kind of…personal, you know." A cast of sadness spread over his face. He stared at the photographs on the carpet. I nodded. Lying back on his bed, I shivered and scratched at my tube top.

"Here, do you have, like, a shirt or something I could wear? This thing is a bit much, and I don't want to go back to my place just yet."

"Oh, totally." He got up, and rummaged around in his dresser. Pulling forth a wad of red polyester, he held it out.

"Don't look," I giggled, straining off my gold sequin top and whisking on the shirt. Lying back on the futon, I pulled the tapestry over us and reached out to him.

He raised his eyebrows. "Okay, sure, neighbor cuddling, I'm not averse. But no fooling around, you remember what happened last time." He crawled onto the bed.

"But of course." I threw an arm over his shoulders. I was immediately taken with how frail he was, his tinker-toy arms held together with wires and strings. I cradled him, his body a butterfly under the immense weight of the blankets, the maternal warmth of mine, the jitter and the teetering twinge of the pills. As a slow, warm breath overtook us, we wavered into sleep.

I followed Limone through a hall to the bedroom, sitting down beside her on the paisley sheets. She pushed back the duvet, and lifted a white-scraped mirror off the bed. She swept up two lines with a health insurance card, and nodded at me.

"Awesome."

"That's kind of what I wanted to talk to you about. You remember the Donny thing?"

"Honey, I see him twice a week."

Limone giggled, "So yeah, I've been thinking about going into business with this."

"You mean dealing?"

"Yeah! It'll be great," she said.

"Great is not the word I would use."

"Oh come on, I stand to make a lot of money, you've seen Donny's new apartment. I could get the hell out of here and do a bunch of free blow along the way." She gestured around to the cracked vanity mirror framed by faded bulbs, the empty pints of vodka scattered with spray-in-shampoo and pomade.

"But aren't you afraid of…" I broke off.

"I can totally do this," Limone replied. "I've talked to Donny, and he said that since you don't want to do it – and, honey, I would really recommend that you work with me here, you have no job and you stand to make a lot of money...which you need right now."

I sighed. I did. I knew that my financial situation, though currently okay, would decay if I kept going at this rate. In terms of morality, legality, whatever, it was a big sloppy blot of randomness and advantage. Yet I had always been proud of not shoplifting, although I appreciated the benevolence of friends who did. There was a subtle – nay, blatant - hypocrisy in accepting stolen gifts from braver friends. All of Jesse's blood-rare steaks. All of those free drinks from bartenders who liked my tits. Similarly, having a coke habit while refusing to hook anyone up or deal was, if not exactly hypocrisy, a bit suspect to my morality of convenience. But the thought of ten to twenty was enough. Much more the fact that I knew Donny had a gun or two in that apartment, and he had told me one night that he would pop someone if enough money was involved.

"I don't know," I stuttered. "I just...can't. I'm afraid of jail. Can we say assrape?"

"Oh come on, you won't get caught," Limone said firmly.

"You really never know." That was always a point of contention, as dealers rose and fell and the hunger continued, does anyone ever actually get caught? Of everyone I knew, perhaps two dealers had been apprehended, but no small-time, half-gram in the compact girlies twittering onward to the afterparty. That was somewhat comforting. But it was possible.

"I won't get caught. I'm too much of a lady. They will never even suspect. I mean, come on, do I look like a drug dealer?"

I surveyed Limone's spiked black hair, silver tube top purchased in a recent London excursion, vintage snakeskin heels, and said, "Mmm, no."

There was a long pause as she cut two more.

I clenched my teeth and felt blood beneath my gums, watching Limone's collarbone shimmer over the acetate. Skin lights like birds in flight, like ivory petal wafting from a shrub, tracing the highlights on her arms. Another line slammed into my bloodstream as the depleted vanity mirror shrugged out its last, the glare flaring out with a pop.

I lounged on the couch at a warehouse in SOMA, watching people come up the stairs. Narrow columns held up the roof, with mod lamps casting blue dots on the heads below. Red sheets divided the rooms. Little privacy. I crossed my legs so as to show them off to better advantage, and leaned back into the cushion. Brady came wandering by, his ruffled shirt untucked and hair awry, and thumped down next to me.

"Hey, my dear, have you seen Limone?"

"That's what everyone's asking tonight; she's the girl of the hour even more than what's-is-name – oh, what is his name, Alex or something?"

"Oh, that guy from The Imperatives?"

"Yeah, he's been lurking by the bathroom in all his little rockstar glory looking for girls to hook him up." I smirked. I had a bag already, and felt smug in my solid connection.

Brady laughed. "I bet if Alex tried you'd go for it!"

"Don't doubt my virtue!"

"Virtue? Oh that's a good one. I'll have to ask Jay about that. Or Blake."

"Don't laugh. Jay's my honey," I pouted.

"He's your child."

I recalled his eager eyes when I made him a quesadilla, sitting cross-legged and pert. Lifting the mushrooms to his plate, the grease passing his anxious eyes, I felt motherly, somehow. Protective. For all that that shit was crazy easy to cook.

"Hey!"

"Yeah, but do you ever wonder if he's using you?"

"For what," I asked, "my meager unemployment check? Fish sticks and vodka, it's a date!"

"I don't know, drugs, connections, someone to get him into clubs for free?"

"Oh, I don't know, if so, it's a mutually beneficial sort of thing. He's got a lovely body."

"That's your call. I would just say watch out, though."

"Oh, sure. But at this point, you know, It's all about pretty toys. Drugs, booze, and boys, is there anything wrong with that?"

"I guess not..."

'Yeah, you know, and then I paint on alternate Tuesdays. Just to keep a foot-in."

"Okay, darling, I know. I just see you out here, and I know you have so much to offer, and you're just wasting it..."

"Brady, I have been working my ass off for years in that office, and I finally have a chance to rock out with my cock out, and I'm going to take it. Cougar playgirl, this is my moment."

"Let's find that bebi, then."

Snaking through the skinny ties and tiny handbags, we emerged by the door. Brady looked quizzically at me, and I opened it. Voices sprang through the stairwell. We descended.

"Limone?" he said.

"Y – Yeah?" her voice shook.

"It's just us. Are you okay?" he said. She was huddled in the stairwell, clenching a phone to her ear. A ziplock baggie of coke was sitting on her red-flowered lap, the crisp white cotton giving way to black arcs like telephone wires.

She turned dilated eyes towards us and said, "I hate this, I hate being responsible for shit. Everyone keeps asking me for more, and I've run out and I keep having to call Donny, and I think he's getting mad at me."

I moved quickly to the lower stair and said, "Honey, you don't have to do this, you're doing them a favor. Think, you're doing the whole – I hate to say scene, but you know what I mean, you're doing them all a favor. You can stop and say you're tapped out for the night if you want to."

"Yeah, I know, but this was, my plan, my job, I want to do this, you know?"

"I'll – um – could I have one?" Brady said, moving down to sit with us.

"Yeah, yeah, of course," Limone answered. "It's like that, I mean, drugs are for sharing, and I want to spread the joy and make everyone happy and stuff, it's just that people get so fiendy and start demanding things, and that's when I get freaked out." She pulled a key from her purse and began to dispense.

The key stopped under my nose, and I sniffed deeply. After waiting so long it fell through me with scintillating sparks. I blinked, feeling like I wanted to talk, really talk, through the irksome barriers of formality. I looked at Limone's anxious eyes and tried.

Three voices – began.

But as the words spiraled out of me I felt them evasive, suspect, the false intimacy the drug produced reducing me to promises and confessions I knew to mistrust. After too many dawns spent spilling to gushing randoms, I knew. The mark of a professional was one who could do a bump and stare back with the glassy eyes of one who feels nothing at all.

As the party spilled out onto the sidewalk, Limone, Alex, Brady and I wandered up the street towards the Eagle.

The same leather bar across from my old loft, I remembered, seeing the trysts from below my bedroom window, and thinking, yow, I'm really in San Francisco! I see flyers for circuit parties and the power exchange all over the place! What can I do to get invited to parties like this?

It was sticky and hot that evening, the black leather slab pushing aside as we streamed in past red lights to a table in the back. The grooved wood slid under my fingers as I watched Limone smile at Alex, feeding him bumps under the table. The Imperatives had DJ'd at the Rosetta that night, and were becoming phenomenally popular. It was crucial, as in all these cases, to act as if you were so blasé that their celebrity didn't phase you, you were simply so used to being around rock stars that a pretty face and a guitar was not instant panty removal. In many cases having cocaine was instant boxer removal. I had spent enough time listening to the egos of aspiring musicians – one lover had actually said to me, "I think...no, I know I am the best guitar player in the Northern Hemisphere." I brought him home for Christmas when I was 19 and he left town in the middle of the night.

At this point I was well-aware that we were all playing specific social games, and Limone's I didn't mind. Beauty, pleasure, adventure, notoriety…it was all disposable, our ticket was youth and sheer will.

I was highly amused to come home one morning to find a pretty British boy in my bed who claimed to be in The Edwardian Stallions. Thinking this was much better than anything the Tooth Fairy had ever brought me, and the Easter Bunny either, I followed that to its end and moved on. He did have lovely hair.

Now, they're the stories I don't tell my boyfriend, the evenings forgotten in the web of flesh. There seems to be a unity, a continuity to all of it
I think it comes from the beginning.
When I got to Reed I was a frisky and nubile little wretch with a blue shag and a miniskirt and no idea how to use them. The pines were wet and mysterious to my first acid flashbacks; I wandered through the dour brick buildings and gargoyles with a vague hint that wearing the shortest skirts possible might find me a better evening activity then writing obsessive letters to my high school boyfriend. The whole dating process was mysterious; our courtship had consisted of him following me home on the bus to Denny's and us painting each other semi-nude.
Somehow I thought that we had excised that pesky virginity one candle-lit night in the poolhouse. He said he didn't want the responsibility, but when I insisted and handed him the Trojan, he put it on, thrust, and retreated, sweaty and panting. I lay there against the filthy sheets and thought – so that's sex? That's what all of reading my parent's porn mags, and the Clan of the Cave Bear are all about? Somewhere I missed ecstasy. Maybe it comes later.
Fast forwards six months: I was sitting at dinner at the Bistro Aqui with my new best friend Christopher and two magical mystery bands. They were in the midst of getting signed by a major label, and this was the seal-the-deal dinner. I had been brought along as bonus jailbait window dressing, a role which I had no problem with.
I was seated opposite a lanky, meltingly attractive older boy who glowed with the phosphorescence of someone too far, too fast, too far for me to touch. With a fur vest revealing his taut nipples, he conversed with me languidly over the ratatouille. He sang in The Unmentionables, I found, and claimed to go by Paul.
Drinking wine out of actual wineglasses, eating something other than the house Mac & Cheese, on someone else's tab, with boys (!), who dressed themselves with much greater fervor than the fleece and Teva's of Reed's goateed stoners…well, I was quite transported. At that point I think my greatest intimation of sophistication consisted of my first winter formal, where I kissed my crush sloppily on the neck after some St. Ides Special Brew. He turned to me and accused, "Are you drunk?" And I caterwauled out of there to the Woman's Center never to return.

By the time we got to the club I'd thoroughly explored what I didn't know about wine. Paul smuggled my underage indecency into the club under his arm like a half-priced bottle of Strawberry Hill. By the end of the night we were making out wildly on a shag rug column. Rough on my back.

Paul returned with me to my dorm room, where he removed the fur vest and leapt into my bunk bed. The walls were covered in aluminum foil in my effort to be a Factory Girl, a décor choice which converted my dorm by day to a gigantic "Miss Suzy Bake-Oven."

It was dark but for my mother's lamp, an art deco nude of a pre-pubescent girl. He dove for my barely-teen twat, and popped the question. I considered for a moment, but the allure of such a glamorous, older boy with his bleached shag and Beatle-boots, brushing against the unknowable roads of tours past and stages won, screams and strums and his lean body against mine, I knew if I didn't go for it I'd be struggling through weeks of pot brownies and backrubs once I finally decided to date again. Besides, I wasn't a virgin anymore, so it barely mattered who I had sex with – right?

Right. Well. As he parted my legs and pushed, it became immediately evident that I was mistaken about that hymen issue. It was well and solid and thriving, and as he pushed harder, and cursed, it ripped and I yelped childishly through the Billie Holiday.

I was floored. I could not admit that I had no idea I was a virgin, gasp winsomely and say, "Wait, let's backtrack a little, let's peck and call it a day," in front of someone who was practically a rock star. How in the name of Edie Sedgwick could I come out with something like that?

After a great deal of struggling and my whimpering, he retreated to the desk and said, "You're just too small for me. I'm too big for some women, you know."

I nodded mutely. He then strummed me his hit single on my roommate's acoustic.

Fast forwards ten years, to an afterparty in Upper Haight. The Unmentionables had just played at the Fillmore, but it scarcely trickled on the edge of my mind. I was just on the post-Rosetta party trek, and had stumbled into this peculiar apartment with antiques and curios on every table and mosaics in the bathroom. It was lovely, with red velvet settees and a backlit liquor cabinet. I was looking into it when a man approached me, lurid drunk. Paul.

"Kiss me, girl."

"What?"

"You're pretty, kiss me." He was slurring his words, veering back and forth. The room slid.

"Um?"

"C'mon!"

"Do you know who I am?"

"Do you know who I am? You're a girl, kiss me. I'm in The Unmentionables. Do you have any coke? I know you do."

"Um, yeah." A mistake, I knew immediately.

"Give me a bump. I'm in The Unmentionables, we played tonight. You must've heard our new record, it's everywhere. There's even a movie about us."

"I don't care how big you are. And I'm not sharing."

"Give it up, sweetheart." He lunged and I jumped back, plunging into the crowded kitchen. He barged after, backing me into closets and pantries, past streaks of startled faces and spilled glasses. I scampered, nervous in the face of someone who'd caused me all of those years of recrimination, embarrassment, and, finally, a sick sort of pride. I tripped on a taxidermy beagle and lost speed. He lurched forwards, blocking my exit, and pushed me back into a bedroom.

"Look, okay, I'll give you a bump if you'll chill for a second and listen to me." Paul sat obediently.

"Okay, you, me, we fucked a long time ago, do you remember this?"

"I don't care, but you're one hot bitch, and I'm famous." He threw up his hands.

A big guy playing cards on the opposite bed said, "If this guy is bothering you, Lena, I can kick him out. We don't want trouble."

"Would you please."

Short of a killer truth-or-dare story, that was the last of him I ever wanted to see.

But in the Eagle, after Brady took several lengthy trips to the bathroom and came back smiling more each time, I felt decidedly fourth-wheely watching Alex and Limone. I was glad when she motioned for us to go.

"I think I'm staying for awhile," Brady said.

"That's cool, do you want to come with us, Lena?"

Limone linked my arm merrily, and lent her other to Alex's pale elbow. We skipped along, past the posters for beer busts and BBQ, and the streaking lights of cars. When the cab stopped, Limone pulled me in, saying, "Yeah, it's okay, we're going to his hotel, you're at – what – the W – okay – "

Alex glanced at me and looked down. He did not speak. As we drove, Limone gabbled about the fabulous hot tub at the W, how we were going to get naked, I smiled, nodded, Alex did not speak. I mentally checked the money in my purse. $2 or so. I couldn't remember if I'd tipped for the last drink.

Pulling up at the W, Alex leaned to Limone and whispered. She pouted. He was firm. The driver leaned back and sighed. Alex handed the driver a twenty and said, in a small, tremulous voice. "Take her somewhere else, please."

Limone threw back her hair amid the mass of dancers, and I saw the strobe glint on her earrings. Long silver strands. Music filled the Rosetta, music pulsing under their feet and over all their heads, the blonde and brown and black, the blonde with black highlights, the black with red highlights, but never the bald, unless ironically shaved.

Somehow Soft Cell merged into Peaches, and Limone said, "If it makes you feel any better, Lena, I always knew Jesse was a bad egg. The first time I met him I was with my friend Iris, and we ended up hanging out with him and this other DJ guy that worked at the Carlyle group."

"Uh huh?"

"Yeah. So we went back to the guy's house, and Jesse was, like, "I'm dealing, here, check out my stuff," so of course we did. The DJ was all over Iris, who had a boyfriend but was eating up the attention. It was 3 am on a Wednesday and I had to work in four hours, but, you know, we kept doing lines. A line spilled down my cleavage – and I was wearing a push-up bra and was, how do we say, more busty than usual..."

I giggled.

"Yeah, ha ha. Anyway, Jesse immediately ducked and snorted it up off my boobs."

"Oh no, he didn't!"

"Oh yes, he did. I was, like, what the hell, and looked up at Iris, who was, like, wtf? That's how we knew he was a bad one."

"That's great."

"So, are we learning anything?"

"I know he's a bad one, in fact, actually, I remember how he used to think Marie Callender's was the apotheosis of fine dining, and kept telling me that he could help my painting because his aunt had done the paintings for the Marie Callender's in San Luis Obisbo and so it was in his blood."

Limone belched.

"What is it?" I said.

"Ew...I feel...ur..."

"Are you okay?"

"Oh god, I think I'm going to throw up."

She had been knocking back those vodka tonics. But the bathroom was full of cokehead girls, pressed tight with frenetic conversation and gossip and burnt eyeliner. You could barely get in the door.

"You can't go in there," I said. "You just can't. It's a gossip train if you even shit in there. You remember when there was that whole thing going on MySpace about Number Two at parties? If you barf in there, you'll never sell coke in this town again."

"Then what?"

"Come on, outside. We'll find a doorway." We wedged themselves through the dancers to the door. Setting drinks on the window ledge, we shoved outside.

Big Al smiled.

"You girls alright?"

"We're cool."

"Okay, be careful out there."

We walked past the penumbra of the streetlights and out into the darkness of Sixth Street. A crackhead bent halfway over a box lurched by.

"Hey, you wanna buy a laptop?"

"No, that's alright."

"Come back if you change your mind. Open all night."

We cruised past the tacqueria's dim yellow glow, red wax pencil scrolling cursive chimichangas and tamales. A woman in pink sweat pants sat in the doorway of the E-Z One-Stop Check Cash. She stared fixedly at us as we passed.

Limone stopped in front of the Metro Limits Lofts, Blake's place, sending me lurching forwards on my heel. A torrent of headlights sped down Market Street.

"It's gotta be here. I'm so out of it. I can't wait."

"It's okay, check it out, the doorway goes kinda far back into the building, you'll be a little secluded."

"Great. Okay, here I go." She stepped gingerly over the rail that held the metal gate, and tripped across some dirty clothes that were scrambled with beer cans along the windows.

"I don't want to ruin this stuff, it might belong to someone." Limone said.

"I don't think it matters," I answered. I heard retching. I tried not turn around.

Two men approached. One wavered in his step, dodging piss streaks on the sidewalk. The other was all too direct.

They stopped in front of me. Gold tooth next to one missing, the first holding a half-pint of something in a paper bag. It smelled like brandy. His hair was half grey, grizzled, strips of leather hanging around his neck.

"Hey, is she okay?" he said.

The second said, "Yeah, yeah, like do you think we should do something, should we, I mean, I can…" He started to walk back into the doorway. I grabbed his arm.

"No, that's alright, really. I've got it under control."

The one on speed flashed yellow eyes and a muscle in his cheek jerked.

"No, really, I mean, I know CPR, I can…"

"No, really. Come on, you can go. I've got it, she's my friend, it's okay." The grey-blue windows behind us cast an eerie light onto the asphalt. Scent of gasoline, crunch of broken glass as I stepped forwards.

"You're sure?"

"Yeah. I mean it."

"'Kay," said the drunk one, taking a swig from his bottle. "Come on, man, I wanna go check out Golgotha." They lurched away.

I took a long, ragged breath. The adrenaline numbed me and it all was so fast, so necessary, then melting away. I heard Limone's unsteady feet come up behind me, and turned to see her wiping her face on a sleeve.

"You okay?" I said.

"No, question is, are you okay?" Streetlights pounding down circles of glare. A rattle of beats from the club, laced with synthetic sitar. *Jesse used to buy speed from Golgotha, a homeless encampment in South of Market. It used to burn the shit out of my nose.*

"Yeah, I guess. It just had to be done. Now let's get the hell out of here, why don't we?"

"Yeah. Let's go back to my house and just chill. I don't think I want anything else." Limone turned and lifted a hand, waving it, going slowly to the sidewalk where she waited, hopeful, until a cab came to a stop.

Chapter 6
minarets in the gleam

The damp carpet walls of the warehouse clenched us in tight as Limone pressed on towards her deal. Orange shag bathmats were nailed on the raw lumber walls, the room barely big enough for the three of us: Limone, Ian and I. Ian was a partner at the Rosetta, his eyes mild and clear, his pompadour and black-rimmed glasses shone. Limone had met him in our nightly rounds, and we had all gone back there after the bar closed. After the maniacs packed tight in the bathroom, talking recklessly, swerving to pick-up, negotiating the afterparty, trying to get bumps off each other and homing in on whoever had a bag.

Limone leaned forwards. "There's an obvious need, there," she said. "You know what it's like, I know what it's like, I mean, people are always asking us if we have any. If there was someone there who could deal safely out of the bathroom so people wouldn't have to deal with sketchy dudes, it would make things a lot safer for everyone."

"Safety, huh?" Ian said, "No, I see what you mean, though. We do have a lot of people in and out, and for God's sake people aren't exactly going to stop doing it, but I'm not totally sure if your idea of institutionalizing it is really a good one." He leaned down to the black trash bag at his feet and pulled out three beers, passing them around.

I snapped the tag on mine, and felt a spring of foam edge against my thumb. I hunched my shoulders and listened, feeling superfluous. Limone had dragged me here like a bedraggled faux-Chanel handbag, and for lack of a better party I had followed. My predatory wiles were rising, however, and as Blake was MIA and Jay was so unpredictable. The appeal of someone who didn't live in a converted Chevy was growing. Someone who didn't have to wait outside the liquor store as I bought our morning mimosas, perhaps, *quelle idée*.

Limone's pulled a bag out of her purse and began dispensing bumps. Ian put a fey hand up and the key passed him by.

"What, you don't?" Limone pried. "What's wrong with you?"

"I used to, but it makes it so I can't get anything done. What with the bar and school, I don't have a whole lot of time to waste talking to randoms or sleeping for twenty hours."

"Yeah, true, it can make it hard to get much accomplished. But you don't work, right, Lena?"

"I do things," I pouted. "I paint, I go to the museum, I read, I don't just lie around in a narcotic haze plotting new modes of seduction – really."

Ian looked at me, taking in the wasted limbs under a sequin tube top, tall boots, stark eyes despite the late hour. He crept a hand along the back of the urine-stained couch.

"So, so, what do you think? Do you think we can do this?" Limone said.

"Yeah, I think it could work. But do we get a cut?" The hand inched closer along the velour pile. I fell back.

"How much do you want?" Limone asked.

Ian paused, rescinding. "Actually, actually maybe not, that makes our involvement even more illegal. We'll let you use the space as a service to our clients and a draw to foot traffic, and leave it at that."

"Awesome," Limone said, new wrinkles skimming her milky skin, "I'll be seeing you Friday."

Ian passed me another beer from his trash bag, as we watched the sun rise from the warehouse roof. A glowing orange ball was lifting a pink haze over the skyscrapers and rows of Victorians, streets gouged out in sweeping tracks, churches sending forth minarets to catch the gleam. I watched him shyly from the corner of my eye, his glasses shining with the glare over a delicate mouth and narrow chin. I was trashed. We had been sitting here for hours, talking, as the pale light came up over the rusty patio furniture, plastic flowers, and Burning Man refuse that dotted the white gravel rooftop.

I turned to him.

"So, like if you check your MySpace or Friendster, there may be hundreds of people on there, but how many of them can you really call?" I gestured to the barren street below, as the career alcoholics began to stumble to the bars, pawnshops putting out their signs, bums tumbling in piles of cardboard.

"I would like to think I have a few."

"I would like to hope too, but I often wonder. I'm not a very social person." I pulled up my top, dropping sequins on the gravel.

"I see you at the Rosetta all the time."

"Yeah, I'm a highly antisocial person who flocks like a moth to a strobe light." I sighed. "I like to dance, I like the illusion of acceptance, I like to get dressed up, but no, fundamentally it's very empty. I don't know, though, I still love it."

"As long as you love it, then you're alright."

"I guess," I said, glancing down.

The sun was starting to rise higher on the horizon, as buses streaked ant-like dots between buildings. I took a sip of the sour beer.

"Hey," he asked.

"Yeah?"

"Do you want to go to your place?"

I didn't question. The dawn light fell around us in a haze as we picked through the rubble, down the stairs, and out to his car.

Taking a sip of white wine, I crossed my legs coyly and watched Ian as he tried to explain the problems of post-modernity. I was utterly charmed. For all that most art-school strumpets like to throw around such diction like there's no tomorrow,

It sure has been awhile. My gold fireplace was glowing with midmorning light as it crept from the curtains, invading as he poured me a second glass.

"So, what did you study at Reed?" he asked gently.

"Painting, Feminist Theory, Film Theory. I'm into scopophilia."

"Interesting. What's your take on Freud?"

"Oh come on. How hysteric do I look?" I shrugged. "I mean, really, I'm actually a little too drunk to talk about this right now. Let's just say that I embody the abject half the time, and the other half I'm repressed by parental strictures."

"You're twenty-eight, didn't you say?"

"Well, it takes some time to get over."

"The good girl complex?"

"Spliced with the bad girl complex. How bad can you be, how far can you go, what will happen if you do such and so. How much is mannered, a pose, and what isn't?"

"I think I know what you mean." He rose from the window and advanced to where I sat. "Like what will happen if you do this…" He laid a hand on my shoulder. "And this…" He lunged towards me, his lips plunging to my lips. I wrapped around him, and the strangely soft hands caressing my sides, his glasses bumping against my forehead. He set them on the floor.

He held my face, thumbs on my lids. "I think I understand you."

"That would be unusual."

I began to unbutton his shirt, seeking the body, the heat, seeking to know what made him arc to come. This one I wanted to keep.

His hands were timid, creeping down my back.

"May I?"

"Mmmm…yes."

He cupped my ass, massaging it. "Mmmmm. Ass and titties."

I smiled. "Oh yeah. You know, I downloaded that song today, and that one refrain is about all there is to it."

"That's why it mixes so well, that's why Kris is so into it."

Little fragments, coming together.

A few days later, I showed up at Tenderloin City Health at six am. Clinic hours started at seven, and they didn't do appointments. It was assumed that those without health insurance had no other demands on their time, and obviously I wouldn't mind trundling my, now painfully ingrown toenail, along the trash-infested streets, at an hour when I was usually still high. This time I was not, just a little hung over, tasting the acid-vodka in my breath.

Things had gotten a little out of hand with my feet, somewhere between mandatory pointy heels and the fact that I didn't feel pain once I had a drink or two. The combination of patent leather and decreased immune system…when I took my boot off the other day, I found that a whole side of my big toe was in the process of rotting off, blood and pus oozing and burbling. I pried the orange crust off, but the fact was that my toenail was determined to grow through my foot.

This had been mounting for awhile, but, having lost my insurance with the job, I decided to follow every low-rent citizen's favorite medical plan, "Ignore it, and maybe it will go away."

Apparently not.

Four hours later, I limped out of the office with a bottle of codeine and a paper bag of condoms. They had cut off half my toenail. But what was I going to do with all of this grape lube?

I climbed out the rickety window, the bare wood streaked with ancient green paint and splintering under my fingers. It was a warm night, the sky streaked with clouds. The floor was littered with creaking lawn chairs, shredded seats hanging low.

I walked across the rooftop towards Brady and Lucas, sitting down and pulling my knees up onto Lucas's skateboard. Gold sandals laced my ankles, hard to walk in, stiletto heels tighter than Capri menthols with black bondage lacing up the back arch. My grotesquely swollen toe, bandaged bloody, hung off the edge.

The party was filling up fast, a Wednesday and Brady didn't work. Being on disability, he filled his days with band practice, songwriting and parties. He couldn't sleep, he could never sleep. Each night they came forth, the party, the moment, the calls that came due. He fell finally around six am, sleeping most of the day, playing his keyboard in the afternoon in slow, keening melodies and then going out. There was always a party. Or three. His phone would whine with the most gorgeous melody as nine came due and the office workers woke from their naps and I got off work and came looking for blow.

Lucas was rocking back and forth on his skateboard wheels. A scrawny boy in ripped woman's clothing, he moved with a gutterpunk grace. The house loomed behind them, lined with mattresses and dank corners. The moon was low and full, shot with arrows of light from the dancing downstairs. I took a swig of vodka and sat down.

"Hey Lena," said Lucas. "Do you have any coke?"

"Yeah," I said. "Let's find the ladies." We shuffled downstairs, weaving through frenzied crowd to a line that rumbled against the walls. Sharpie slogans dashed across the frame of a painting hanging behind them. A mottled mold of a face emerged from the wall. Streaks of blue and black paint fell over what looked like a hand.

The door opened, and we entered in the wake of shrieking girls. The windowsill was lined with Loteria cards, and a row of tea lights were burning on the edge of the sink. Lucas sat down on the toilet lid and said, "Here, sit on my lap."

I slid into his arms, and he plunged his lips onto mine. Tongues swirled. I pulled away, laughing. Brady stared out the window at the light well, and the open window across the street, where an old man heated a can of soup on a hot plate. A hand came up with a bump for him, and he took it, then looked out again to where the man was pouring the soup into a bowl. Cracks around the edges.

His phone rang.

"Fuck." He pulled it out of his pocket and looked at the screen, seeing 'Roger'. "Walking corpse! Why does he keep calling me? I swear, we only hooked up once!"

"Must've been good," said Lucas, wiping his finger along my lips and smearing it onto his own.

"No, it wasn't." Brady thumped the phone back into his pocket, unanswered. "I only went home with him because the guy I wanted to go home with went home with someone else. It was the end of the night, and he had coke, so I figured, 'why not?' It was disappointing....and now he won't leave me alone!"

In the dim yawning light, there was a bang on the door.

"Are you done in there? Jesus!"

"Right, right, okay. We good?" We quickly straightened collars, hairdos, lipstick for two and hopped up to go.

Streaks of grime fell down the window, the concrete slab outside standing in for a yard. There were no yards in the city. All you got was a doorstep with an iron gate flat bare against the sidewalk, maybe a couple of steps if you were lucky. Lucas' lucky squat was a one-bedroom with his cozy spangled nook in the living room, collages on the kitchen wall. He crawled through the window and let Brady and I in. The "A" on the apartment door a green-glazed copper. Opal paint peeling off the door under a low-hanging yellow light, a flight of stairs leading up and a hallway going back, a man muttering in Portuguese somewhere very far away.

Inside, I lounged on the low-slung couch, leaning back to where the curtains draped longer than the windows, red velvet like hair. Brady crossed his legs neatly at the ankle and breathed deeply. Reaching a hand up to the coffee table, he smiled as he picked up a guitar pick.

"So you have been practicing?"

"Oh course I've been practicing." Lucas pushed the door shut, anchoring it with a brick. He pushed back his hair and lifted a six-pack of PBR from the bag.

I took one and settled back in the sofa.

"I've got a new song, actually, check it out."

"Awesome. Go for it."

He strummed a few chords, then settled into a tune. Beginning to sing, "Sucking on a big old dick, gang bang and then we all do it doggie style." he faltered, nervously, and stopped.

"I don't know. Not tonight. I'm not done with it yet."

"Dammit, Lucas. "

"Sorry, whatever, later."

"No, no, it's cool, sorry. I shouldn't get mad over shit like that. It's improving."

"No, you shouldn't"

"Right." They drank.
"Do you have anything?"
"No-thing."

Brady lingered at the hors d'oeuvre tray for a moment.
"I can't figure out why you bother making these little niblets," he said.
I looked at him. "They're tasty, but everyone here is too fucked up."
His fingers lingered near a stuffed mushroom, when a voice near his ear said,
"Oh, those are good."
"Oh, hello."
"Hi, I'm Ian. You have the most beautiful fingers."
The corners of Brady's mouth curved up a little bit.
I turned away.

In the bathroom, beside the hula-girl curtain, Brady sat on the toilet. A Valley
of the Dolls record cover hung above him. Anne, Jennifer and Neely were sitting on
the rosy bed in pink nightgowns.
"Hey could you lock the door," Brady said.
He put his hands on Ian's ass, and pulled him towards him. Massaging his
jeans, gliding upwards to feel his warm back, he dove a finger down to slowly,
gently, probe his asshole. Ian felt his cock stiffen. He hadn't been with a man in
awhile, and as Brady's narrow chest rubbed his groin, and his teeth moved to deftly
pop open the buttons of his pants, he began to pull Brady's shirt off.
It's been awhile since I left the middle buttons undone.
Brady took the other man's cock in his mouth, and slid his tongue along the
underside, tasting the pre-cum's sweetness. There was a certain dusty latex flavor,
which did not detract, as the aubergine head thrust to the back of his throat.
Ian felt his cocktail party tension dissolve. Wrapping his fingers in Brady's
hair, his head fell back and mouth dropped open as Brady glided a finger up his ass.
The tiny hairs on the bathroom floor, the Trader Joe's Refresh shampoo, the
daguerreotype of Louise Brooks, the molten pleasure that shot through his cock as he
began to cum. On Brady's purple velvet smoking jacket.
"Oh, shit, I'll never get this out."
"Dry cleaning?"
"Ah, not exactly a priority right now."
"Maybe a gentle cycle with some green tea?"
Brady glanced up.
"It'll still show in black-light, though," Ian said. "Sorry about that."
"I've got a show coming up, too...oh well."
"Let's have another drink."

Ian snuggled up to Brady on his futon.

"It's all because of that cock-blocking fag-hag Lena," he said, wrapping his arm around Brady's waist.

"That's uncharitable!" Brady said.

"No, I'm kidding, it's just that….she seems to have some sort of abandonment complex. She's really needy."

"Oh, you are sleeping with her? I thought you were just at the party for the blow."

"No, I don't like cocaine. I have a…collector's interest in Lena."

"Oh really?"

"Well, come on. A man needs to keep his options open. There are a lot of foxes at that bar."

Chapter 7
pawnshop of one

Sixth Street was alive. I slid out of a cab and strode over to the entrance, under the pink neon rose. Big Al nodded carelessly as I thrust my shoulder through the doorway, hoping, as I crossed the door girl, hoping my dubious passport still held. Fucking the owner wasn't much of a fifteen minutes. She didn't stop me, though. Three dollars more towards a drink.

I saw Ian bartending. Wavering, I raised a hand meekly, not wanting to be too forward, too demanding, too entitled. He stuck limes in three Coronas, slamming them down, and turned to me.

"Ian. Will I see you tonight?"

He shot tonic in two glasses, splashed vodka, and turned to me. "What?"

"Are you free tonight?"

"I don't know, Lena, I'm really busy here. We're mobbed. Give me some time, let me see, and then I'll meet up with you later. Okay?"

I lowered my head.

"Okay. I understand. Really."

"Really?" He coiled two spigots against each other, and passed me an olive.

I took it from his fingers with my lips. Pulling away, squashing the pimento beneath my teeth, I turned to the ingénue who sulked behind my arm. "And who are you?"

"Kareena."

"And what do you do, Kareena?"

"I work at Villains, I'm a buyer."

"Fabulous, I'm a vestigial appendage upon the welfare state."

"You what?"

"Nothing." I turned and arched across the dirty tile, pacing reckless down the bar as the new and young closed in and I felt the relentless moments like an anchorweight of endless moments closing closer towards the end. My end. Whether playgirl or promissory note, I knew I could no longer kick coke poster hussy about like a bubble-bath of promising invites. There had to be some way to get out, barring self-internment on the bong couch with VH1. What to do? What to do with the rest of my life? I glared at Ian, making Mai Taïs for a flurry of girls, and sashayed down the bar.

In the crow, I saw sunglasses I recognized. A sideways shag, track marked arms, he came rocketing towards me as I shied away.

"Lena! Cuntrag!"

I ran away, tumbling elbow to knee to the warmth of strangers as I slid between their arms towards the bathroom. Jesse. Fuck. I cursed my cabfare here, my silly hope of fucking Ian. Facing down Jesse in the sordid heat of the dance floor, the palms and hipbones jostling as he grabbed for me, and I pulled away. I scrambled to the bathroom and fell in to a host of strangers as they stared and one held out a hand. It was Audrey.

"Rough night? You didn't even say 'Hi' to me!" she said.

"Sorry. Jesse's here. I'm sketched. I think I have to go, like now."

"Oh sure, Petunia," she said. I glanced around, falling into pure reptilian terror tactics. How to get out. How not to be seen.

Panting, I pulled my chiffon-clad ass off of the sink, and ran off into the murky bar.

Outside, Kris Danger threw records joyfully and shoulders bobbed in the sweaty crowd. I pushed my way through the dance floor, to where Ian leaned by the door.

"You busy?"

"Are you leaving?" he said.

"I have to. Jesse's here."

"I can have Al kick him out," he said. "You know we don't want him fucking with you."

"I can't ask you to do that. He might buy drinks. Probably afford them more than I can. Besides, I've had it, I'm freaking out, the fact that he's gotten this close to me…it's too much, I need my safe, cozy bed now. This world is not a good place."

"Take it your way, then."

I put up both hands as if he might stop me, and took off into the bright invisibility of the street.

The phone rang the next morning. I picked it up and heard my mother.

"I just wanted to see if you're coming to Easter this year, we're having it in San Diego this time. I was thinking something brunchy."

"Sure, I hadn't thought about it, but yeah, that sounds fine."

"Good, good. It's a shame about that Jesseie character-"

"Jesse, mom."

"Why don't you try joining the alumni association, maybe you could meet someone there, or, I don't know, Telluride Association, they keep sending out volunteer pamphlets…? Great chance to hob-knob with someone other than those…characters."

"Telluride was a summer program, mom. High school. We're talking eleven years ago. I don't think anyone's going to remember me."

"You should give that some thought."

"It's fine, mom, really."

"But are you thinking about what you…I mean, honey, what are you doing over there?"

"Oh, you know, just being me. Doing my thing."

"Um…does that involve…a job? Are you…in school?"

"I'm thinking about stuff, mom. I'm talking to my therapist about it." I gritted my teeth and tried to sound sincere. I wanted so much to devolve into a guilty child and just tell them what was going on, to be absolved and delivered, picked up and taken to bed, but it was impossible. At a certain point I had ceased to tell them things, realizing they could not deliver me at all. All they would do was worry, and all I could do was try to solve it myself. I waited for an answer.

"Just come to Easter, then, and we'll talk."

There was a nervous silence and I clicked the phone shut. The sun had completely set. Taking a sip of cold coffee, I set it down anxiously in the damp circle on the table. Strangely alert, I felt I could hear all of the buzzes and clicks of the power lines around the building, echoing the sparks and surges in my room, the chimes of the microwave, car alarms, to the neighbor's lights across the courtyard that suddenly, ravenously, burnt out.

The Boxster sped down Van Ness Street, the glimmer of passing cars streaking by, as I leaned over the armrest. Ian was driving, idly, circles under his eyes from the long night. He wiped his glasses with one hand and changed lanes. I was too awake as usual. Many nights lately I'd waited for him, often turned away after a few hours by an "I'm tired, not tonight." I was so hooked that I had almost stopped going to afterparties, eschewing the jittery purgatory to sit night after night in my spot at the bar, free Fernet in hand, ginger by the wrist, sipping slowly as he polished and wiped.

My life had closed in, somewhat, I rarely saw Audrey or Brady anymore.

The mist condensed silver on the windshield, and Ian pressed the defrost button. Puffs of night sky began to clear away the fog. A Chili's passed on the right, the yellow and red neon diffracting in sodden glares, drips sending down bright bars. I stretched my hands out to the heat emanating from the floor, turned to him, and said, "So."

"So. How's Limone withstanding? I see you guys out there all the time."

"Oh, it's fun. Hectic, crazy, people always grabbing at her, but that's the Rosetta. If it wasn't packed it'd be tough for you."

"I think I could handle it. It's not my life, you know." He smiled ruefully.

"What is, then, if you could answer that? What do you live for, anyway?"

'Pretty big question. Huge, in fact." He turned onto O'Farrell, passing a dumpster heaped with fetid take-out and bottles. "Well, I don't know. School is more important to me right now. I'm graduating next semester and I've got to keep it together. Late nights, well, at least I have afternoon classes."

"Ah, so I have the Art Institute's registrar to thank for my sex life. Fantastic."

"Pretty much, yes. Maybe you'll get a signed print out of it, too."

"Oh come on, an installation."

"More like a website, I'm not New Genres. Think, it can have little icons of your lanterns and coffee cups, and lots of links to Indian food!" We passed the New Century theatre to a flurry of spangles and thighs.

"Do I have to be naked?"

"No, that's another kind of website. Unless, of course, you want one of those cam-things so random men can see you, like, alphabetizing your shoe collection or obsessively downloading Kraftwerk songs, or sleeping face-down for 20 hours."

"Hey, I don't do those things!"

"Come on, you totally do. I've seen them. They are organized by color and heel height. Don't think because I'm a guy I don't notice these things."

"Yeah, that is weird. Do you sniff my hair care products, too?"

He blushed. "No. I just use them. Your pomade is better than mine. Oh, look, parking place!" He swerved to a meter beside a dyed-carnation florist and began to parallel park. I got out and slammed the door behind me, jerking onto the curb. Tipsy. He came around, flicking the remote lock, and took my shoulder. Together we ambled down the stained concrete past a donut shop, two Thai restaurants, and three liquor stores. The sky was just fading into dawn, sending an ice-blue shimmer across the trucks and down the delicate filigree of the apartment facades. The dark windows shone like a hundred pupils dilated in the dying night.

I gazed out of the streaky cab window, fingering the edge of my suitcase. San Diego loomed closer, always an abstract until I actually stepped out of the train and saw the palm trees and the plasticine sky. There was always something unreal about it, as if a honeymoon ad in the wedding magazines I used to read had stepped forwards and mated with the Real World Miami.

It would be welcome at this point, however, having seen too much of the Rosetta bathroom closing ivy tendrils on Limone. We would sit in the wire barstools by the stall, and the room would fill with anxious partiers, frantic for what she had and dispensed so easily, as the two of us took leisurely sips from our lemon drops and conferred. Soon Limone would have a box full of money and no bags left to sell, and we would go to the dance floor. Strobe and disco, electro and drama, then Ian's vigil or an afterparty, and eventually sleep came late if ever.

My phone rang. Grappling to the bottom of my purse, I heard Limone on the other end. "Lena, Lena, are you there?"

"What, hon, are you okay?" The cab volleyed rapidly through the industrial district, warehouses blinking by grey and orange with construction workers and empty lots.

"I'm at Donny's," Limone said. "Listen, things are fucked, can I borrow two hundred dollars?"

"What? Limone, I don't have a job."

"I need it, Lena, I don't know what I'm going to do. He's pissed, I somehow gave away too much, and…"

"Okay, okay, I guess, but you better pay me back, I mean, if you don't I'll be really screwed. I don't get my unemployment check until next Monday."

"Oh, thank god. Listen, where are you, I'll meet you."

"I'll be at the Amtrak station in South of Market in about ten minutes. I can wait maybe half an hour, and then I'll have to get on my train. I'll try, sweetie, just hurry."

"Okay, god...Donny, okay, I'll be back, okay." The call ended, and I stared anxiously at the phone for a moment before putting it away. Limone cutting lines like that so readily, thinking she had an unlimited supply, and every bag empties eventually. Even when Donny advanced her $500 worth a week, she was always supposed to bring him the cash on Tuesday after the weekend's excess. Something must have slipped this time, something must have slid by with the spangling Technicolor haze of intoxication, the shiver of it, the desire to share and welcome.

The cab jolted to a stop at an orange kiosk, and I got out, passing the bemused man a ten and lugging my suitcase to the curb. My luggage weighed a ton, and had a harsh plastic handle that bit into my hand, causing deep welts and swelling as I lugged it past the families with their open faces and scrambling kids. Sifting between commuters towards the ATM, I felt the secret driven like a steel splinter beneath my fingernail. It marked me, but it was a mark I was not afraid of, for I knew failing her was far worse.

Leaning against the soda machine, I scanned the bobbing heads for Limone. She was late. The salt water taffy machine beside the pretzel case was winding tighter, tighter, pink and turquoise swirling into new loops like my nerves wending tighter from the reading on the clock. 5:19 swept the hands above the concession stand, and I was beginning to feel shifty and ridiculous standing here in the Amtrak station with the $200 wadded recklessly in my pocket. The leather was bulbous around my hand, and I shifted it, sweating.

Limone approached, ducking as if each hand would rise to strike. Emerging near me, she raised her head in greeting, with a twist to her red lips and a shrug. "I'm sorry, I didn't expect..."

"Yeah, well, I guess this sort of thing happens, but, Limone, you can't do this again. I can't handle the stress, and I can't afford to bail you out like this. But, whatever, come on." I walked across the pitted concrete to the restroom.

Inside, the dampness clung to the orange stalls and radiated outwards to our pinched expressions in the mirror. Coke jowls. Malnutrition. It stuck to my hands as I passed her the wad of bills and plunged my fists into the sink to catch the last drops of cold water that were falling, falling, gone.

Teetering through the aisles of the train, heading to San Diego, I watched the streaking lights of diners and McDonalds, supermarkets and Subway, against the darkness outside. I caught glimpses as I searched for the dining car, passing college students in hiking boots and businessmen with the omnipresent New York Times. Orange decals sprung up, followed by a tubular staircase that looked more Swedish Modern than Amtrak 2000. I climbed, and soon fumbled down a narrow hall to the dining car.

Everything seemed to be anchored in some way, from the entrenched benches and tables to the cardboard cupholders and trays. I inched my way in, swaying with the jolts of the train, and lurched up against the counter. An old man in a bow tie and white collared shirt polished a futuristic tea set.

I smiled.

"Why, hello, little lady, what can I help you with?"

"Um, wait a sec…" I scanned the menu. Hot dogs, pretzels, hot pockets, etc… "I'll have the bean burrito, oh, and you have cocktails…I'll have a gin and tonic."

The man smiled benevolently and flipped open a tiny gin bottle, pouring it in a plastic cup and topping it with an iridescent flash. I took it gratefully and settled into a built-in bench by the window. Staring out the window at the stars, I took a long drink of gin and let my body go limp, easing out the tension and worry of the last couple of months. The people in the room fell away as I let myself melt into the black velour spanning the sky, pinpricks for stars letting through the glare from a world I could never see. It was all too overwhelming, the black circles under my eyes in the morning, the shaking of an empty bag on a mirror, yielding a soft wisp of dust, the luxury and plentitude of fullness and then the agony of that last waft. The sense that Jesse was lurking around, that I didn't know how to protect myself; if perhaps I could just muster the will to turn aside as if I was above him, when I knew I was really just as dirty, just as tainted, just as much a creature of appetites and rages and lusts. The train lurched, spilling a splash of tonic on my fingers. And Ian, elusive yet lurking, always, behind the bar dispensing drinks, grabbing my sleeve for quick cigarettes out front, whispering for me to wait while he closed. Always the mirror of the Rosetta bathroom reflecting back and back again, limbs flailing like patio furniture in a depraved garden party. All of us caught, all of us caught between pleasure and horror, between the icicle brilliance of a bump and the bottlecap-struck tar echoing beneath our feet as we trailed home.

As I ripped open the package of spring mix, my Mom said, "Oh no, not that one, use the baby spinach."

"Huh?"

"The Diet, the South Beach Diet. We've got to make a spinach-arugula-walnut salad, Easy Chicken in Wine Sauce, I think that's on page 216, and…oh, okay Italian-style Spaghetti Squash." I looked down at the cookbook, marked with post-its.

"Okay, okay. But why is there no garlic in this?"

"Oh, that is funny. I've noticed there's this sort of "mayonnaise-centric," stuff in here, they rely heavily on salt and pepper…Agatston seems to think he's rediscovered Atlantis with the olive oil…."

"Hm….but does it work?"

She sighed, and looked at me. "You know, I'm trying. And he's trying too. It's just that when we go out, you know, he won't follow the diet, it's chimichangas and Cadillac Margaritas, and ice cream, and then he wonders why all of this South Beaching isn't working."

"Bummer."

"Yeah, it is. So this time we're on Phase Two, and he's made some improvement. I'm just hoping that you can help me out with some of this, there's so much preparation."

"Yeah, it looks like it. Lettuce roles with cilantro mayonnaise? That sounds kind of gross."

"If you want to throw some garlic into that spaghetti squash…I mean, just for authenticity."

"Won't Dad freak out?"

The night of their wedding, Aunt Bianca and her fiancé had stuffed garlic powder in Mom and Dad's luggage. After spending valuable honeymoon sex time scrubbing it out, Dad was sworn against the stuff. My childhood was punctuated by walking two steps into a restaurant…not just Italian restaurants, and my father bellowing, "Is there GARLIC in here?" I was mortified Regularly.

"I've been adding a little to the food here and there, usually half a clove when it calls for a whole. It's just so necessary!"

"That works."

"Oh, and can you hide that jug of Carlo Rossi he's been working on."

"He still drinks that stuff? Wow, Dad's punker than me."

"Yeah. He brought out a bottle of two-buck-chuck when Gerard Thistle came over, and we had to have an intervention."

"Oh my."

Dad jogged in the kitchen, his grey-haired legs topped with teensy neon running shorts. He wore a white T-shirt reading, 'I'd rather be a Dumb Shit than a Smart Fuck,' pushed up on one side to show a heart rate meter. White tube socks and running shoes completed the look.

"Hello girls! How was your train ride, Lena?"

"Oh, Hi Dad. Pretty good."

"Wait, wait," he bent over, sweaty. Holding something between his thumb and finger, he turned to us and said, "Is this a pubic hair?"

"You're the one in shorts, dear." Mom began tossing the salad. "Are you going to change for dinner?"

"Oh, you know, I just feel so good after running. I mean, isn't this shirt great! My brother gave it to me."

"Oh. Yes, I recall. Why don't you open the wine, Lena?"

The next morning, I wandered downstairs and put on coffee. It was Easter, and, although my last – and final – Easter basket, had contained panties in little plastic eggs, and a copy of Anne Rice's "The Claiming of Sleeping Beauty," I was 13 and not amused. This time, I figured they would scale it down. I was still a little confused as to why they had thought a waterbed was a good idea for a twelve-year-old girl. Chugging an espresso, I thumbed open the South Beach Diet book at the appropriate post-it and thought about egg-white omelets. Quichecups, maybe?

Mom came in, and said, "Would you like some oatmeal, dear? We've been making it with these frozen blueberries, it's really delicious."

"If only they hadn't discontinued them!" said Dad, coming in. "I wrote Ralph's a long email, telling them how we go through seven bags a week, and that this was just indicative of the general mendacity of grocery stores today, and you know what they did?"

"What?" I said.

"They brought them back! And the store manager sent me this great letter, hmmm, let me see if I can find it..." He turned back towards his office, a converted bedroom now crammed with computers, a servers, and stacks upon stacks of legal documents.

Dad was an attorney. He used to have an office downtown, there had been several partnerships, and then he was assaulted by a prospective client. The man got past the secretary and bashed him in the head with a telephone. He was out to kill. Dad suffered a concussion, fractured skull, and multiple bruises. Spent some time in the hospital. Then he decided to start an airline, and tried to assemble capital for 8 years. 9-11 happened. He lost the office. After spending a few years getting really good at computer solitaire, he turned to military consulting, and was currently working on something classified involving pirates on the Bering Strait.

"Now let's see..." Mom opened the refrigerator, and pulled out a bottle of champagne. "I wouldn't normally, but it is Easter. Could you make some orange juice, dear."

"Mmmm! Great idea." I began shuffling around the fridge.

A few mimosas, in, Dad started spiking them with Grand Marnier. The conversation got more interesting.

Empty oatmeal bowls were strewn around the kitchen table. I leaned back in my chair.

"So, Dad, I can't believe I never asked this, but why do I have mom's last name?"

"It's true," he said. "The Glenwood's took a different path. It all starts in Reno, Nevada."

"Doesn't it all." Mom laughed. "Yeah, we'd been married about six years, and -"

"My Pappy, well, you know how he got shot in the head when they were elk hunting, back when he was a kid…. They took him home, the doctor came in from town, and said, 'Make him comfortable, he ain't gonna last the night.' But he did. Later on, yeah, he dropped out of high school and went to war, got shot again, met your grandma and just went ass-end-over-teakettle over her, she was so pretty then, all these blond curls…and then he got a job on the oil derricks, and a couple of big pieces of iron fell on him – sustained substantial head damage that time, and then when he recovered he got a gig as an airline mechanic. Had that for a long time."

"Fascinating." I said.

"Anyway, at one point when they'd been married awhile, he was in his sixties, he went batshit-crazy and went after Granny with a butcher knife."

"Oh my god! That's…that's….I never knew this."

"This was before you were born. She made it, she ran to the neighbor's house, and called 911. Pappy was in jail for awhile, diagnosed schizophrenic and then Granny signed out on his parole. He only lived a couple of years after that, and Granny wore pink to the funeral."

"She looked good," Mom said. "The case was on the news a lot, though, and we felt that it would be better to give you my name. Ben took a little convincing, but I'm good at that." She smiled at me across the table. I drained my glass.

Chapter 8
the limone lark

I rang Donny's doorbell the day I got back, waiting behind the gate as he buzzed me in.

"What up, Le-nah?" He beckoned me in to the room, past a giant bag of weed and a glass coffee table weighed down with bongs and take-out. He sat down and began to flay some fish and chips, dipping glistening hunks of cod into tartar sauce. "You hungry?"

"Oh no, that's cool. I'm on the cheese and crackers diet."

"Up to you. So what are you trying to achieve, here?" The room was alive with lush aquariums, full of purple Angelfish and Koi.

"The ushe. I have to ask you, though, what happened with Limone? She's my friend, you know." A sea anemone beckoned green tendrils to a rouged center, ready to digest.

"Oh, yeah, I feel bad about that, you know. I know she's just starting out, it's just that she took me for about $450, and that's some serious cash. I wasn't about to really fuck her up, I mean, come on, I'm not that kind of person. But I just didn't want her to go diddling it around to all your little hipster dudes and shorting me when it really came down to it. That's all." He laid big hands flat on the table.

"Well, yeah, I don't know, I mean it's totally your thing, all I know is that she borrowed $200 from me and I was really freaked out."

"Lena." He met my eyes.

"What?"

"Come on."

"Okay…"

"So, how much do you want?" He picked up a piece of battered cod.

"A forty."

He moved to the back room, easing down next to a Tupperware of coke. Lifting a tablespoon, he poured a dash, and then another, into the bag. I settled down on the black leather. As I waited, a chinchilla came bubbling into the room in a plastic ball.

"Oh my god, it's so cute!" I squealed. "Look at his little face!"

"Oh yeah, that's my little one. Got him a couple weeks ago."

"What's his name?"

"Pablo Escobar."

"Oh shit."

"Yeah, huh. So here you go, fake it till you make it." He handed me a gram. "Oh yeah, and by the way, I'm going to Thailand in a couple of weeks, taking a vacation, so I'll give you some numbers. This guy Miles that I know."

"You're awesome."

"Just watchin' out for you."

Brady told me the following later, much later, but this is how I know it now.

At the party, Brady and Ian walked down an underground hallway to the tiny backyard that the block shared. A few stunted trees hung over a BBQ, and feral cats roamed around dishes of kibble. Bright windows speckled the dark walls around.

Ian pulled out a pack of cigarettes and handed one to Brady.

Taking one himself, he lit the other man's and sat down on a wicker bench.

Brady paced, watching the smoke drift upwards, hearing the shrieks from inside.

"What sort of art are you making right now?"

"I'm getting really involved with fonts. Like, there's this great magazine called Plazm, that's basically just packaging for this great lettering."

"That sounds fun. I'm having a lot of trouble with my band. Lucas just can't get it together with paying for the practice space, and the whole factor that we have to practice in Oakland makes it all the more difficult."

"That's a drag," Ian said. He bent a finger at Brady. "Want to have a seat, you're making me nervous."

Brady sat. He felt Ian's hand come under the back of his shirt, and massage his lower back, then curve around to cup his waist. The sweat at his belt buckle.

He reached over to cup Ian's balls, the warmth under the denim. Their lips met. Kissing spasmodically, Brady moved down his jaw to his neck. He popped open Ian's pants and pulled out his cock, jerking it and rubbing the tip with his thumb.

Ian moaned. His index finger dove down Brady's crack, rubbing and working his asshole. He licked the finger and stuck it back in. A lit window on the wall went black.

They buckled against each other, Ian pulsing in Brady's hand.

Brady climbed off the bench, his knees in the dirt, and ran his tongue along the head of Ian's cock. Plunging shaved balls deep in Brady's mouth, Ian gripped his hair and pumping his face on his cock.

A cat brushed against Brady's back, mewling. He felt the soft fur on his rear and laughed, more a gurgle than a giggle.

"God dammit!" Ian said.

"It's a hummer!" Brady said.

"Okay." Ian fell down and pulled the other's pants down, freeing his uncircumcised dong. He worked the foreskin back and forth, as if it was a fascinating new toy.

Flat on his back in the dirt, Brady stared upwards to the sky. The kitty licked his forehead in tender scrapes. Ian hooked his arms around the other man's knees and pulled him upwards, so that his cock was rubbing into his anus.

"What do you think?" he asked.

"I'm into it."

"Got a condom?"

"Shit, I don't actually. It's cool, though." Brady answered.

Ian smiled, and began to push. Brady willed himself to loosen, and felt the rod fill him. His own cock was stiff against his stomach. He reached down and stroked it.

The cat began licking his eyelid. Ian pumped harder, forcing his way into the tight, grainy rectum.

Brady moaned, his body convulsing.

"Mraorw!" Fast cat away in the dark.

Cum in spatters on Brady's stomach, a star of orgasm shooting out his heart.

Ian clenched him closer, thrust again, and pulled out, his stallion member shining in the moonlight. Jets of cum on the grass below.

At the time, I was with Limone.

Climbing the four flights of stairs to Limone's place, I watched the molding glide by under the mosquito-buzz of the light. I tapped lightly on the door, beneath a Pucci postcard, and Limone let me in.

"Honey, so glad you could make it."

"No problem. I just wanted to make sure you were okay," I followed her in.

"Okay? Okay? Well, I guess I'm okay, I mean, I don't really feel very excited about the world right now...I'm in debt to Donny again, though he's being cool this time, thank god. Everyone thinks I'm losing my mind, I think I'm losing my mind, I got a nosebleed this morning..." Blood-daubed tissue were wadded by the vanity mirror, stark stage lights illuminating lipstick and massage oil.

I shrugged. "Well, nosebleeds aren't too bad..."

"Yeah, I know, they're just visually alarming. Just kind of makes you look in the mirror and wonder what the fuck you're doing, like, this is so not cute anymore."

"I know, I know. It's a bit scary. But they tidy up." I looked anywhere but the tissue. "But no, don't think I'm downplaying this shit, believe me, I'm not exactly feeling cute either. ...it's Ian, I don't know, he's working all the time. It seemed real, but now it's starting to seem like more of an after-bar hookup thing."

"What else is there?" A shoe tree dripped layers of heels, ice blue to black patent and buckles in between.

"Well, I heard this strange rumor that guys sometimes take girls out for dinner, but that hasn't happened to me in years."

"I think you're asking for too much," Limone said, checking her hair in the huge gilt mirror. "Feel lucky if he has a place to live."

"Yeah, you're right. But it is kinda annoying to always sit around for a million hours as he cleans the bar and then we go to my place by four. And I'm not even sure why it's always my place. But that's quibbling, sorry."

"Yeah, hello? Real problems?"

"Okay, Jesse. He's living with Jay in a van in the TL."

Limone turned to the mirror again.

"And you're fucking Jay too?"

"I like a little danger. Jay's just so goddam delectable. I love that rosy blush they have at that age."

"Pedophile."

"Whatevs."

"But on that Jesse tip, just get a grip on it. Try to talk it out with him."

"Well, I the last time I ran into him, I way too freaked out to deal with it, I just ran the hell out of there. You don't know what he's capable of"

"You don't really think…"

"I do know what I think. I think he's dangerous. I think I need to watch my back."

"That bad?"

"Isn't that what I've been trying to tell you! Yeah, that bad. Knife fight bad."

"Well listen, try to be strong, okay. Remember you have people backing you up, it's not just the two of you in the Tenderloin anymore. Just go out tonight, and don't get too fucked up, and try to have a reasonable conversation if you see him. But don't go where the bouncer can't see you."

"Fuck-tastic."

"Look, I'm trying here." Limone threw a final spritz of Bumble & Bumble into her shag, and pulled on some black flats. "Let's roll."

I stared at the crumpled tissue, thinking of my own bloodstains in the bathroom trash, crimson fading into brown into the souvenirs I hoped my lovers wouldn't find. The mornings bleeding through to dawn light, the days fading into the next.

At the party, I hung limply to the sidelines, my cowl-neck hanging too far, and my boots too severe. Stopping by the kitchen counter, I lifted bottle after bottle, each empty and light as they jerked upwards to my touch. A young girl looked away as I lifted a half-full glass and sipped the last dregs of wine. Bottom-feeding. I had spent my cab fare home on drinks, my booze money on coke, and was now waiting to see how far cleavage could get me. Double A did not always equal triple X.

Across the room, Ian smoked and talked to Brady. A cone of blue light hung over them. Relieved, I wended in their direction. Stumbling past Audrey, I finally fell to the wall beside them.

"Are you okay?" said Ian. He pulled off his glasses and rubbed them with a black t-shirt.

"Oh, hey. I was, well, I don't know. Not a good evening, I guess. I'm just not feeling it. I feel, I don't know, played out or something, like I should just stop doing this. Do you have any coke?"

He stiffened, "I never have coke, you know that."

"Oh, right. You're right."

Brady put a hand on my shoulder, "You're sure you're alright?"

"No, totally, yeah, I'm fine," I said, giving Ian the eye. He straightened, seeming put out. "Was I interrupting something?" I murmured.

The men gave each other meaningful glances, and moved apart. Ian slipped next to me, and leaned over.

"Lena, we were talking about the bar. Business."

"Business, always, right."

"He wants to DJ on Thursdays; we're trying to figure it out."

"That's cool, whatever." I shifted my head from side to side against the dismal glitter of the strobe light. "Are you all worked out now?" I muttered.

"Lena. Get it together. Are you always wasted?"

"Who isn't?"

"Okay, okay, yeah. I get it. Just try and pull yourself together, okay, we've got shit to do."

"Well sor-ry...didn't know this was so important. It's just another party, come on."

"Just maintain, okay?"

"Okay, right." I clenched my chin down to my chest, frustrated. "Whatever."

"But no, really, is this really what you want to be doing for the rest of your life?"

"No, seriously, it's not, I know, Ian, I know I need to get it together, I want to do something, really, I've just got to fucking get it together."

"Like hell you need to get it together. Most definitely."

"What the hell?" I said, "I know things are a little hectic right now, I know things aren't good, look, I'm sorry if I can't be the most perfect, pro-active girlfriend for you, but I'm sorry, I just have my own shit going on right now, and for all that that may mostly concern an eight-ball, I'm sorry, I try. I do care about you, I do. A lot. I wait at the bar for hours for you to come fuck me."

"Lena. Try to show a little discretion. Come on, let's go outside."

"Okay, okay." I followed him down the hall, down the long stairs to a patch of tile and the outward gate to the street. Outside, the moon shone over Victorian turrets and broken beer bottles. We wandered down the block to a doorway. I reached down his shirt to his collarbones, running sharp nails across it.

"Dah-ling."

"Don't try that Dah-ling shit on me, Lena." He threw my hands off his chest.

"What?"

"You just want to slide by on the surface of things, when will you understand that you've got to get deeper than that? I am not just boy #365 to you, at least I shouldn't be. I know you've had a few. I should be the one that matters, the one you are actually going to think about, not a blank seduction for another naked coked-out night. Think about it."

I fell backwards, hugging my shoulders. "Look, I'm sorry, I was just trying to…"

"I know, I know, I know what you were trying to do, it's okay, we all try to seduce, but come on, how long can you do that? How long can we cycle on like this?"

"I don't know what you mean?"

"Come on, you do. How many bumps can you do in the bathroom before you know it's really over? Sure, there are people that do that past their twenties, but we all know that the new kids are needling us out. It just bothers me to see you wasting yourself like that."

"Look, I'm sorry if I have no meaning or purpose for you. I try to be a decent human being, I recycle, I call my Grandma, I give to Planned Parenthood, even with their little omission, I'm sorry if my life goals don't conform to yours, Mr. Serious. I try."

A cop car drove by, sirens echoing past the stucco and Wisteria façades. Ian took me by the shoulder and said, "Look. Just do something, anything, with yourself."

"Who are you to ask that? Look, I'm just trying to get a job at this point, mustering a zeitgeist is not exactly in my day planner."

The corners of his mouth twitched. "Well, get back to me when you've got it figured out."

"I can't believe you're doing this right now."

"Just talk to me later, okay," he snapped.

I turned and wobbled down the street. The treacherous muck of gum-wrappers and diesel exhaust wrapped around me as I shivered, pulling my blazer around my waist and taking quick, mincing steps that fell to pieces as I tripped and skidded sideways on my ankle. Gasping, I pulled up and began to slog away again, hoping I could make it back home.

I walked down the hall, and deposited myself on Limone's bed. I glanced at her, noticing the amount on the mirror, but stayed quiet as she dealt out a rail and pointed it towards me.

"Dah-link?"

"Oh. Right. Thanks." I ducked and swept it up. The shimmer was blurred by anxiety, the bliss blazed out by the tolerance…but yes. I smiled and lifted back up, resting my elbows on the bed. "But what about you?" I asked.

"Oh, you know," said Limone, "I got my own way. Don't look."

I looked away, waiting as I heard a soft clang, the hiss of a lighter, a long pause, and then a gasp. I looked up to see Limone with a needle to her arm, belt tightened, head back as she stuck it in.

"Oh honey, How long have you been doing this?"

Limone went limp with release, her blue eyes dilated, her long frame splayed across the floor. I bent down and cut myself another line from the pile. It was going to be a long night.

And there were more and more long nights, as I sat on Limone's bed watching her blur out under the needle, remembering Jesse and the unraveling pearl of blood that went shooting up the syringe as the cocaine sped in.

Taking a deep gulp of my Fernet, I surveyed the Rosetta. It was a Saturday, full of the tousled and taunting. The neon cobra above pierced through the smoke, as I stared up at it like one would a distant star. Above the huddled hair products, above the abraded noses and leers, out that door and up to that streetlight-blurred sky I knew there were stars; distant, beckoning, welcoming. Free.

Limone came up behind me, falling against my shoulder. "Come with me for a sec, to the ladies."

She wavered back through the pouncing dancers, while I fell behind. She knocked heavily on the restroom door. It stayed firm.

"Open up, this is my office," Limone yelled over the music.

The door parted momentarily, and we wriggled in. The room was filled with eager, grasping hands. They pulled her through to the back counter and set her on a wire stool. The pale jade walls were scarred with tags and flyers. I pulled myself up on the other stool.

Limone did not look good: a gray-green sheen was forming on her face, while her voice careened upwards. It ricocheted off the chandelier, sliding in sour glissandos down the ivy strands.

She pulled her purse to her lap and began doling out grams, as hands full of twenties waved hungrily. She opened one of the bags and took a bump, then passed it to me. The room filled with nervous laughter. The ivy wound tighter. I took a key-bump and sealed the bag. I wet my finger and daubed it along the crease, then licked it off.

"Limone...do you need help with anything?" I asked, passing it on. The door opened, and more people poured in, more and more, as Limone lifted her key and thrust in the bag. She took a long sniff, and slid it back into her purse.

"Hey, what about me, eh?" a voice sprung up from the back of the bathroom. "Pack my beak at an alarming rate!"

"Yeah!" The crowd surged forwards, pushing her back against the counter. Pupils dilated and face pasty, Limone clutched the countertop, trying to crawl on top. Like an antennae of silk she pulled herself up, wavering, kneeling and shying away from the mob.

"Leave me the fuck alone..." She yelled, "You people don't know how hard it is to do this, to handle your demands night after night, to deal with your cracked out bullshit. You're not famous, you're just tweaker bitches and scenester twats who think you own the place because you have no where else to go. Fucking hipsters. You beg for my shit, and then you get all weak, and insecure, and I have to sit here and listen to you trade phone numbers with people you're never going to call all because you think you've had this great life changing moment with them, when really, fuck you, you're just babbling away in a piss-smelling cave surrounded by crackheads and filth. Fuck you, and you and you and you! And you back there who yelled, yeah, do you know how much I owe my dealer because I've been nice to people like you?"

She fell back against the mirror, breath fast and unsteady. Skate stickers scraped with lipstick hung against her hair, as her face fell to the side and a precipitation halo formed from her breath. The crowd muttered.

The bathroom door opened, and Big Al came barreling through.

"What the hell is going on in here, now git, party's over. Leave the poor girl alone. And you, there with the mullet, this ain't 1982." His arms shone with sweat as he cleared the way through to Limone's body. 'Is she okay?"

"She's breathing," I said. "So she didn't have a heart attack." I leaned over and shook her gently, as she opened her eyes. Violets.

"What the fuck?"

"You passed out on us, honey, too sketch."

"Well shit, you let me faint on this? Do you know how many people have pissed on this floor?" She lifted naked shoulders from the tile.

"I try not to think about it," I said.

"Thank god I didn't wear the Von Furstenberg."

"Oh, you stole that, anyway."

"I know. But, shit, those bastards, they seriously would have carved us up into little gram-sized pieces and smuggled them out in their handbags. I'm getting the fuck out of here."

"Aw...It's the end of an era."

"But, no, it's like, I mean, I've got to get off this shit, my pulse is still all tweaked out and I'm all paranoid, and I'm so in debt as it is. This wasn't exactly the money-making proposition I thought it was. I'll be lucky if I get out of here without pawning my computer to pay him back."

"Oh honey." The bass reverberated through the walls.

"Yeah, and Lena, it's gotten bad, it's gotten really bad. I wake up and do it, I do it in my room when no one's around, I do it when I go out and then I do it at the afterparty. There's no one there to stop me. There's this vacuum. I can do whatever I want and it just becomes more and more. And the shooting's no good." She stared upwards pleadingly, "I'm going back to my mom's in Marin."

I lifted her hands, pulling her up until we were standing. The chandelier shone warm dapples on our hair, matched by the smell of shit and antisepectic cleanser. We ambled out the door and into the treacherous confines of the bar, as the toying synth called us back to the fold.

Walking down Montgomery Street past the Bank of America building, on the way back from picking up my pills, I heard the tones of the calliope keyboard. The carnival whirled as melodies blurred, one starting before the other had stopped. Carousels and evil clowns ignited in my head as I passed, smiling with the realization that, no, I did not have a psychotic breakdown every time I hit the Clay Street Walgreen's. Hiding between two SF Weekly dispensers, the musician adjusted his glasses and lifted his fingers for another melody.

I walked on. The sidewalk was sparkling, and people sped past with a purposes. In Limone's absence, I was on hiatus from the bar. Trying it out. The skyscraper's dark windows lifted endlessly above me, each one invoking another human caught in fluorescence with a computer and desk. And a phone. A large, multi-extension phone. Treading lightly, I tried to block out the rising feeling of emptiness. Ian had not called. I had thought of nothing else. A khaki shoulder shoved into me and I stumbled, tripping into a severe matron with a rolling bag.

"Hrmph!" The grande dame grunted, and I went on.

From the stairs of Montgomery Station, I fell immediately into blossoms. Lilies and Zinnias and bright Gerber daisies, the painful red roses and dignified stems. I descended quickly and went closer, my cheeks burning as I screwed my eyes to the pavement.

As I fingered the petals of a daffodil, I knew that Ian would never buy flowers for me, nor Jay, or Jesse either. I was an independent woman, a free agent, a…alone. I watched a man leave the stall with a bouquet held gently, knowing that it was not meant for me.

A thin wisp of accordion music came up from the station. White tulips were perched with open baby mouths in a carafe. I leaned down and picked up a cluster, cradling them. No one would ever do this for me. Perhaps it was better to do things for myself. I was independent, right, I didn't need a boyfriend. I was a modern feminist who could live as I chose. My man-candy gave me what I needed. And that was all. Tenderly, I stroked the petals.

An elderly woman and her husband were lifting a suitcase down the stairs, helping each other with easy familiarity. To know someone that well, to know their blood and the capacity of their bones, to have the capacity to work as one in a task that should be daunting… Blinking back tears, I carried my purchase into the shop.

It was early March, and a few wilted Valentine's Day arrangements were still visible in the back. A barrage of potted sconces spread across the wall, as the woman took the tulips and began to wrap them in plastic. Plucking a stem of ivy, she encased them in brown paper and stapled the edges.

"Are they a gift?" she asked.

"No, no, they're for me," I blurted. The woman hunched over and let them drop into my hands.

On the bus, the blondes and suits gouged their eyes into me. Slumping over the package, I inhaled their questions as the wheels throbbed. It was half pity and half inquiry, I decided, putting aside a vote for paranoia. Surely they could see through my dejection and lowered eyes to the cold mornings taking up the whole bed. Hiding in the muck and dampness on the rubber floor, I endured the half hour ride with my hands folded.

When I opened the door to my studio, I stared around at the spent, discarded clothing and newly amateurish paintings with an eye to toss the whole thing. They were all just reminders that I had been laboring all these years for what, for the achievement of some dubious aesthetic through collecting trash? Through smearing colors to seem fulfilled? Through gathering books and records and clothes and beauty shit that in the end did nothing at all? I was not any better, My things did nothing for me. I was still alone, still twenty-nine, still throwing myself into an adventure in masochism because it was all that thrilled me. In the way I needed. While she spent my nights tracing studies of Brady's face.

I took a deep breath and ripped open the flowers. Spreading them out on the kitchen table, I saw that each stem was satin-swathed and luminous with green life. I picked up a blossom and inhaled a dewy field catching the light in acres and swans. Children and dogs running through it. Children that would never scream in a flight or convulse in greed at Target, but maintain the miniscule perfection of solemn toddlers on the cross-town bus.

Settling them into a pint glass, I filled it with tap water and set them on my bedside table. There. I was an independent woman. The luminous petals lolled in soft circles over bursting stems. I toyed with an stalk. There. I would not be afraid. Although I would stalk the dawns alone, there was a silence there that embraced me, and I would survive into the day.

Chapter 9
razors, stubble & rouge

Elbows bent to the bar, I hunched over my shot. It was after hours, the bar almost empty. A dim halo backlit the hard alcohol, shining silver over Ian's back as he wiped down the sinks. The bartender grabbed lemons and olives and yanked the containers to the mini-fridge. I looked down the dark wood, plastic scraped with initials now glistening from the rag's last swipes. I picked up a straw and tapped it, lightly, against my glass. So much for hiatus. Pulling my eyes up slowly, I stared sadly at Ian as he bent to talk to Al, their heads blurred in shadows.

Ian straightened and turned to the bottles, drawing Saran Wrap over them gently. He moved over to me and watched as I tried to smile, then bent forwards.

"So you stayed."

"I had to. I wanted to talk to you. I...I... know I was drunk the other night, and being an idiot, and I'm sorry."

"Apology accepted. Yeah, I'm kind of sorry about that too, no, not just kind of. I was being a little harsh, I was stressed out over Brady's DJ night and some bar stuff I don't really want to get into."

"Like what?"

"Let's just say the Limone thing has accelerated some...issues for us."

"I see..." I muttered.

"Yeah, but then when I saw you just being a victim of it, of circumstance I guess, just drifting along and not trying to change things, I got angry, and I lashed out." His eyes were soft behind the glasses.

"Yeah. I know thing's are fucked right now, but that's my problem, and you don't need to get involved with it."

He reached under the bar for ice.

"I don't need you to deal with my problems," I said fiercely. "I can deal with my own shit. I guess what I'm asking for is a more consistent response."

"I know, I know," he said, "It's just that I'm really busy. I have a lot on my mind." He shot spouts of gin and lime juice into the drink, and took a sip. "Hmmm. More lime."

I drooped.

"Just try," he said.

"I – okay."

He took another sip.

I withered. He looked up.

"I'm moving in with Brady. I can't afford the studio anymore."

"Really?"

"Yeah, we're trying to get out of the Tenderloin, it's just too depressing, after awhile."

"You'll be happier. Wait for me tonight."

The bartender moved in and said, "Hey, do you have the key to the back?" Ian turned to the cash register and rustled around, then followed the guy to the storage room. I watched him go, clicking my fingertips against the side of the glass. I rocked my feet back and forth, twirled the dark liquid, and took another sip. It would be a long wait, and it would be best to nurse this gracefully.

The next day, walking up Van Ness to Geary Street, I saw a darting body picking butts off the sidewalk. Jesse. He stuck one in his mouth and lit it quick, tossed it down and leaned against a bench.

I swerved on instinct, trying to look like I'd left the baby on the bus. Stepped into an alley, splashing in the drainwater. He hadn't seen me yet. I hoped.

Tossing in my bed, I threw my head to the pillow, let the stuffing settle, and swiveled to new contortions. Jesse. Razors and shower-rails hung sullen in the closet, with hangers of ridiculous clothes. Maybe if I moved, he couldn't find me. I stared straight ahead into the static of my night vision. Lately, if I stared too long at any one spot, I would see a spider coalesce out of the scribble and advance towards me. I kept my eyes closed hard at night.

My phone rang, and I sighed. Not on the bedside table, not on the floor, the sound increased as I reached for my purse and dumped it out mercilessly. I always answered the phone when it rang late at night, knowing it was either a party tip, a booty call, or a cracked out friend needing consolation. All worth attention.

"It's Limone!"

"Darling! I didn't think I'd hear from you, I've been all worried about you, in fact."

"I've been getting better. They're fattening me up, seriously, now that I've been easing off the drugs I've been getting a little tum-tum"

"Hey, beat's emaciated. I'm just so glad you're alright."

"What's been happening with you, how's the Rosetta and stuff?"

"Oh, the same...you know...it never changes, except you're not there. I miss you, though, it's getting lonelier."

"I'm sorry, sweetie. I miss you too. I'm teaching myself HTML as a cure to boredom. That and hanging out with Iris, this girl I know from high school. It's different, though, the scene here is so different. The guys are so douchey and beefy...someone handed me his business card at this bar the other day, and I was, like, you mean you're not a DJ?"

"Employment...I've heard of it. Not a fan."

"Me neither. I've been thinking, if I can put together a cool enough website, something like rotten tomatoes or something, I could maybe do that instead of clipping asshole hipster hair sculptures. It just seems more sustainable."

"That sounds pretty fun, actually. I'm all about agoraphobia. But listen, if you ever feeling like coming back to the city, I would so love to see you. Let's go out some time."

I clicked shut the phone and crawled under the covers again, seeking the sweet haziness of sleep. To climb iridescent goblets to hotel rooms with waterslides on the pillow, slipping downwards to anchors under docks lined with marionettes...I closed my eyes and slipped away.

Brady, Lucas and I rattled down Mission Street. Drunk and happy, we were headed to El Farolito after the show. Coming out of the darkness at the 24th street BART Station, the fluorescent glow and steam trays rattled as we joined the line at the 24-hour taqueria. Little cups of salsa were piled in pyramids along the plexi counter, and swiped as often as they were stacked. The smell curled inside me and made a fist. I hadn't eaten since the day before.

"Special quesadilla, por favor." I said. Green salsa with cilantro shreds.

In the back, on a yellow booth, Lucas pulled a forty from his bag, and took a drink. Long, golden liquid going down.

"You have to hear our new song, I fucking love it, Brady wrote it."

"Oh, thanks," he said. "I fucking love this burrito."

"It loves you back."

Stuffing meat and cheese into my mouth, I said, "Well, yeah, sing it! That'd be awesome."

Brady rocked back and forth, took a drink from the forty, and grabbed Lucas' hand.

Sitting in the back of a limousine,
All stretched out, if you know what I mean.
We've got some money, and a little bit of time,
And If we had a little more, than we could go for a ride.

I'll be your Mistress, or, and if you want hardcore,
You can go for more, like you've done before.
I'll be your Mistress, or, and if you want hardcore,
You can come for more, like you've done before.

Lying in a bed in a hotel room,
Not much to say, but a whole lot to do.
Living it up, just the best that we can,
Because I know you gotta jet by quarter to ten.

I'll be your Mistress, or, and if you want hardcore,

You can go for more, like you've done before.
I'll be your Mistress, or, and if you want hardcore,
You can come for more, like you've done before.

Second place is my favorite space
First is a bore, and third is a chore.
First will suffice, while third is just right
Let me be your filthy secret to-ni-i-i-ght.

Wealthy Whore Entertainment

The last note hung in the air, as their hands dropped. My paper plate was grease-marked, and I could feel the acid scratch of truth through my heart.

Donny passed me the twenty, and I swooped to take the line. My nose flared with pain as I inhaled, lifting quickly to pull up my top. I had stopped over before going to the Rosetta, and gotten waylaid by free drugs. They lay like gasoline tangos on the mirrored coffee table, under the of the anemone.
"So, how's the chinchilla?" I asked.
"Chinchillin."
I laughed, as the rodent scuttled in the hamster ball as if the most exquisite carrot lay just beyond the subwoofer.
"I used to have one of those, this cute lil' rattykins."
"A rat?"
"She was great, really! Little scaly tail wrapping around your wrist, little nibbly teeth. Mine was called Heartsy"
He laughed. "I had a dog, your basic Weinerdog, real yippy. Took him on my paper route all the time."
"Paper route?"
"Oh, yeah, wait a sec, in fact, check this out." He got up and disappeared into the back room, emerging minutes later with a children's book. His large hands cradled it like antique glass. Sitting down on the couch, he opened it and leaned over to me.
I rubbed my nose fiercely and peered at the cover. "The Paperboy?"
"Yeah. I used to deliver *The Chronicle* to this old handicapped guy, and I would water his plants and shit, and help him out, and then he wrote this book about me. Read it." He passed it to my lap.
I paged through watercolor illustrations of a young black kid, waking at 4, waking his dog, and setting off while the bakers were cooking their wares. Watching as the child leapt over stores on his Schwinn, I turned to shots of him throwing papers through sprinklers and chain link, the dog running behind. Finally, he came back to

his bed, bag empty, and turned to dream of spokes and barks and great, hurtling sprinklers. I closed the cover and looked at him.

"That's beautiful."

"Thanks. He was just this sweet old guy, and then he gave this to my mother one day, and said he wanted her to have this. She kept it for me, and gave it to me when I was twenty. I'd love to know where that guy was now, probably dead, but hey, it's pretty cool anyway." Donny was beaming, with a contentment I rarely saw. His broad cheeks shone as he leaned to the coffee table. I ran my hand across the glossy cover, feeling the creases of age in the laminate, thinking of it resting in a drawer for fifteen years of eiderdown and cotton balls. Another's memory, the memory of him encapsulated like a secret history, passed on intermittently to an unknown rhythm.

The Jetta sped down Market Street, making a hasty detour onto Valencia. The Mission was swarming with people, the restaurants bustling, drunk hipsters roaring out of the bars, the real residents making their way. Restaurants sided with modular furniture boutiques and sushi bars, martini neon hovering over men selling H at the 16th Street BART Station. I watched Limone's hands fiddling with the CD player, her mouth moving with gossip and wisps. Since she'd moved back to Marin, she'd been letting her natural hair color grow in, a chestnut shade that hung in waves over her shoulders. We were on our way to Bordello, this time, veering around in search of parking.

"God, I've got to move back into the city, this drive is killing me!" Limone said.

"I suppose living with the parents would kind of cramp your style. I couldn't do it." The bright signs of liquor stores fluttered through my vision.

"Yes, totally. I though it would be great to move back in, and, you know...clean up and shit....and yeah. Plus, when I lived in that place in the Tenderloin, I could never park anywhere, and the parking tickets were insane. The city's fun to party in, but, I don't know, living here is fucking depressing. Wipes your soul."

"Oh, I know, but I still want to stay here. Sure, it's hard. Getting that place in the Haight with Brady almost wiped me out, but it's so intense and exciting, you feel really alive here. Plus, you can do pretty much anything you want, and get away with it. I love that."

"Yeah, I suppose. Marin is just making me crazy. It's nice to have the free food and laundry and no rent, but it comes with a heavy dose of, 'Oh my God, are you wearing that to work?' I mean, come on, It's just hair."

"At least you have work."

"Oh Lord, I gave a ninety year old woman a Brazilian today. Being an aesthetician is not all that. I'm working on that web project, though."

We cruised past a Mondrian-squared dentist's office, the orange and aqua swiped by moldy white. The air was thick with exhaust and urine. Two men with ragged beards slugged from a bottle on the stoop of a discount furniture shop.

"Here," Limone said. "Let's find a seedy alley and do a bump."

"Alright."

The car veered over to a dark crevice behind a coffeeshop, and we pulled in. A mural spread along the concrete, coating the wall in the faces of Vishnu and a mirror-inlaid sun god. The orange was dim in the dark, and the mirrors reflected nothing but blackness. I looked far into it.

"How are you and Ian, anyway?"

"Okay." I dug around in my purse, avoiding the question. "I don't know, I have this huge uncertainty about him. He exists in this night fog of someone I can't pin down. He's so ultimately desirable to me, obviously, he's way more solid than Jesse, he's actually not a sociopath, but at this point even the idea of a solid relationship seems slippery. Unattainable, even." Pulling out the bag with a half-guilty sigh, I handed it to her. "I don't know, I just want to wake up the next morning and have someone still there."

In the light of the dim restaurant doors and the dumpsters, Limone was a bundle of comfort. She lifted a light hand and set it down hard. "Hon, there are men who have jobs and will not beat you. Who might even marry you."

"Are you sure that isn't just what your mom told you, and it only applies to the – sorry, unspeakable – class strata who are d/d free, no baggage, and under 22?" Folding the baggie into my makeup bag, I leaned back and stared at the bare hints of stars above the neon. "Darling, I have so much ho-baggage." The faint whispers of light were so thoroughly drowned that it seemed ridiculous to even search for the Big Dipper or the Pleiades. Orion had been my favorite constellation since sixth grade, when I was Athena in the school play and my best friend played these stars. Ever since, I would try to find them, but in the city's glare it was usually impossible. Only the green café sign slashed with red let us see.

Leaning over the balcony to the scarlet curtains and Moroccan lamps, I surveyed the dance floor. Bordello was more than packed, bodies jostling shoulder to shoulder beneath smears of eyeliner. They danced recklessly and flirted the same, and amid the strobe and jolting beats, it was easy to fall into all sorts of debauchery. I watched knowing that last week and the last I had fallen hand to hand to men here, but all of it fell away as easily as silk.

Next to me, Limone sipped a Stella Artois and laughed into the air. She rested her elbows on the railing and lowered her head, then turned to me.

"Hey, do you want to sit down? I feel so obvious up here pining over the little hotties." From our perch on the balcony, the bottom floor of the club spread out below them, spots of white and red shooting over dancing bodies. A fifteen-foot screen at the far end roared with fluctuating pixels, fireworks superimposed with celluloid beauties on split-screen.

We turned and snuggled into a plush couch, leaning back and watching the strangers blend into red. A Kraftwerk/Spice Girls mash-up was playing, the lights darting over outstretched hands.

"So, darling, how's things." I asked.

"Oh, well, I dumped Derrick, did I tell you that?"

"No! What happened, I though you were all into him. Wasn't it, like, a month ago that you were raving to me that you met a boy at the Coffee Cat? I mean, mraowr!"

"Raowr, Raowr, Cougar-time, I know, I thought he was the greatest...I mean, he was Swedish, you know how I feel about blondes. And he was really intelligent."

"I don't know, I remember that time you guys came over, and he spent the rest of the night babbling about why Sweden was better than the US and how his business model was superior to all others. I just about died."

Limone laughed. "Well, I thought the business part was interesting."

"Business major, that's what I said."

"You know, yeah, well..."

"Oh Limone, it's okay, it's nothing to be ashamed of."

"I guess, I just feel sometimes like I'm a big sell-out. You know? Since I gave up the drug trade for e-trade."

"Everyone needs to make a living somehow, and the fact that you're working on something you enjoy is great! It was totally time to quit dealing. Don't you remember...come on, remember! Nosebleeds, Donny on your case? Things were really fucked. But then, look at me, living from temp job to temp job and pretending I can be an artist is pretty ridiculous too. Artist equals coffee in this town. Bartender if you're lucky, titty-dancer if you're not."

"Thanks. I need to be told that, sometimes. And don't get down on yourself like that, you can still bring some slides to Southern Exposure and try to get a show or something. Don't give up, you've done it before. There's so many galleries, coffeeshops, you know, clubs even."

"At this point I have very few illusions about making my living at it. I mean, I was told this at school and I've been told it again, painting is a dead art. Representational, figurative painting, especially. Dead. Useless. Nobody cares. I mean, sure, I read Juxtapoz, and there's some cool shit in there, but so much of it is so subculturally mannered, you know, like rockabilly pin-up-girls on bowling pins, or ultra-mod Tiki bars. It's so LA It's like, if you don't have Betty Page bangs and bustiers, your work isn't relevant."

"Well, how important is context versus what you want to be doing? Does it make you happy? Then does it matter how it fits into some sort of weird illusory movement or whatever?"

I sighed. "Movements aren't illusory. They just aren't part of the world we spend our time in. I know that, here, the pointy vs. round shoe debate is bigger than any sort of subversion of the male gaze through the Guerilla Girls, the male gaze is par for the course to get most things I want, and perhaps even my old Riot Grrl aesthetics are a little outré as of now. You know how when people on Craigslist say, 'I'm a 30 year old grrrl.' It just doesn't work. But ArtForum's too expensive to stay abreast of, when I'm working my ass off just to eat."

"But, I mean, who cares about that stuff?"

"People do. There is a world out there of people I have never seen who debate this stuff, whether it's the exploitation of outsider art à la *Pecker*, or the subversion of the picture plane, whether there can at all be any value anymore to representation. – or flat art at all, like maybe it's all unhangable and unbuyable?"

"What? Then what is it?"

"I don't know. My last installation involved a light-up plexiglass table with a bunch of jello molds jiggling and glowing."

"Jello shots? That sounds like a party."

"It was....yeah! A happening. But, yeah, sometimes someone will come along, like Mark Ryden, and reengage my hopes that all those skills I have of copying – and, really, it's just copying – just stealing from life and forgetting to credit the source – but that representation is valid, and can be relevant, and then..."

"Whoa, whoa, Lena, who came along and fucked you up like this? Everything I've seen of yours I liked. It's catchy, human, people can relate. What's wrong with paintings of cool people?"

"Modernist fucked me. I had this art teacher in undergrad, with a hook on one arm, and all he painted was shapes, little colored shapes, with black lines between them. They all looked like stained glass. I remember I was working on this canvas once, all of these different scenes like postcards on Byzantine gold, with a Virgin Mary at the center, and the story of a woman tying up a man and shooting him...when in a state of grace, when grace is lost...And he would come around, each week, and tell me, 'Lena, you have to stop this, this type of art-making is over. You will never go anywhere with this, gallery-owners will laugh at you. You need to go abstract.'

"That's really shitty. But, I mean, I remember Reed, they couldn't exactly stop you, could they?"

"No, they couldn't. I was pretty stubborn, I just kept on making those *diabolical* people. When I tried to paint in the abstract, I just ended up with smeary shit that I couldn't make any sense out of. I wanted meaning. Even if it was just the glamour of someone's sexy legs, some buildings, a cigarette. That was all I knew."

"Huh. But how did people react? It sounds like this teacher may have been on some weird trip."

"Fucking Modernism! Fucking Clement Greenburg! Well, I remember one time, I was in this critique for a sculpture class, and I had this sort of – you know those Jesus candles?"

"Oh yeah, El Anima Sola. Lonely Soul. That one in your room."

"Yeah, that one. I cast my torso in plaster and rigged up these cellophane torches and covered the top with plastic flowers and baby doll heads, and this hippy dude said it looked like something a crazy person would make in their garage."

"What the fuck?"

"Yeah, I was, like, excuse me, you made a fucking clay pot. Wow, your friend has a kiln. You mean you got stoned together and ate some lentils and played with clay? Do you want to have snacktime now? Play hacky-sack? Naptime? I'll call your parents to come pick you up."

"Well, you have to admit, its a little Courtney Love."

"It was the nineties. I liked Hole. It was about "The Body.""

"God, this does sound kind of bitchy."

"Crits always were. My problem was more that Kitsch, which was what I was really super-into, was seen back then as, please, I quote, "the most degraded" part of modernity, this trite, banal, tacky nouveau riche casino bullshit. Vegas-y. My teachers wanted solid blue canvases. I wanted Liberace."

"You do walk around like you got attacked by the sequin factory, but, really, that other stuff is where people say, "My kid could do that.""

"Yeah. Modernism was, in a sense, about being really, really boring. Have you ever tried to read *Tender Buttons* without a nap in the middle? I have to drink and sound it out."

"But come on. The real thing is, does painting, your way, satisfy you?"

"I don't know. I still love doing it, it gives me this sense of peace I don't get anywhere else, but while I'm scraping away in my room it's more therapeutic than interactive. I mean, sure, I've done shows, and been written up in magazines and stuff, but that was back then. As of now, millennium o'clock, nobody cares."

"Well, if that's what you're going to believe..."

"Hey, let's go get another drink," I said, jumping up. As we threaded our way down the stairs and into the mayhem of the bar, I closed my eyes and tried to block out the guitars. Opening them, I saw that Limone was handing me a gin and tonic, glowing blue in the blacklight.

It was late afternoon, in the apartment I shared now with Brady, and the pearl grey sky was hemmed into the fire escape over flowering cherry trees. White blossoms like snakeskin spots, like a Xerox enlarged a million times until the image blares into shattering pixels. Staring at them on a screen, pixels blared into squares of a thigh and a tambourine.

Two raw sienna couches framed a table draped in maroon. A moon mirror hung above. Brady wandered out from his room and sat down on the couch. A little too thin now, he hid his wasted limbs under glittery women's blouses and scarves. The frayed hem of his smoking jacket hid a tracery of scars. He leaned into the couch and closed his eyes.

I heard the rustling and peered out my door, still wavering from the night before. My head was scrambling, hair disheveled. I approached and set a hand on his shoulder, saying, "Hey, sorry if I kept you awake last night."

"No, no, it's okay. Stumbling in late."

"The ushe." I sunk to the couch next to him. "I don't really want to get into it. "

"Mimosa?" he gestured towards the fridge.

"Urg, no, that's okay, I can still taste the booze. Coffee's all I want right now."

"Up to you. How was Bordello?"

"It was decent..." I stared limply at the dripping ashtray and drifts of bottle caps on the table. "Limone was having a boy crisis, so I was trying to cheer her up. We spent most of the time on the balcony working through it...that and my art garbage. Once we got up, the crowd had pretty much dissipated and no one was dancing, so I took off pretty soon after that."

"Sounds fabulous."

"We had a good talk. Everything else was just decoration."

"Well, The Dummies are playing in three weeks, so you better come to that." He stretched a hand along the side of the plush, smoothing it with nails bitten to the quick. Outside, Haight Street was revving up for an afternoon of record swapping, the street punks and princesses tossing insults to the wind. A sheer white curtain filtered across a lamp with the beadwork ripped off. I moved to the coffeemaker and began to grind the beans.

Amber light fell across Delfina's Restaurant, trapping the patrons in syrup. Brass lamps with rainbow slits hung from the low ceiling, stretching back like a Mafia hideout. Ceiling mirrors reflected the back room, where Ian and I were perched on gold cubes. Haunted house wallpaper hung bronze over scarlet carpet, wrapping the sparsely populated room. A slight whiff of vinegary-wine trailed the walls. There was a large fish tank behind the bar.

I tapped out two lines on the glass tabletop and gestured over to Ian. He took one gingerly.

"I thought you didn't do that?" I asked, taking the other.

"Well, I guess I started," he said. "Temptation, I don't know. I used to back before we got the bar. I just felt like I wanted to get serious for awhile. But hey, whatever, you know." He raised two hands limply, as the murky red blurred out to envelop them. I took a long sip, closing my eyes.

"Wait, I have to go to the bathroom, I'll be back." I rose and wandered off, past Audrey's table. The girl looked up, and our eyes met for a moment, passing through bedrooms and phone lines and dark crowds and bathroom mirrors. I touched her shoulder momentarily and passed by.

A hallway opened at the back of the room, spanned by a low swinging door. I entered. Retreating double-time down red steps, I stopped at the kitchen door and looked in at the blue-white land of colanders and tureens. There was ice in the butcher knives, this iron clean, as I stared at the empty room. Even with people around me, even with Ian, I felt this isolation, this distance. All the late nights could not erase this feeling.

Pulling away, I went deeper into the building. Suddenly, a scrawny hand reached out and grabbed me by the wrist. A lattice of scars traced the thumb.

"What the hell?" I yelped and pulled away. Looking back, I saw sharp shoulders under leather, stubbled razors for cheeks, and Jesse emerged. He looked down at me, the sunglasses lost, and I could see the deep wrinkles etched around his eyes. He was a lot older than he had told me, I realized.

"What do you want?" I sighed.

"I need to talk to you. You fucked me over." His gaunt face.

"I fucked you over? Come on."

"But, you have to listen to me!" He lurched towards me. The restroom sign buzzed.

"I don't have to do anything, Jesse."

"But you do," and his eyed flared with that old viciousness. "You kicked me out on the street, bitch."

"You're a sociopath!"

"So you couldn't take it?" he said. A chill gust came in from the back door.

"I prefer to live my life in a slightly more orderly fashion, yes."

"Oh yeah, that's what I've been hearing. Sure, Lena," he sneered.

"Okay, things have been kind of fucked up lately, but, I'm getting it together. I mean, what the hell have you been doing?" The buzzing was overpowering.

His hands clenched involuntarily. Slip-knot rope. "Well, I hung out with Jay for awhile, then I went to Seattle, and met a girl, and then another girl, but then I heard I got into FIDM, so I'm living with this chick Vanessa now, and working on a fashion line. Kinda post-punk."

"Wait...You...worked? You got into any institution anywhere? You put together enough complete sentences to make an essay that wasn't smeared shit? You showed up for SATS and didn't clock the administrator for making you sit down and not use crayons?"

"Fuck you, Lena. I'm capable of a few things. All they wanted was a portfolio, and Vanessa helped."

"I wish you'd figured that out when you were with me, that would've helped a damn lot. But no, Jesse, it never would have worked out, because you're a violent bastard, and I was getting really sick of being slapped around and all the craziness, and the speed, and you just being such a mean motherfucker all of the time."

His eyes traced my hair, blurred. "Come on, Lena, think about it. We could get back together. It would be different." He ducked his head, stepping back momentarily into the shadow. "I've got my shit together now."

I wavered, remembering his arm on my shoulder as we slept. Waking up in a summer night with him to compare nightmares with. Striding through the Tenderloin arm in arm, with a half-pint of jack and the union of two fuck-ups against the fierce and glittering world.

His pinball eyes bore into me.

"We could," he said. "We could try."

The sharp path of a razor past the hula shower curtain, diving into the algae strands at my feet. An ashtray blown through lightbulbs smoking blue and metallic.

"Don't you want to be my Sedgwick? My Nico?"

"Yeah, and end up dead before my time? You're no more Warhol than Kris Danger."

"I'm gonna be bigger."

"You might want to get some talent first. I'm going back to my boyfriend, he's waiting for me."

I turned away, seeing the long stretch of hallway beckoning me. I started to walk, and as I walked, the red walls closed around me and I could only see the patterns on the wallpaper, the gold flowers and loops, mountains to climb with my hand tracing the velvet. I let his stare fall behind me as I climbed, quicker now.

I heard footsteps, felt a hand on my shoulder, he grabbed me, wrenching me back. I fell forwards, scrambled, punched, grappled for his shoulders and missed. His hand covered my mouth. I kicked him in the balls and he yelped and fell backwards, enough for me to wrestle away.

I ran through a side door, and found myself on a long, narrow passageway, with concrete walls and a plank rising to another room. I slid my hand along the wall and tip-toed down to the milk crates holding down the plank. I lifted myself through to the cubbyhole, wiggling my shoe free from the plastic lattice, and saw the open top of the fish tank that sat behind the bar. A tub of mixed nuts sat above with a wad of lettuce hanging in the water.

I moved closer, awestruck.

The blue eels, streaked with lemon, the crimson beta, spliced with white, all wafted delicately above the ground. Duct tape lined the cardboard top. I stared at the fish.

His long nails gouged into my shoulders as he pushed me forwards. With my nose an inch from the water, Jesse ripped my skirt up and pulled off my polka-dot panties. He dropped them in the fishtank, and I watched them drift slowly through the algae. He was hard immediately, gripping my hair with one hand and shoving his cock in my ass with the other.

I was getting ass-raped with the fishies. How did I get here? The numb nose...my body cold. The embarrassment of being caught at Delfina's with this loser...and by Ian...and, oh lord, Audrey would not be kind. I would be 86-d. Better to just wait until he finished.

Finally he squirted what felt like a gallon of Hep C cum in my anus, and for good measure shook some down for the fish. My face against the water, I watched the eels nibble at it.

Jesse slapped me on the ass and said, "There ya go, Tiger, bet ya forgot what that was like!"

Blank...blank...cold. No presence was survival. Distance was strength.

"It's not the same with no lube, asshole! I mean, come on, didn't they teach you anything in the military? I have to go now."

"I'll call you!"

Grumbling and commando, I took off for the dining room.

Behind me, the creak of the back door opening, and then a slam. Silence. A peal of laughter came tinkling down the stairs as I climbed to escape.

Ian was still at the table, looking around as if to catch me creeping down from the chandeliers, lurking behind the bottles, carousing invisible with the specters within. I went to him, and Audrey's laughter clawed at my ears as I sat down on the red cube and said, "Sorry about that, I got held up."

The warm, sticky trickle from my thighs to the sparkly vinyl.

"Yeah, I thought you took off. I was weighing humiliation versus ditching you here and feeling vaguely shitty about it later. Lose-lose."

"Oh...it was nothing." I snapped open my clutch and pulled out an Altoids container, clicking it open to get the bag. "Here, let's have another."

His forehead wrinkled, as he took off the glasses and opened his mouth to speak. The chandelier bulbs whined.

"Look," he said. "I need to tell you, I'm moving to LA at the end of the month. There aren't any jobs here for graphic designers, short of flyers, which isn't worth my time."

"What about the bar?"

"What about it? I'll let Kris deal with it. I'll be back here and there for business shit."

"Oh. Shit."

"There's something else. I live with my girlfriend."

"Nice."

"There's something else. You know your friend Brady."

"Yeah, I'm quite fond of him."

"Well, he, well, we, well…we got to talking one night, and ended up fucking in your bathroom. I thought I should tell you before I took off."

"I need to go," I burst, "I need a very large bottle of very good vodka." I got up, walking down the steps to the restaurant. It was empty, white tablecloths glowing under silverware. Sourdough and marinara hung in the air.

The foyer was quiet, low bar scrubbed bronze. The rainbow lamps shone dimly.

I went outside.

Leaning against the metal gates, my breath was hard as my pulse. The sky was black and violet. Next door, the donut shop glowed with maternal warmth, the red and yellow shining over a closed taqueria. I was alone. The liquor store lit the corner with lottery tickets, the Korean BBQ place hung its menu behind glass. I walked across the sidewalk, over the black gum-smears and urine pools, to the asphalt. I bought a bottle of vodka, and slung it under my arm.

I stood in the middle of the deserted street, my boots on the yellow line, my head turned upwards to the sky. A haze of mist fell down. I opened my mouth to the fog, breathing in, breathing out. Staring beyond the soot and metal, staring down the avenues, I saw above in that blazing circus of streets the will to go on.

Chapter 10
at dawn, to go on

I opened the window to listen to the rain. The wind blew up across the red chiffon curtain and empty bottle of Blue Nun. Jesse was coming over, and for all that a 6:00 am call for a coke run should've floored me, I did it for him.

When his cab pulled up to where I hung on the gate, I strode up and paid. I had been out all night at Bordello, my money going to shots of Fernet and margaritas, and I somehow tried to justify it as I skipped upstairs with him watching my bare legs. I was wearing a denim mini-skirt that was a little too last spring, and round black heels. It was 7:12 in the morning and I had not been thinking too hard about style, smearing concealer under my eyes and shellacking my short hair, shaving my twat, wondering why I did all this for someone who had forced me to have sex with him, forced me to have unprotected sex with him, put me at risk for disease, beaten me up, almost and almost and I skipped up the landings with his hand around my waist and my purse a little bit lighter.

He was tall, Jesse was, 6'3", with a charm to his rambling words that made me take him back a week later. We were alone and together.

As soon as we got to my room he stopped rambling about his FIDM design partner, Monsieur Demi-Gallant, going to Singapore, taking all of his T-shirt ideas with no contract, about everything being based on trust, and began to take off his pants. Trust. That was what he had said two days ago, said when he took the condom off and stuck his dick inside of me, said, "I am teaching you about trust, this shows that I trust you and whatever you have I have, and whatever I have you have. I am going to show you you can trust me by pulling out at the exact right time and coming all over your pretty face."

At that point I had squirmed, and cried, and begged him to stop. I had twisted and pulled around and wanted to yell but I knew that Brady would hear and condemn me for letting this dodgy fucker back into my life. I should know better. I didn't.

Jesse took off his shirt and tucked himself in next to me. He said, "Do you have it?"

"Yeah. Miles was a little pissed, but he said fine, he knows me, just not to make a habit of it."

"You know it's no big deal."

"Yeah, and I know you only call me after four am, so that's your deal. I take no responsibility."

"Are you going to cut it up or not?"

I did, pulling up an antique hand mirror and splicing up two lines. We did them, and I hoped with the sniff that it would still get me high. I was aware of my own vulnerability. It wasn't as if my phone never rang. He was just so convenient, somehow.

The light was coming through the window that I couldn't see, draping across the room, red from the curtains. My nose felt scraped out, I had been doing too much lately and the electric-thrill of it seemed dull. But I was accustomed to taking what life gave me, going from the next thing to the next thing as if an assembly line or an old freight train was chugging me onward. Automation. Never autonomy.

Jesse grabbed me and lifted me bodily to a lower part of the bed. He sunk his lips into my neck and wrapped his arm around my waist, and I could feel his cock hard against my thigh. I kept my eyes open, watching the porcelain lucky cat endlessly wave its paw on her bedside table, next to a glass dish of earrings and several half-full glasses. Water or vodka, I wasn't sure, likely melted ice from either. He lunged over me and whispered, "My baby pigeon likes it hard, hmm…"

"Oh, yes, daddy," I tried to whimper. It came out whole. As he pressed down over me something began to rise, and my cunt got wet, and the anger as the rain stabbed against the window and the lucky cat waved tenuously, delicately, and something truly furious began to rise within me as he pulled up my skirt and said, "Oh, now who do you belong to?"

"Jesse" I squirmed upwards, more solid now, what had been effervescing away now coming forth fiercely. "I don't think…" Suddenly the sparse trill of his phone ricocheted through the room.

"Baby Pigeon, would you see who that is?" I obeyed. The face read, "Vanessa".

"It's your girlfriend," I said harshly. He squeezed his eyes together until tears ran out.

"Oh shit, oh shit, I've got to go, Lena, listen, hold that thought, I'll call you later, I'll – "

"You won't call me later, I know you, you'll call me in two weeks when you want to get laid. Don't go, I, I want you to hold me for once, I want to cuddle, what about what we used to have, why can't you?" He was already pulling his pants on, the sheets damp with sweat, the light stark and bright now as it inched towards eight o'clock. I huddled on the bed, wrapped in a purple blanket, staring up at him with fury-dilated pupils.

"You said you would stay. You never stay. You never want more than to get here and fuck and then leave. You made me go all the way to the Mission to get this shit for you, and then you barely say thank you and cut out again. What the fuck?"

"Look, she's my girlfriend. She takes precedence."

"Thanks, thanks a lot. You bastard, do you know what you've done! I used to be your girlfriend!" I lunged at him, looping my arm over his neck and hanging there, trying to keep him with me for a moment longer. He threw me off.

Charging down the stairs, he pulled on his blazer and said, "Look, I'll call you."

I ran down the stairs and threw myself at him, forgetting he was two feet taller than me, forgetting the grace I thought I'd learned. It all dissolved in desperation, for the ecstatic dissolve of lust and all the pants pulled on second after. For the door slammed as the sun rose and I found myself alone in damp sheets, as the week passed with isolation and finally the call when I'd forgotten.

I followed him down the stained staircase beneath the lurid glare of the bulb and into the street. As the front gate slammed and he strode away from me, I stared at my hands and something broke, all dignity, all grace, all solemn strength broke and I ran after him in a frantic patter.

His face was set, sullen, glowing with that lurid smolder that I loathed and loved. The lapels of his blazer snapped back in the breeze as he said, "Look, leave me alone, I have to go. I'll talk to you later."

"Well, what, do you want to hang out later, will you call me?"

"Yeah, okay, fine, I'll call you."

"When, when do you want to hang out?"

"Later, okay, later."

"When?"

"Tuesday?"

"Fine."

I turned now, embarrassed, and dashed across the dark street to the safety of my gate. My building was looming, solid as matrimony, the iron scrolls folding inward as I pushed past the door and ran, through the dank green hall, up the stairs and past the shattered glass door of my apartment. No one was around. Limping slightly, sobbing, I tip-toed to my room and fell on the bed. Scattered shoes, a plastic fan, and several pill bottles fell in my wake. I pulled up the velvet comforter and closed my eyes.

In the burrowing and the warming, the serenity and the curling, my eyes snapped open. It was dark. I pulled off the sleep-mask and saw that the room was bright with morning. Lifting as if something might break, I pulled up on the pillows and tried to remember what had happened. As I stared at the mountains of blankets it all came clear. Jesse. Losing it. Humiliation. My vision blurred and I fell back against the dirty pillows, trying to go back to the previous moment. That grace before you realize what your life really is. Bitterness. I sunk under the sheets. Closing my eyes, I tried to black it out by sleep. It wouldn't come.

Finally, I pulled myself up and climbed out of bed. Creeping silently towards the door, I slid into the kitchen and opened up the refrigerator. Pulling forth a bottle of cheap champagne, I grabbed a glass and walked down the hall to the back stairs.

Climbing through the mauve-slatted stairwell to the roof, I watched the brightness fall through the landings. Finally, I pushed open the rotten hatch and emerged on the roof.

The gravel and tarpaper bent under my feet as the brilliant sun embraced me. The air seemed alive, and as I stared into the cerulean sky, the horrors of my night dissolved. One more step, one more step, and I was over the low wall to the full expanse. There were no railings on the edges, and the avenues slashed through the apartment facades like violence. I sank down, and watched the tiny cars flow over the tiny streets, escaping, the windows and balconies and smokestacks and clouds. I reached down to the bottle and ripped off the foil, wrenched off the wire, and pushed at the plastic cork. With a whoosh of foam the champagne frothed up, pouring over my hands. I would stay here for as long as I could.

Fumbling through my termination paperwork from Devechio and Associates, I pulled out the sheet about 401K liquidation. There was a number on the bottom. Oh God, I really didn't want to talk to them again...but I would. I had to. My money was almost gone.

I dialed slowly.

"$1,500? Yes, and can you...please?...FedEx it?"

I stepped glibly off the 49 Van Ness bus into a swarm of pigeons. I was on my way home from yet another temp job, skipping bus to bus on a Friday afternoon. The sun was still plucking plexiglass slices through the auto body shop across Market Street, the olive & brass streetcars heaving by, the buses lurching soot up and down their many stops. All-Star Donuts glowed with bear claws and frosting. I gulped exhaust and dodged a huddle of children as I turned up an alley to a hidden niche.

I had a call to make.

Ahead, a teenage couple were embracing in front of a Camaro. The firebird was half-obscured by spray paint. The woman's hair fell over one eye as she kissed her partner.

I began to dial Miles. Clutching the phone in one hand, I leaned out to the screaming street to a cluster of sparrows.

The couple ahead of me ducked behind a chain link fence and disappeared, arms linked. The Camaro was dusted with pigeon shit. Crushed cans littered the asphalt as I dodged razor-scooters and shopping carts, watching the clouds wheeling above the streaking cars and the shuttered Rite-Aid. Teetering to the bus stop, I headed for the Castro.

Entering Duchamp's, I swung past the swaths of white orchids and the grand piano, and sat in the back. Miles was late, and the bar was its usual sway of business cards and overpriced cocktails, Calamari and drastic drag chanteuses. The wood paneling between the mirrors and vases was scarcely visible, the knife edges on the leaves imperceptible. I wasn't sure why he always wanted to meet me here, something about the inevitable martini specials, the sense of elegance that persuaded him. I enjoyed it, for that that I had to factor in a $10 drink to his $50 bags, a lot more than Donny's $40. His stuff was better, though, not cut, and he didn't keep the strict 6-10 pm hours that Donny did. Donny was gone, though, he was in Thailand again, and so I did what I could. Good to have options.

A blonde in black tie took my order, and I settled in for the wait. The purple and red stained glass window was carved in circular imprints, the whorls like a preschool snowflake. They reminded me of the kitchen tile in my parent's house, and as I stirred the newly arrived Tom Collins, my head drooped in sadness.

1983 San Diego

My mother bent over the orange circles of the tile, red orbs central, robed by orange and hard edges of white. Squares. She daubed her fingers against the frozen corn scattered on the floor and said, "Lena, really, you weren't supposed to be watching Jem and the Holograms, especially not a marathon, you were supposed to be watching the Love Boat or Bewitched, or even Donna Reed, but especially since okay TV snacks are frozen corn and purple cabbage, not Twinkies that you filched from the neighbors."

Me in my pink 'Children's School' sweatsuit. My purple Velcro Kangaroos crunched corn.

"I'm sorry, mommy, I spilled. It was up too high."

"It's not about telling me it was my fault, honey. It's about you doing it right. In the big adult world you don't get second chances."

I picked up a handful of the silver-iced corn and stuffed it into my mouth.

A delicate man with a scarf in his hand strode up to the table, and I perked up.

"Hey, you remembered! I love this scarf!"

Miles plopped the soft bundle into my hand, and took the a seat.

"Hey, oh God, I have had all sorts of girl trouble this time." His narrow face was smooth and his eyes flashed laughter.

"Oh no," I said. "Do tell." A waitress approached.

"Surprise me. Something good, okay, Tanya?"

She laughed and turned away.

Piano chords drifted from the back room, and someone began to sing. I dug about in my purse for my wallet. Plucking forth two twenties and a ten, I crumpled then in my hands and leaned forwards. He met my eyes. I slid the handful under the table with an awkward lurch, and he took it.

"God, I will never get the hang of this hand-off thing. I always feel totally obvious."

He showed his teeth in a quick smile. "You'll get it. Now...here!" His hand darted out gracefully and deposited a gram in my purse. The waitress set down a martini with a sliver of pineapple. Miles perked up and took a sip like a third grade birthday. "Foofy drinks are the best. So anyway, yeah, there's this girl I've been seeing, and, my God, she is making me crazy. She expects to come over every night, and, I'm sorry, it's just way too much."

"After two weeks? That's pretty excessive."

"Yeah, I'm starting to feel married again."

"Have you ever been married?"

"Engaged, twice, both times called it off."

"Yeah, I was engaged too. Wasn't that a bad idea."

"Wow....But I don't know what this chick expects me to do with her."

"Get married, have a bunch of little demons?" I set my glass down with a thump. He gasped. "Why do you say these thing, woman? You must be trying to kill me. No way am I having babies with this girl, I am thinking of ending the whole thing. I swear, when she comes over I can't sleep!"

"You're...ah...occupied? M-m?"

"No, it's not in terms of us doing shit, it's more like I just can't sleep because there is someone in my bed, I can't handle it. It makes me stay up."

"Goddam. And you're drinking again?"

"Yeah, true true. I was nervous about a deal." The smokers outside shifted in the stained glass, leaving blurs of grey.

I toyed with my napkin. "What sort of thing, if you don't mind me asking?"

His arms fell down around his glass, and his face sagged two inches towards the table. "Oh, let me tell you. Well, there were these guys coming out of Mexico to sell three pounds to some people who were flying out from the East Coast. This costs about $50 thou. I was middle-manning, of course, and so the Mexicans were supposed to call me. I was going to go to Oakland with a duffel bag full of money, pick up the drugs, and deliver them to the other people."

My stare became wider.

"I waited for the call for three weeks, anxious as hell, and finally when it came, I was reaching for the phone under my bed, and they hung up, leaving a message but no phone number!"

"Oh my God."

"Yeah, I was totally destroyed. I sold $1,000 worth of ecstasy pills to the east coast guys, at a profit of only $300, when he could have made twenty K for myself. They went to LA to try to buy there, and I was left at home all stressed out and freaked out. So I gave up all my straightedge shit and started in with the drinking."

"Yeah, that's when you drink. Absolutely."

"God. And it wasn't even that really good coke you had, that came from these young gangster girls who were a total pain in the ass to deal with, so obnoxious, so difficult. I really prefer dealing with adults, usually I deal with, like, forty-year-olds or something."

"I had no idea you were so...involved."

"Yeah..." he looked up from his hands. "It's a pain in my ass, I tell you. These people, they just don't know how to handle themselves."

The piano glided in relentlessly, carving away the day, carving away the dwindling evening. I took a deep breath, staring at the wood grain whorls in the table. Twining, aligned, momentarily linked together. Then apart. A tall woman in a chignon and black turtleneck came breezing through the doorway and into the bar. I folded my hands in my lap and considered my exit.

I clenched the iron scrollwork of the gate, leaning out onto the damp sidewalk. Grass blades were creeping around a lost mattress. Bottle shards littered the dirt. I saw Jesse as a dark mass moving towards me, blurry, hazy, emerging clearer as he pulled off my scarf and swung in the door. I fell into his shoulder as I knew I always would.

He slapped me on the ass as we jumped up the stairs.

Upstairs, he slammed down in our salon chair and sulked his arms around a knee. The row of candles behind him swayed, their flames bobbing. The curtains lit haloes against the rain-splattered window. Jesse dug fingernails into his knee and clenched his teeth.

"You won't believe what happened to me," he said.

"What? Tell me, tell me." I peered into the mirror, finishing my makeup job.

"I'm not supposed to tell anyone."

"What?"

His face contorted in pain.

"I got a call from the detectives today."

"You what?" In the mirror behind me his body shrunk.

"They asked me who was dealing dope, and said if I wouldn't tell them they'd throw me back in prison." His mouth was an open sore.

I swerved, dropping the mascara and falling into the cinderblock walls and glass dividers in the visitation rooms. Did I qualify to visit? I didn't even know. Would've if we'd gotten married.

Advancing cautiously, I said, "I know you used to deal in Vegas, but that was ages ago. Are you middle-manning again and keeping aside a twenty, like you told me to? I know people will still trust $60 for a bag."

"Look, do you believe me or not?"

"Jesse, I do, it's just that you've given me reasons not to trust you before." I babbled at the ceiling, avoiding his eyes.

"Hug me, squeeze me?" he whimpered.

I dashed forwards, enfolding him in my arms, and he lifted me to the vinyl cushion easily. The oceanic quiet of the building draped us, creaking in its electro-fitted hinges; a drop in a sink somewhere on the second floor, the whirring of the heater was barely perceptible.

"You're so small."

"Don't."

Wrapping myself over him, he folded his hands around me. I wanted so much to protect him, resenting my smallness, my helplessness against the amorphous detectives and the unimaginable world of shootings and madness and handcuffs and destitute horror that lurked on the other side of the TV but never in my world. Jesse touched on that world, I knew. Homeless, boosting, dodging bullets and such. I knew. My arms were all I had to comfort him.

"My little boy." His gaunt cheeks were rough with stubble and his liquid blue eyes welled, the sunglasses lost. He sunk his head on his chest and folded in like the last page of a book.

"I'm putting people away, Lena. I'm ratting out career criminals, people who are addicted to dealing, people who run organized gambling, and have their own hookers. They're my bros half the time, and I feel shitty, but I have to do it."

"Jesus. I don't know what to say."

"Thank you for being here." Tears squeezed from his eyes.

"What are you going to do?"

"Go away. I'll have to move away for awhile."

"Is there a witness protection program?" At this I backed off and thumped down on the bed. He waved a hand dismissively.

"We'll see." He leaned back on the recliner and squared his shoulders, mustering his strength, trying to appear commanding and kingly on his pedicure throne. Ours.

"Hey, take off your clothes."

I gasped and began to unbutton my blouse.

"Slowly…no, quickly. As fast as you can."

I pulled off my top and flung it stripper-like to the winds, wanting to placate him, to help him forget. I felt suddenly dutiful, as if our usual booty-call philandering had been overshadowed by the drift of larger things. Things I could not control like the nuances of conversation or swells of steamed milk.

"Now slowly." He slid a hand down and began to unbutton his pants. One by one I clipped open the buttons on my jeans and slid them off.

"Oh! Those are my favorite panties!"

"I wore them for you," I dimpled, exhaling softly.

They were strips of cream lace. He ripped them off. Leaping on top of me, he shoved my legs apart and pushed his cock into my cunt.

"Jesse, use a condom," I yelped.

"Come on, I'll pull out." He thrust deeper.

"No, I mean it, use one."

"C'mon!"

"I don't trust you," I hissed.

"What the fuck?"

"I do this for my own reasons. And you have given me reasons not to trust you." I stiffened under him, batting at his shoulders with my hands.

"C'mon, baby!" He clutched my ass.

"Jesse!"

"Beg for it, I know you want it," he hissed above me.

"No, no, I don't, now this is good, this feels amazing, but you have to pull out now, please, I'm begging you."

"I'm not going to."

"Please! I'm not on the pill yet. I hate the pill. I will, but - !"

"Yes, you'll go on it, but for now you can just take the morning after pill, now take it, ah, ah, beg for it, now."

Jerking my head up and down I tried to twist away from him and failed. The empty wine bottles shone amber and silver.

He thrust into my pussy and came, his head rolling back and his mouth contorting. Holding his shoulders, I let him fall gently onto my body, saying, "Jesse, Jesse, oh god, baby, no, oh, sweetie, please, oh god." Underneath the thumb-tacked fans and 3-D glasses we were small and soft in the dark. I reached down and felt how much fluid there was everywhere, realizing what it was I was both terrified and weirdly moved. This was him. This could be a baby. I hated babies. I had never wanted children. Especially not as an unmarried, underemployed dilettante with a junkie-narc for a mate. Who I, suddenly, loved. Although, as he pulled out of me and fell back, gasping, on the sheets, he cared so little about me that he would peruse my body like a newspaper and toss it into the street to wilt in puddles and pebbles when he was done.

The window was open and I could hear the soft hiss of sleeting rain and the mariachi from the window opposite. The room was dark. Jesse was a mute bulk in the night. Climbing up, I wiped the fluid off clumsily with a blanket and climbed on top of him.

"I'll get the morning after pill. Please, honey, it's okay." Although I knew this would repeat and my cycles were as erratic as the BART train, I knew, this time, this time, I would forgive.

I swung off the 71 Haight-Noriega bus to the broken sidewalk of Fillmore Street. Lowering my eyes, I pointed myself towards the Walgreen's burnt-out sign. Past the cracked bus shelter and back-lit pictures of cereal boxes, I walked into the drug store like the whole of the city was watching me. Although my more brazen side believed this was all in life's due course, I felt a desperate shame and sadness, almost as if there was actually a child I was excising. I had taken this pill many times, and my frantic fear of pregnancy and its attendant death of my lifestyle always fought with this strange desolation. Padding past the racks of fake nails and the security guard. I knew I was getting older. Thirty. I knew I was losing chances. I knew this was the wrong time. It was unimaginable, as I strode past the Oil of Olay and Nubian Beauty hair straightener, the calcium capsules and gel-padded insoles. There was no way I could have Jesse's spawn. But I hung back when I reached the pharmacy window, watching the uneven teeth and benign smile of the assistant as he weaved from bins of pills to the counter.

I looked through the tax bulletins as I gnawed my nails. The dreadlocked girl in front of me took her bag and withdrew, and I stepped up to the counter. The man bent his head to the side and said, "May I help you?"

"Yeah," Leaning forward, I whispered, "I'd like the morning after pill. Plan B? Please."

"Oh! Okay, let me get you the pharmacist for this, she'll get you the paperwork." He backed away and disappeared behind the computer. A rack of cold caplets, blue Abreva tubes, nail fungus solutions, and lip balm hung on the counter under announcements about Medi-Cal changes.

Moments later, a young woman emerged from the divider. She had gelled curls and sympathetic eyes, and as she handed me the clipboard her long hands flicked the release forms lightly.

"Alright, have you taken this before?"

"Yeah, yeah, two months ago," I winced.

"That's okay. Here, just fill this out and we'll have it ready for you in about fifteen minutes."

I took the clipboard and retreated to the chairs below the condom rack.

I limped out the automatic door with the "Plan B" clenched tightly in my hand. Tucked against the Walgreen's wall was a blanket spread with goods to sell: two Barbies with filthy pink dresses, their blond braids stabbing odd angles, a gold-trimmed child's sombrero, a teddy bear in leprechaun lederhosen, and a Leonard Cohen record. A walkman with no headphones sat neatly at the end. I paused to stare at the diminutive hat, bending forwards as the cardboard pill pack stabbed into my hand. The later afternoon sun streamed over my shoulders to set the Barbie dresses sparkling, the gilt rick-rack against the black velvet hat alight with ripped edges.

There was a volley of words from the Low-Cost Meat Market, and I straightened up, moving past newspaper dispensers to the crosswalk. The bodega ahead spoke of plantains and pomegranates, and I steeled myself for the jostling ride home.

Huddled in a cream-toned booth at Silk, Brady and I waited for Jesse's fashion show to start. The MySpace invitation had shown up in my inbox the week before, and for all that I fretted and whined to Limone about showing up a lone stalker, I went anyway to see what he could possibly come up with. While we watched from a corner booth, the hip-hop club's unfamiliar coterie were playing out their raindeer games across the crowded dance floor.

"Five fifty for a gin and tonic, that's such bullshit!" I said. Brady laughed and rapped his Budweiser against the table.

"Yeah, this was four, it's preposterous... How do these kids have the money to afford this, anyway?"

Looking at the Cal sweatshirts over aerobecized pecs, the fresh, healthy faces and exposed thongs, I said, "They must not go out as much as we do...like not, every night, and not spend all their money on drugs."

"Right...how easily I forget. It just wouldn't be any fun that way, though." A giant Fabergé egg of a lamp sent yellow glow through the stools. Most of them were empty.

The smoke machine hemmed us in as we joined the crowd. Edging past the bartenders into the back room, we shoved our way to the front. A makeshift runway bisected the room, with a DJ spinning records on one end and a commanding drag queen pirouetting on the other. She pointed her hand towards the back door and said, "I give you "Street-walking Cheetah," Jesse-Cat's spring collection. Check it out!"

With a flourish, she sashayed her shoulder pads off stage. The lights dimmed, and I nestled closer to Brady, tucking my arm under his. He could be my date for the night, my beard. Small, curling blond hairs on his neck had escaped the black dye. I smiled softly, and turned to watch as a statuesque androgyne stalked out in a leopard print catsuit.

One by one they came, tossing glitter and grapes, their bodies lithe and unforgiving, their clothing flimsy with an eye for the flesh. Golden eyes flashed. A deconstructed wedding gown in black burlap stabbed by on steep heels, a chastity belt/crusty bumflap hemming the bodice with Discharge, Anal Kunt, Aus Rotten, patches. *God, even sewn with dental floss.* Streamers of bicycle tire and lace formed the skirt.

The bride was a lean size 0, the neckline plunging deep. Her nipples pointed skyward through sheer mylar. She was laced up tight, lips pursed red. Eyes, demure under thick Winehouse liner, bent to a bouquet of gardenias.

I burned.

She stopped in the middle of the runway, swirled, and tossed the flowers across the crowd. Roaches swarmed from the petals.

'Oh, this is just so now!" said someone near my elbow, taking notes.

I weaved my head from one position to another to peer onto the stage. The Twot's "Damaged Goods" thundered to a stop, and Jesse strode onto the stage, his jaw jutting in pride, his long hands clenched around a flask. I wilted in the crowd beside Brady, who squeezed my shoulder. Puddles of sweat were forming on his neck. I wiped my forehead and watched him mug for the camcorder, flashbulbs, some girl's camera-phone.

I rubbed the sweat between my fingers, fluent like the linseed oil that was drying, forgotten, by my window.

Grabbing Brady's arm, I said, "Let's get the fuck out of here, I don't want to deal with congratulating him, if he even deigns to speak with me. This feels so deliberate."

Looking up, I saw that Jesse was leaning against the bar and laying down a drink ticket. He looked up as his drink hit the steel, and our eyes met.

Brady pulled back, leaving me in a whirl of empty bodies. I stared, trying to work up some warmth, trying to step forwards and greet him like this had not once been our dream. Like we were simply friends. But his eyes only settled on mine for a moment and then turned away, the liquid blue slicing through the room to other soft shoulders and narrow hips. He picked up the beer, flipped the bartender a tip and plunged back into the crowd.

As our cab wheeled through the Lower Haight, tracing ramshackle Victorians past cannabis clubs and Urban Forage raw foods, Brady leaned over to me and said, "Maybe he didn't see you."

In the warm darkness my tears were still visible, lit by smoke shop neon. Smudging my liquid liner in tiny pouts, they had crept to the rims of my eyes and gone no further.

"Come on. I know he saw me. There was that flash, you know, kind of like when you paint in the eyes on something, that flash of recognition. You know it's there, and they know it's there. You can't hide at that point. They see you." Incense and pipe tobacco came up from the cushions.

"Take your pills."

"I'm not crazy. You take yours."

"You stop taking mine. Okay. But, I mean, wasn't that chick in the embarrassing Anne Rice get-up his girlfriend or something?"

"Yeah, I think that's Vanessa. The belle of the fucking ball. I hope she gets a pre-nup."

"There, the misfortune of others. It can be very comforting. You can find better." With a nod, Brady leaned towards the driver. "Here, here, by the Dragnet."

Handing him a bill, Brady pulled himself out of the car and reached for me, "Come on, sweetie, don't give up yet. Zed Leopard's spinning, and that's always a good time."

On the curb, I noticed that the sidewalk was empty. The neighboring bars were holding fast to their awnings in the stiff spring wind. Vestiges of ancient flyers stapled against black plywood.

Pushing the door open, we crept into all-consuming fog. The smoke machine was apparently on full speed, as guitar thuds whirled sight unseen. Invisible walls, a smattering of chairs to the left, and as I wandered in I saw a huge punch bowl set up with test tubes and beakers, full of emerald liquid.

"That's the punch," said the bartender. Dipping a scoop with a ladle, she held it up. Effervescent. Leafy. Sort of a foamy Superfood.

"Sure, I'll have some." I said. Wiping a smear of black down my face, I dove back into the fog and groped along until I hit the dance floor. Stepping up, I saw that Brady was dancing in the strobe, the light blots against his body. There was no one else there. I had seen a few huddled forms by the tables, but the dance floor was empty, and empty was paradise. Moving towards him, I threw my hip to the side and slid a foot across, then another, then my hands, then I was dancing too.

The floor was empty, and I reveled in it, swaying, throwing one hand across to slip by Brady and then another. The smoke came in gusts, hiding him for a moment as I whirled away. There was no one there. And then there was.

Zed Leopard emerged from the DJ booth with his hands above his head and said, "Kids, hey, someone came! I'm so happy I could pee myself." Throwing himself across the floor, he pumped his arms in salutes and ended by twisting himself into the splits. He fell back onto the concrete, out of breath.

"Nice." I said, tilting my head. Those layers of denim and tiny T-shirts held many a discovery, I knew.

I had met Zed (back when he called himself Louis) a year ago in the bathroom of the Rosetta Bar. He was shirtless, exposing a swath of inked cursive across his birdlike chest, and holding a switchblade.

"Hey, it's my 21ˢᵗ birthday, does anyone have a bump for me?" he said, flicking the knife open and closed. It was very sharp. And he was nearly naked. I just had to do it.

Stepping up to the sink, I opened my purse and said, "Well, what do you know, I think I do. Come closer." He kissed me as the key fell from his nose. "Happy Birthday." He backed me against the sink, as disgusted girls began to file out of the bathroom. But, for all that we kissed all over the Rosetta, he still refused to go home with me. Some flimsy reason I had soon forgotten.

And a goal I had never achieved. But, as I weaved and bobbed to the thrums, I watched him move from floor to record flip to a trajectory in my direction.

Grabbing me by the shoulders, he said, "You finally left your house, I'm so glad. Now we can work on that cat hoarding problem." I watched his hair so as to miss his face.

"Whatever. I go out sometimes. Really. I go see The Dummies a lot."

"Well, when you do, you should call me. Really. I miss seeing you around."

"That's sweet...Zed Leopard, is that what you're calling yourself these days?"

"Shh...it's my name! Don't tell. Look, I got a bracelet!" He flashed a friendship bracelet thus woven.

"Whoa. You are serious about all this."

"Of course I'm fucking serious. Hey, listen, you wouldn't happen to have any blow, would you?" he grinned.

"Well...actually, you know, I do. Here, let's go to the ladies."

He held the door open for me as we slid in. Leaning against the filthy sink, I pulled out my makeup bag and began digging around.

Dipping in with a key, I held it out to him. His eyes closed as he took the hit, and sniffed hard. The mirrors reflected two dark heads, two bent backs.

"Whew!" he said, wiping the back of his nose with his hand. He jumped up on one knee. "Okay, okay, yeah, now you. Let me watch."

"What else would you like to watch? Voyeur!"

"Oh you know, love those dumpsters. Nothing like hiding behind a dumpster when you've just had three shots and watching the firemen speed by! It's like being on acid! Except better! Because then you can go back inside and try to pick up on girls."

Shaking my head in the fluorescence, I stuffed my keys back into my handbag.

"Oh hey, hey, have you seen my other tattoo?" he said. "My best one? Here." He fumbled with his shoe, ripping off the Vans and throwing a pasty foot on the edge of the sink. In the cold light, against the black-smeared sink, the scrawl across his foot read, "I heart pussy."

I laughed helplessly. Doubling over, I backed towards the toilet and sat down on the lid.

"Yeah, you love it, huh, you know you do. I'd get more, but my girlfriend at the time said she was going to kill me if I ever did that again, so I didn't."

"No, that's...fucking awesome. Really. You are actually punk as fuck now. Feel special." I leaned against the wall, throwing one hip out and tilting my head to the side.

"Oh, right. But no, here, wait, hold still." He smoothly backed me into the wall, putting both hands against the sides of my face and placing his lips on mine. Thumps came from the dance floor outside. Smoke against flashes of light. Brady swayed somewhere in the distance. A urine stench.

Opening my eyes as he pulled away, I said, "Wait, you, what? I didn't know you..."

"You didn't know? How could you not know? I always talked to you, didn't I?"

"Yeah, but you never made a move, and I was too shy. I didn't think you would like me, because..."

"Because why?" he wrapped his arms around my shoulders.

"Because I was too old."

"Oh, come on. Now, I should probably get out of here before the record ends. But, hey, I think we should go home together. Do you want to?"

"Yeah."

Taking my hand, we emerged from the girl's room into the misty depths of the club. Sliding off into the fog, he was gone instantly, and I stood there for a moment shading my hands through the stripes of gossamer light.

I draped an arm along the edge of Zed's transformers sheets, looking up at the rows of Japanimé figurines and the squat copper Buddha lying next to two straws.

Fire alarms.

Or not. Sex with Zed felt like sex with the little brother I didn't have. He had remarked that I needed to lose some weight. I was 28, 5'4" and 108 lbs. Not everyone was an imp like him. What a little shit.

He had tried, though. We had both tried. When I switched to on top, my favorite way to grind, the only way in which the elusive clitoral orgasm was possible, he got all confused. Said I almost broke his pelvis. Too much of a tiger.

He was sweet, though, stroking my cheeks after.

It was a wonder we didn't both implode from anxiety.

Perhaps time to call Jesse. At least he knew what to do.

As soon as Jesse walked into my room he took his pants and shirt off, and sat on the bed. I walked over and sat on his lap, murmuring, "I've been lonely without you."

"Oh have you, Baby Pigeon. You sure sounded like it on the phone." He thumbed the hem of my shirt and lifted it over my head, revealing a black bra. Throwing it to the side, he said, "Oh hey, do you want some drugs?"

"Sure...I have to work tomorrow, but I can deal."

"Cool." He lunged off the bed for his pants, lifting them and pulling a packet of white powder from the back pocket.

"Oh, check it out, I got this great new mirror at a garage sale!" I jumped up and dashed across the room, pulling a square, gilt-framed mirror from underneath a chair. It seemed made for such things. Proudly setting it before him, I leaned back and watched him dispense two lines.

"So, what was up with the fashion show, huh, I saw you, but you didn't say anything to me. You totally ignored me, in fact. By the way, thanks for the blow."

"Yeah. Well, it was totally 'House of Jealous Lovers' that night, I couldn't exactly talk to you. Vanessa was all up on me, it was all I could do to keep her from kicking your ass, and so, sorry, I had other fishies to fry."

"So wait, how'd you two meet, anyway?"

He cut two more. "Don't ask me that, you don't want to know and I don't want to tell you. Less talk, more pretty."

I dipped my head to take the line. "Right. Well."

"Are you on birth control yet?"

"I couldn't!"

"You know you're in trouble. You do know that, don't you?" He clamped a hand on my shoulder.

Two weeks ago

There were five of us in the sweaty, shag-carpeted practice space, passing around cans of Pabst Blue Ribbon, talking rapidly in that low patter where connection matters more than content. I was sunk deeply into conversation with an older man I'd never seen, who was talking about his work in San Francisco's free clinics. These places had saved me. I stared up at him with true Keane saucers.

Edward was a real saint. One of the few who forsook money and power to do the dirty work. A hero. I took another drink from his beer.

Later, I sipped my six am Chardonnay and crossed my legs. His apartment, an immaculate one-bedroom with hardwood floors was all I could have hoped for. We sat on the leaf-green loveseat while he told me about the challenges of ethics and the lessons of patient death, spliced with appropriate gravitas.

I could see the down comforter on the four-poster behind him. Oh, Noe Valley.

"Oh, here, I have something to show you," he said, moving into the bedroom. I followed him, noting the polaroids of toddlers on the dresser. His?

He began to talk about some rare anatomy book he'd saved from an estate sale, and I listened with the upturned eyes of someone who does not see.

He turned to me.

"You can sit. Here, sit, here, have a pillow, yes, there."

I sat gingerly. He slid beside me with a feline grace that was both alluring and repellant. He reached up and began to rub my shoulders.

"Oh, your back is tight. Here, let me give you a massage. How does that sound?"

"Sure."

He reached for the ylang-ylang oil on the bedside table, and slid his cold, clinical hands under the back of my shirt. Lifting, he pulled it farther and farther up until I was topless. I lay on my stomach, and he rubbed my back like he was running an examination.

"Aha, no bra. You do have lovely breasts. In fact..." He delved.

I hated his dry, sterile hands, the way they felt like a doctor, not a lover. I looked over her shoulder and saw the shine of glasses over thin lips.

Gritting my teeth, I wove my thoughts into infomercials of wedding ice castles and closed my eyes as I fell into the sheets.

Soon, the stripes of shadow fell over our sleeping shoulders, with my knees tightly folded away.

I loped down Haight Street, boots scraping across the sidewalk past mannequins like rhinestoned harpies in the half-light. I cruised past the Chinese take-out place, and thought how good an egg roll would taste.

"No, focus, come on. Focus on the task at hand," I muttered. I was on the way to the free clinic to get my tests done. Mistakes had been made. The Christmas lights on the poplars flickered, flashing into darkness for a moment.

A homeless kid sitting in a doorway lit a lighter, said "Come on, put on a happy face! Got a quarter?" The space around his head was stickers on slashed glass. Silver.

I shook my head. If I had money I'd be at Kaiser. Pure Beauty loomed above, the blue letters bright in the white neon. If I had money I'd be going in there.

A teenage volunteer took my pulse. The tiny room was cramped with flavored condoms in bowls, brightly colored signs in ten languages discussing the necessity for safe sex and the need to report abusive relationships to some hotline. Mistakes had been made. I sighed again, as the cuff tightened around my arm and my fingers began to tingle. The girl was elfin and delicate, and I wondered how she could possibly deal with the lumbering, disturbed, possibly violent people that must come through here. How, indeed, she dealt with the stories her patients told her. She was taking notes in my chart in cautious, circular handwriting, and appeared to be dotting the "I"s with stars.

"So, what brings you to us today?" the volunteer said.

"Well, I wanted to get my tests done. I mean, it's been awhile and you never know, and – "Hearts and stars, Petunia, what the hell do you think?

"Is there a specific symptom or incident that you would like to discuss?" Demoralized, I leaned forwards to whisper, all too aware of the laughter of the off-duty staff in the other room.

"Well, I..." Suddenly a middle-aged man emerged from behind the elf and caught my eye. Pinched lips, silver glare in the glasses, a knowing expression, and those cold, clinical hands hanging at his sides.

It was really time to cut down on my nightlife.

"I couldn't get an appointment at the free clinic," I lied.

Instead, I had run away.

"I tried. They're understaffed, they said they couldn't even schedule me in, but I had to call back in two weeks at eight am."

"And when I find out who put that mark on you! You're in trouble for that, too." He touched the scalding red blotch on my neck.

"It was just...it wasn't anything, I just hooked up with this guy, and..."

"I don't want to know. Don't tell me. Just know that you're in trouble. You'll remember when you're punished." He let me go.

Curling up naked on the sheets, I said, "So you can't afford my Plan B, but you're going to Coachella?"

"Hey, hey. Walker helped me with that, okay. I had to go, to advance my DJ skills. I need to study from the masters."

"Right. Whatever the fuck other "skill set" you want to pick up. Why don't you go to DeVry and learn a real skill? You owe me $40.00"

"Baby, I'm giving you coke, shut up."

"'Kay."

"Let's fuck, okay, I'm done with this." He reached for me. I grabbed a condom from the drawer.

I sat on top of him, and as he slid in I thought about all I was compromising then let it all slide away in a wave of hot flesh. Riding him, driving my knees to rugburn, I thrust my clit against his pubic bone and thought for a moment that I came. Tantalizing, exhilarating tension thrilled through me as I thrust again and the trill of his phone rode up from the floor.

"Wait, wait, I have to get that." He picked it up, and as I fucked him with rapidly decreasing fervor he grunted monosybilically into the phone.

"Walker. Yeah. I've got the stuff." A pause. "No, I can't get it now, listen."

I fumbled to a stop and glared at him.

"Jesse. I am not going to fuck you while you are on the phone. Come on, manners, here?"

"Okay, okay, listen, dude, I'll call you back in a second, okay?"

He threw the phone under a chair and flipped me over, picking me up and reversing me. At the end of the bed, the white pile twinkled on the mirror. Jesse pushed me up as he fucked me in the ass and said "You know what to do."

"Okay, okay." Jostling against the low dresser, I gripped the straw and cut myself a white trail.

"Ah…" I leaned back into his cock, and said, "You know, Jesse, this is kind of like my version of Disneyland."

"Ha! Would you do the Minnie dress with no panties?"

"I kinda see Snow White's Evil Stepmother. Now, she's got a good look."

"Yeah, yeah, I can see it." He fucked me deeper. "Yeah, take that cock."

I moaned, "Oh, Jesse, do you know how much I love you, how much I cherish you?"

"Less talk, more pretty. Play with your tits."

"Okay." I fondled my left nipple. The afternoon sunshine playground toyed on the floor. The TV roared from Brady's Comedy Central fix.

"I'm sorry, I'm so, so sorry for what I did."

Shards on the floor.

"Yes, yes you should be. The question is, how are you going to be punished?"

"However you see fit."

"Oh, I know." I could hear my neighbors revving up their music. My hands were ground into his chest. Opening my mouth in a gasp, I moaned and fixed my eyes on him.

"Anything."

"Miles. Tell me what you know."

He gripped me in warm, knowing hands.

"Jesse! How did you... Look, he's just my drug dealer, I don't really..."

"You know. What did he tell you about his last big deal. About those Mexican guys." The lost tulips were rotting in their glass.

"Jesse. Really. I don't know anything."

"I know you do. I need to know."

"I can't. Jesse, stop, this is weird."

"Lena, Lena, come on..." He gripped my arm. "You know things."

"No."

"Okay, fine. So you'll be punished."

"Fine. I said that was fine."

Flipping me over, he ripped my legs apart.

"Look, you tell me, or we'll do it this time without a condom, I don't care what happens."

"Shit, Jesse, I mean, come on, you don't want a baby."

"I said you'll be punished. This is your punishment." And he plunged his cock into my pussy, dry with fear. Driving in and out, I moaned and he threw my legs above my shoulders.

He slapped me hard. "Tell me! I need to fucking know this!"

"No, fuck off."

He shook me, slammed my head against the mattress. "You're gonna tell me, or you're gonna regret it."

"I don't do that!"

"I'm going to come inside of you, and you're going to beg for it."

"No, Jesse, no, I told you, I can't fucking take the morning after pill again!"

"Get on the real pill."

"I'm trying. I'm broke, and I can't get into the clinic. We can't do this now!"

"Then tell me about Miles."

He thrust into me over and over, banging my head against the wall. It was too hot to stop, and in a way I didn't care. My fear intensified. I could hear Brady talking on the phone with Lucas, worrying about rent for the practice space, about Ely's latest speed binge, about the pedophiliac overtones to his last song. The white sheets flew back.

He put both hands on my neck and squeezed.

Harder.

My eyes snapped open.

"Okay."

"Are you ready?" He pulled out for a moment, resting his purple cockhead against my thigh. It dribbled.

"Please don't."

"Okay, then. Tell me."

"Well, okay. Miles is my drug dealer. The deal you're talking about involves these guys from Mexico selling to guys from the East Coast. Three pounds. He was middle-manning, taking a duffel bag of money to Oakland and picking up the drugs, then delivering to the other guys. Are you happy now?"

"How much was involved?"

"I don't know, $50,000 or something? I don't remember these things."

"Did he do it?"

"No, he didn't get the phone call in time. He lost the sale. Now will you leave me alone? I'm sorry, I feel like shit, I shouldn't've told you that."

"He's not going to give a fuck after we're done."

"Excuse me?"

"Less talk, more pretty. Spread your legs."

I lay back, letting him take over. Giving myself over to him, giving up control, I let myself be swept up in the heat of it. The fuzz and holler of the television fizzed out, as he thrust into me and I didn't even wince when he stiffened and stabbed and came into me with a fierceness I'd never felt.

Brady's forehead was glazed with sweat. He leaned back against the wall of the Rosetta Bar bathroom as I fumbled in my purse. The dismal glare of the green chandelier lit a shelf for two drinks and a mirror scrawled, "lucid" with Revlon Cherry Mood. My electric blue eyeliner was drooping on the edges. Brady reached out and rubbed the corner of my eye.

"You're smearing, there. Have you been crying?"

My hands darted for the key. Holding it out to him, I whimpered, "Only a little. Only a little."

"What happened?" He sniffed and raised both eyes. "Aaah." Fluttering his hands back, he said. "Tell me."

Cracks in the mirror slicked silver across the wall. I reached up to wipe my eye.

"It's stupid."

"Come on. Is it Jesse?"

"No, it's just…well…okay, yeah, it is."

"Come on, what did he do this time? I have to tell you, why…why do you put up with him, anyway?" Grey water streaked down the walls. Electric blue. Green glass.

"I don't know, I just…there's just something there I can't deny. I know it feels like a cliché, I'm well aware, but there's just something there that I can't escape. I need him. To own me. He needs me. To help him. Or maybe he just needs to fuck me, okay, maybe. But I need him, fine."

"Is it fine to you?"

"Well…I know I want something like a real relationship, and he's the closest I've had in ages. I know I've told you how he can be a dick sometimes, yeah…. Well, this time he fucked with my head really bad, basically coerced me, extorted with my body information about my dealer, and I don't know why, I know he does some weird shit, that I can't say, but…I'm scared. I don't know what's going on. I also could be pregnant, but that's kind of a minor concern."

"Lena. You need to get on the pill."

"I have an appointment on Tuesday. At Tom Waddell."

"Good. I don't think you should do this necessarily for Jesse, but just for your own piece of mind. I mean, it kind of sucks…"

"Yeah, I'm afraid I'm going to gain thirty pounds and not be able to leave my bed."

"But maybe not?"

"Or maybe not." I wrapped my hands in my skirt. The soft fabric bent easily to my touch. A murmur of young girls fluttered outside. There was a knock on the door.

"Right. Take care of yourself, quiche-cup, okay?"

"Okay." I grabbed the handle and bent it up, striding into the bathroom and flouncing out the door with the bitter veneer I'd learned. Brady followed in my wake.

From a bench in Golden Gate Park, I cracked my knuckles and flipped my phone open. The silver clamshell winked. Cupping it gently, I dialed Miles.

The phone rang, and rang again. The lavender silver of a eucalyptus, with long dark leaves, perched on the iceplant ridge like a lovely widow.

There was a long tone, and Miles' voice mail.

"I'm not available right now, please leave your name and…" I watched the grey-blue trunk of another tree, extending branches like pale necks and a drape of black leaves at the nape.

A low tone sounded.

"Hey, um…I need to talk to you, it's not the usual, it's kind of sketchy, like, I mean, not in the usual way, I mean, we're not sketchy, I mean, yeah, it's really fucking urgent, and I'm really worried about you. Please call me. It's Lena."

Climbing out of a cab, I walked across Haight Street towards the Happy Donuts. The mango smoothie ads reared up in all their washed-out and dirt-speckled goodness behind bars. The streetlights glowed amber haloes against the mist, the cracked-out aching sidewalks. I turned my eyes down to the yellow line against my feet, and heard the rumble of a car.

Jumping back, an unmarked black sedan came roaring past me and ground to a stop against the Guardian dispenser. I lurched and retreated to the opposite sidewalk. The Zona Rosa taqueria was stalwart and empty in the twilight. Amoeba neon glowed from across the street, sending empty messages of hope and comfort in import remixes.

Six feet three emerged from the passenger side. Jesse. There was no mistaking the gutter-punk slouch, the flicker of a hand doffing a cigarette and shaking someone's hand. It had to be.

I crept through the mist and thrust myself at him as the car drove off. Happy donuts shone.

"You. Should. Not be. Out here. Right now," he said.

"What? I'm coming home."

"You better go home. And I mean right now."

"Do you want to…I mean…come?"

"No, I do not want to come. I wasn't here. And you did not see this. Go home. Now." He turned away.

I looked down at my hands. They were smeared with soot and lipstick. My nose cracked with blood.

Chapter 11
electroshock redux

The beaded fringe of the lamp fluttered in the dawn-light as I pulled out a Depakote and slid it over to Brady.

"Here, try that with the pill-cutter."

"That is such an ingenious device. Where did you get that?" Limone said.

"Oh, you know, down at the free clinic."

Brady stuck the big blue pill into the plastic box, beneath the razor blade, and slashed it in half. He turned it and cut again, and again, as I sniffed the last line of Vicodin and watched my hands jerk. This was routine, I reminded myself, chill out. I took a drink and leaned back, picking at a chicken-soup crust on the cushion.

The doorbell hit off again. As Brady glared, I got up and let in Jesse, silently cursing myself for letting him hang out so much

"How was Bordello?"

"Well, ever since they've hired me I've gone over really well…   Except today I mistook Kris Danger for Method-Man, and it all went to hell."

"You should at least have known who he was, it's not like he isn't one of the bigger DJs here."

"I only know who people are if they're actively involved in my life. And he's just backdrop. Backdrop with a bigger following. Do you have any drugs?"

I sighed. "Yeah. Here, we've got some fun pills. We couldn't get coke."

"Right on, let's have it." Jesse followed me to the couch and squirmed in. Brady cut four, and we inhaled. I was used to having a tolerance, but my heart fluttered. I rose and leaned cautiously on the edge of the couch.

"Are you okay?"

"Oh, yeah, it's cool. I just have to check something in my room."

"Okay, well, hurry back."

I wobbled down the hall and through my door, collapsing on my bed with a heavy breath. This was peculiar…I was used to stimulants, downers, whatever I could get, nothing surprising, why was I suddenly so fucked up? I huddled around a pillow, as my heart began to pound frantically. Outside, the voices of my friends hung like seagulls in the air, too far to reach. It was as if my heart was pulsing in my chest, my ears ringing loudly in a high-pitched clang, with a waver of sonorous wailing. I burrowed into the covers, pulling them over myself. Why this, why now, why was this happening? I had things to do, I had a temp job on Wednesday. I had to deal with Jesse, who was going to be really pissed. They would all be. Freaking out was not conducive to discretion. I would give them all away if I went to the ER now. Especially with Jesse's situation, that could be serious. My heart was racing. I had to get away from them, leave the house, protect them. Terrified, I yanked open the bedroom door and ran, shoeless and coatless, through the living room.

"Lena?" said Brady. "Are you okay?"

"Got to…go…an errand?"

"It's four!"

"Be back…later. Later." I scuttled down the hall, yanked open the broken door, and was gone.

As I ran down the stairs, I had a powerful feeling that I must hide things, protect secrets, and I began shredding Limone's business card, a flyer of Brady's that was in my purse, and stuffing them under other people's doors.

"What, who's there?" came a deep male voice from the second floor.

Terrified, I ran down the final steps and into the street. Outside, there was a light mist drifting through the streetlights and the neon of the restaurants.

A forlorn glitter fell from passing cars, as I inched up towards Haight Street. There had got to be a way to take a cab, maybe, to get away somewhere where it would be safe. I couldn't be near my friends, from where I'd give them away. I felt around and realized that my wallet was empty. Moving past the ovoid mirrors of the hair salon, I fell against the SF Weekly dispenser, my knees caving in. Glassy disasters whispered from the windows. I threw my arm in the air.

After a long wait of cold breaths, a cab came trundling past, and pulled up in front of me. I fell against the door, opened it, and was inside.

"Hey, I don't have any money and I'm having a breakdown, can you take me to the hospital?"

"What, you want to go to General? That'll take money."

"What…fuck…I mean, or you can just kill me, that's probably easier for everyone involved."

"Get out." A bearded face glared.

"Shit." I vacated, and the cab drove away. The night was lonelier than ever now, the shops shuttered, the feather earrings and flats shut up behind iron gates, no one around except for the roaming gangs of homeless kids. My heart was still pounding thick and wild, and I knew they would find me, they would find out, they would find my friends ensconced in their comfortable den with their powders and pills, they would find out about Miles, about Jesse, my secrets would have to die with me. To…die. To die. That would have to be it.

I scanned the empty street, the wailing in my ears increasing. There must be some way. A grey Volvo advanced towards me. Taking a garbled breath, I lunged, ran forwards, and with a glance at the terrified denizens, threw myself over the hood of the car.

Rolling over the top, I caught a glimpse of the stars and the streetlights, before I bounced against the trunk and down to the asphalt. Gasping, I lay there for a moment, assessing my injuries. A few scrapes. I got up, and dashed back to the sidewalk as the car raced away.

Another car appeared, and I tossed myself against it, again, only to slide off the back as my purse flew through the air. I heard screams, and after a long pause as the delusions closed in, the red lights of an ambulance rounded the corner and a tech was shaking my shoulder.

"Are you okay? Can you hear me?"

"Don't tell, don't tell."

"Can you hear me?"

"Oh, god, please, take me in, I can't do this anymore."

"Do you have health insurance?"

"Sort of, I'm on the San Francisco Mental Health Plan. But, please, don't let them find me."

"Okay, alright, now, here," and the man in the blue coveralls gently rolled me onto a stretcher. Another man came around and they picked me up, and settled me into the back of the ambulance. The crisp white interior, the bizarre tanks and lights, all of it was a monstrous flash as I closed my eyes, opening them momentarily to catch the last glimpse of neon winking to a close.

With a wave of nausea, my eyes flashed open again, to see a needle stabbing into my arm. A blue curtain hung around my hospital bed, where I was tucked into a backless gown. There was a flurry of people around me, a nurse with a pinched mouth depressing the syringe.

"What's that?"

"It's adrenalin. For your heart. We've got to get your heart back to normal, you're having an arrhythmia."

"I what?"

"Just lie still and shut your eyes."

"I.." and I threw my hand over my mouth. Another nurse thrust a grey basin into my lap, and I threw up violently. Streaks of shame creased behind my eyelids as I remembered what I had done, where I was, where I would go.

Lifting my head, I said, "Okay, okay, that's all," and fell back on the pillows.

I felt scratchy sheets and an unfamiliar chill. Lifting my head, I saw that I was in a dormitory with three other beds, all empty. The walls were pale gray-green, and windowless. My stomach clenched, as yesterday came back. The floor was brown tile, and a small table bore a folder entitled "Your time at Langley-Porter: Tips and Helpful Hints." I lifted it gingerly and settled against the flat pillow. The pages that followed told what I was scared of – I was in a psych ward at UCSF. Fantastic. For how long, I didn't know. I turned pages anxiously, looking through rules, visitors (allowed after the second day), and honeyed platitudes of healing spliced with clinical absolutes. It quickly became clear that there were those who never left this place. There were those who were kept here against their will.

Wincing, I set down the folder and slumped into the hall wearing two hospital gowns pulled over my front and back.

A nurse stepped up abruptly, looked me up and down and said, "Lunch is in the cafeteria, down the hall to your right."

I walked along the curved, windowless hall, with doors on either side. Eventually I came to a nurses' station with bored-looking clinicians talking on the phone, peering out at the patients in the glass-walled cafeteria, and paging through files. One was filing her nails.

I inched forwards, my hand twitching, and said, "Um…hey. I was wondering how long I need to stay here? Can I leave now?"

A nurse in blue scrubs said, "And your name was?"

"Oh…Lena. Lena Cosentino."

"Okay, Let me get your file." She shuffled through a drawer. "Alright, Cosentino. Looks like you were brought in last night, possible suicide attempt, seventy-two-hour hold. So you have about three days. And, sorry, you can't leave until the clinician deems you psychologically fit and you have been formally discharged."

"Oh…"

"For now, they're having dessert. Group therapy's at 2:30, and, let's see, it looks like you haven't had your tests yet, so do that after lunch. You should have a schedule in your orientation packet."

I stared bleakly at the cafeteria, and began to walk.

The walls of the cafeteria were stolid grey. I felt them clench me in as I lifted my spoon from the tray. Every inch, every motion through that air was excruciating – to know where I was, that I was a prisoner, that my worst fear had come. I took a bite on the vanilla pudding and set the spoon down. I had never acknowledged the reckless pleasures of my life. Drugs, pathos, Jesse's hi-jinx, sex – however horrible it was, it was mine, and I was free, and that freedom was gone.

What I wouldn't do. I glanced around at the matrons in beige polyester, the slack mouths of the patients as they sat and grimly inhaled their food. The beige plastic bowl clattered weakly on the tray as I set down my last bite. I had only the hope that someone – Limone, Brady, and really only those two – would get me out of here.

Then my gaze slid through the air to a set of eyes with a vicious, bitter flame.

The girl was sitting diagonally across the yellow tables, by the hygiene posters. Her brown shag looked ripped, her fingers bore into the decaf tumbler. I felt a lurch, a fall, a feeling that this was someone I should know.

Our shoulders bumped, edging out of the cafeteria towards group therapy. I looked up from the carpet and saw the girl throw her head back. She turned and stared at me.

"What're you here for?" she said. "Burroughs this a piece where he goes, 'What're you here for? We are all here to go. Go into space. We are all here to go.' So you, what about you?"

The boy ahead of us folded his misshapen limbs narrower than shoulders should go. Glassy eyes on the woman ahead, her feet crusted with sores.

I turned to the fierce girl and said. "Sure. I'm here to go. Upwards and inwards. What's your name?"

"Coco."

"And what are you here for?"

"OD."

"What kind?"

"Heroin."

"Well. Mine's similar."

"And that got you here?"

"God, I don't know what got me here. I was having a fine time with my roommate and my sort of not-boyfriend, maybe unfriendly-with-benefits, you know, four am and, you break out the pills, and suddenly I just lost it."

"Yeah, I was with my boyfriend in our apartment and shot up and then I was here. It was all blinking lights and sirens and IVs for awhile, and then suddenly I woke up in this gray room with someone's schizophrenic nanny."

"God."

"I tell you."

They turned a corner.

"Okay, guys, sit down, we'll be starting in a moment," said a bald man with a purple dolphin sweatshirt. We sat. Prim orange plastic seats lined the perimeter of the room. Unyielding glass stood between us and the lush San Francisco hills, the eucalyptus and Spanish tile. The glossy panorama of sun. I rested both hands on my knees, picking at the dingy hospital gown.

Coco, for all her hard eyes and reckless hair, was wearing a hospital gown with a pair of Diesel jeans underneath. She was barefoot. Pedicure.

I had read in the hospital guidebook that shoes were not permitted. Or belts. They had taken both from me when I was still sedated. My temp wages had not permitted me much paraffin. Tucking my legs underneath me, I gazed adoringly at my new acquaintance.

"Okay, alright, patients of Langley-Porter, the group therapy session has officially begun," said the man. "Now, who has something to share with the group?"

The woman in the corner raised her hand and nodded her head in assent.

"I tell you, I heard them demons again. The ones I hear. You know. They were telling me things, things I can't tell you, secret things. Things about this place. Things about what you do in this place."

The bald man lowered his head in answer.

"Thank you, Helen. We appreciate your opinion." He looked around the circle. "Anyone else?"

The disabled boy with the haunted eyes and the brown shirt flapped a hand. "Yes, Toby."

"I...I...I felt a hand."

"Yes?"

The group leaned inward.

"And it told me...it...it touched me, and..."

"Yes, Toby?"

"It told me you guys are perverted!" He dissolved in giggles, spit on his chin. Coco glanced at me.

"He always does this sort of thing. Some sort of retard sex pervert, I tell you. I think he's about eighteen and having all of those hormones set upon him with no outlet. I mean, who's he gonna fuck? You? Me? No."

"Quiet down over there," said the mediator. "Do you have something to add?"

"Just that I've been clean and sober for 37 days!" said Coco, lifting a fist in the air. "Yay for me."

Clapping filled the air. All of them, misshapen, lucid, pleased, rough, bending in happiness.

A slight smile bruised her cheeks as she fell back into her chair.

I teetered into the drug test counseling with a fear clenched deep in my teeth. For all Coco's encouragement, I was worried about this session.

I was obviously an addict. Obvious to anyone. Only soon would they come after the rest of us. They were torturing people in Guatanamo, why not here? I knew what had happened to Francis Farmer. I knew about electroshock therapy, Artaud had it fifty-some times back in 1948s, when they didn't know what it would do. His toothless, broken body, deemed irredeemably insane, why not just keep shocking him until something broke free?

There were sex clubs in the city where Doms played with electricity, but this was not play. If they knew, if they found out, if they could trace the lines from my body back to Jesse, and Brady, and Miles, and the rest. Even Limone, she was so almost in the clear, she would get taken down.

I wasn't sure how long I could hold up if the trodes went on. A razor slicing, knuckle by knuckle.

My mind was racing as I slid into the scoured room. These medical rooms, how they scaled the boundary between the scorched clean and the dinky. The filth and mold still slid in the ceiling, where the sponges hadn't managed. A thin, twitchy man with a toothpick clenched between his fingers was staring at my chart.

"Um, hi...?" I tried.

"Lena Cosentino?" he said.

"Yes?" I wove my way between the tile.

"Alright, I'm looking at your chart, and it looks as if you have an unusually high concentration of Vicodin in your system, at least you did at the time we took you in."

"Huh…"

He looked at me.

"Well, I was taking some for back pain. I've been under a lot of stress."

"Are you sure? There was also a lot of Depakote, indicating double-dosing."

"Yes, I'm prescribed that. 2000 mg."

"That's a great deal."

"I rapid cycle, and this…this…overstim thing? Things are hectic. The mood regulator helps me.

"Well…I guess. Just keep it in line."

"Oh, I will. On the straight and narrow."

"Right. I mean that."

"Yes, sir." I slunk out the door.

I crept along the olive tile back towards my dorm. The adrenalin heat slid into exhaustion, tingling down my arms. Perhaps coke did zip out of your system in twenty-four hours. The green and gold grating of my heating vent scraped golden on the wall as I curled in the thin-sheeted bed.

I wandered down the hall barefoot, the hard-pressed carpet giving little. I passed open doors, but none of them seemed inviting. Pulling the hem of my hospital gown, I looked up to see a nurse standing by a phlebotomist's alcove.

The woman had a kindness in her eyelids, in the flicker as she looked me in the eye.

"How are you?" the woman asked.

"Hi…um…fine. Listen, I was wondering if you can tell me, what can I do to get out of here as soon as possible? I don't belong here, you see, I'm not crazy, I'm not like these people." My head jerked from side to side as I checked to make sure we were alone.

The nurse drew closer.

"Okay, honey, what I can tell you is that you need to clean yourself up. Really. They look around and they see who looks like a normal person, like they are functional. So go ahead, take a nice bath, put your clothes on instead of the gown, and tell your psychiatrist that you're ready. It might take a few days, but you'll be in better shape that way."

"Really? Wow, okay. I'll do that. And then there's this…" I peered behind me, then realized that would make me sound even more paranoid. That wouldn't look good on my file. "Yeah, okay. Thanks."

As I moved through the hallway, I turned back and saw Toby marching doggedly towards me. I sped up and took a right towards the bathtub room, then looked back from behind a row of vertical pipes. The gray-green paint had dried in irregular clumps, and they dug into my fingers as I looked back and saw that he was still coming.

I darted along the hallway again, glancing backwards. He was still there. I turned right again by Dr. Howard's office, the carpet scratching at bare toes. The iron fluorescence glared down. I pulled up my drooping jeans. Damn low-rise. I glanced back again.

He was still coming. I gasped and turned down the hall again, coming around the long sweep towards the common room. With the nurses I would be safe.

As I turned, watching how the plaster spliced the walls, beige above, brown-red below. Wasn't red an anger-producing color? A glimmer of Stanley Jr. High, painted in glaring yellows and neon green, flashed into my mind. The art theory of the seventies said these colors were calming. Right. They knew what they were doing when they painted the Behavior Modification Room a lurid orange, a color that I still thought led to fury.

Perhaps this explained all of the beige.

Flicking my head back, I ran across the carpet, falling forwards when I entered the nurses' penumbra. Okay. Now to look nonchalant. I pushed open the common room door and settled down on the couch by Coco.

I curled on the sofa, my fingers twisting in the pile. An ash grey like the suits I used to work with. Would I ever work again? I had no idea where my phone was, or my shoes, or my belt. Suicide prevention?

My pants drooped suggestively. Why, why had I bought the extra-low-rise? That was the last time I took Limone's advice. I pulled them up over my hips as Toby came in the door. Door, wall, the whole surface was transparent, giving the nurse's station ample eye. Two women sat there filing their nails and teasing out the latest Bennifer gossip. They staring implacably at the back of our heads as Toby sat next to me. Coco flicked the channel to what looked like *National Velvet.*

Elizabeth Taylor's soft childhood face hung bright over us as she stroked a chestnut pony. Green eyes flashed in the static. The old TV was stacked with dusty videos of musicals and children's films.

"What a shitty selection," said Coco.

"Can't imagine they'd have *Return to Oz.*"

The boy was absorbed in the movie, his jaw working up and down.

That face blared down at us again.

I remembered. A few months ago. Leaving some forgettable boy's house with half a gram and without the keys to my house. Doing the walk of shame in through the SFMOMA, the best place I could think of to kill the four hours until Brady would be home.

But that painting, that Warhol had been there, ten feet high, rabid pthalo green background with a black silkscreen over and over and ever and ever, Liz in National Velvet. Her childlike arms around a horse. It had been so real. It had glowed above me as I took a step back, wiped my nose and sniffed an clinging clump of powder and with a pop it was Liz and Liz again.

And Coco was shaking my arm and saying, "Lena, are you okay? We can go, I mean, if he's bothering you."

"Wait, no, what?"

"Read to me!" Toby said again.

Lifting a newspaper from the battered table, I flipped through it.

"Let's see, well, okay. Do you like movie reviews? Let's see what they have to say about…"

"Mwah!" Toby pointed at a couple kissing on the page.

Coco giggled.

"Oh." I turned the page. Glancing over my shoulder, I checked to make sure the nurses were watching, and said, "Okay, alright, what's happening with your diet. Anyone here have any diet complaints? Says we should eat more blueberries."

"Ass-to-mouth!" Toby yelled, stabbing his finger at the "Savage Love" column. I looked at Coco. She looked at the nurses, their faces turned away.

"Okay, Toby, well, I think we…"

"Mwww-ass and titties!" Toby lunged across the newspaper, grabbing. Coco's hand flashed out and pushed him back. I jumped off the couch, dropping the newspaper in a heap on the floor.

We darted out of the common room to the open, waiting hall.

The sign on his door said "William Howard, M.D." I sighed and pushed it open.

There was a cramped office with brown tile on the ceiling and a grey-bearded man tapping his pen against a file. I craned my neck to see, and he slid it under a stack of documents.

"So, Ms. Cosentino, how have you been feeling today?"

"Fine. That is, sane. I'm not crazy. I got a little…well, I was under a lot of stress, I've been fighting with my boyfriend, there haven't been very many temp jobs, I've had trouble getting my medication…I thought I was pregnant." I considered mentioning Toby, but I knew paranoia would be read as delusional.

"It's like that Hitchcock movie Gaslight." Bonnie said. "Jesse isolates you and tells you what he wants, makes it seem like you are the paranoid one, and he is in control."

"I see." The Doctor said.

"Yeah, it's like, I'm fine, though. Now. I don't need to be kept here, I'm not dangerous, I'm not going to commit suicide or anything."

"Yes, it says here that you…"

"Yeah, I was under a lot of stress, as I said."

"Okay." He closed my file. "Well, your problems seem like those of a normal woman. I need to ask, though, have you been hearing voices, seeing things that aren't there, anything like that?"

"Oh no. Never. That never happens to me."

"Good, good." He toyed with the mug of Laffy Taffy. Lifting a banana morsel, he held it out to me.

"Oh, um, thanks."

"Now keep having good days, and you might get out of here sooner than you think. We just need to make sure you've stabilized."

The third day, a nurse came to my room and said, "You have a visitor."

"I do?"

"She was your emergency contact, and she wanted to see you." Her grey eyes stared back without touching. To move within this circle of hallways and never acknowledge the patient's humanity. That must be in the employee handbook.

The door swung shut, and I was in a tiny, windowless room with Limone, who looked more worried than I had ever seen her.

"Oh my god, are you okay!"

"Yeah, yeah, I'm fine. It's been a little scary, but I'm hanging in there."

"Oh God." The walls were army dirt-ditch brown.

"Yeah. They told me I might get out tomorrow if I seem like I've stabilized. I'm trying to be as normal as possible, but, seriously, there are some people in here that are enough to make you crazy. I actually feel more in danger in here than I do in San Francisco. Just on a normal day."

"Oh, honey." There was a high-pitched whir coming from the ceiling vent.

"It really does suck, yes. But how are you?"

"Well, I'm okay, but Brady...well...Brady's not doing too well."

"Wait, what's going on with him?"

"He's sick again. We don't know what it is. Jesse was trying to get him to go to the hospital and bring back some morphine, first time I've seen Jesse get motivated for anything, and then Brady told him to butt out."

"Oh my god. My boy."

"Your booty call. He really was getting annoying, though, he was getting way too involved with the place, and telling Brady what to do in his own house, like not to let his vegetables get rotten and instead give them to him to eat, and a bunch of stuff like that."

"Well, that's Jesse. Crazy-ass control freak."

"Well, even Brady depleted, he's king of his castle. But enough about that, you'll be home soon enough to sort it all out, right? Then you'll want to go back here to where it's all safe and quiet."

"Not likely."

The door opened, and the nurse with the grey eyes and ponytail came into the room.

Leaning against the door, she said, "Alright, fifteen minutes is it. You have two more visitors, and then art therapy."

"Two more! Oooh! It's like cake! I wonder if Jesse actually…"

"Lena, let him go," said Limone.

"Ladies, ah…" The nurse raised her hands. Limone mutely followed her out. I glanced around the tan-tiled cubicle, settling myself in a chair behind the rickety table. Pressing my hand down on one corner, the blonde pressboard teetered in one direction, then rocked back in another.

There was a knock on the door.

"Lena?"

"Zed? Zed Leopard? What are you doing here?"

"I though I'd come see you." He shifted nervously from foot to foot. Blue Adidas.

"But how did you know I was here? People don't…know, do they?"

He laughed.

"Well, I posted it on MySpace…"

"Fuck!"

"No, no, I didn't. Don't worry. Secret's safe. I found out from Limone when she came to Catastrophic last night."

"Well, I would hope she's not blabbing my secrets all over. Jesus. She was just here, too."

"No, don't be mad at her. I wanted to know why you didn't come. And I pried, really, a lot."

"She was drunk, she gave it up. Okay, but please don't tell anyone else, my reputation's already pretty much toast around here. I should move."

"Don't move. We'll miss you."

"You are so sweet, do you know that."

He looked down.

"Well, you know, well, I dunno. So when do you get out?"

"Tomorrow, I think. If I'm deemed not to be a hazard to the public. Shit, it's pretty terrible to have to think of things like that, I'm sorry."

"Oh, don't freak out, it's okay, it's okay. You're not dangerous. Leopards are dangerous!"

I laughed a little. "Okay, okay."

"Yeah. And, maybe, when you get out, do you want to go to the park with me?"

"The park? Like, for what?"

"Like for a picnic. Get some beer or mimosas or whatever it is you girls like to drink in the morning."

"Well, when I drink in the morning, I have André Brut with Minute Maid, pulpy."

"Right, I'll get that."

"I can't believe you asked me out in the psych ward. That's sweet."

As he started to reply, there was a loud knock, followed by a nurse, followed by Jesse.

"Ow, gotta go," said Zed.

"So, I'll leave you," said the nurse. "Fifteen minutes."

As the door closed behind them, Jesse turned to me and said, "And what was that?"

"Ah, hey. A friend."

"O-kay. So, have you had the electroshock treatments yet?" He sat down across from me.

"Ouch, no. I hope that's not in the program. They've been telling me I get out tomorrow, I'm trying to be extra-good."

"Do you want a twenty? I have some with me, keep you motivated towards recovery."

I sighed. "I totally can't. I'd be fucked. Do appreciate you coming here, though, really, I mean it."

"Good, because I hope you know how brutal the MUNI ride is to get down here."

"I don't even know where I am."

"You're at UCSF, Baby Pigeon."

"That's two stops from my house."

"Yeah, you could jump out that window and fly home, were we in a different world, but we're not, in which case call me tomorrow when you get out."

He rose to leave. Coming around the edge of the table, he hugged me and I felt a sudden jolt of tears. I curled up against his chest, fighting the wetness in my eyes. It was warm and safe here. I never wanted to leave. I could hear the nurse saying, "Okay, okay, that's enough."

He pulled back and released me to the grey walls. I watched him as he left the visiting cube and moved to the hall. As I wiped the snot on the back of my hand, I felt the tears on my sleeve.

"Well, Lena Cosentino, you have been evaluated, and we think you are ready to be released."

I bit the back of my lips and blinked back tears again as I swung my legs and looked up again at Dr. Howard.

"You mean I can go?"

The classroom clock ticked above his head as he dug a single finger into the Laffy Taffy. Lifting a grape bite, he held it out to me.

"Yes. Your emergency contact, I believe Limone is her name, is here to pick you up. The nurses will have your things. Proceed to the front desk and collect them."

I took the Laffy Taffy and wedged it in my pocket. Yanking the jeans up over my now-stubbly stomach, I smiled, ducked, and turned to go. I pulled down my shirt. The doctor closed my file. As I reached the door, the scrape marks on the doorframe made me pause.

I looked back.

He was bent over a new file with a pen lodged firmly in his mustache. I grabbed the back of my jeans and lurched out the door, through the dim hallway, to the edge of the nurses' station where I saw Coco, daubing at what looked like track marks.

I ran towards her.

"Hey, hey Coco, I'm getting out!"

She looked up, her eyes red and sore. "Good for you, doll. I'm stuck in here for another thirty days."

"Are you okay...?"

"What they don't know won't hurt'em." She pulled down her sleeve. The fluorescent lights buzzed incandescent. She flipped her chin up. "I want you to be happy. You go out there and tell this Jesse character to treat you right, okay?"

"Yeah, yeah, I will."

"Yeah, I met him in the hall, I can see the attraction."

"Every girl loves a train wreck," I sighed.

"True. Just please...well...will you call me when I get out?"

"Of course, here, I'll give you my number. I want to hear from you, I want to know you're okay."

"I'll make it."

I folded my phone number into a square and pressed it into her hands.

The nurse gave me a paper bag with my belt and purse and phone – at last, six calls from the temp agency. That would take some sorting out. I tucked them under my arm and bent to pull on my socks, realized I'd run out without shoes, sighed, and stood up again.

Walking through the corridor behind the nurse-elect, I looked side to side at Toby, rapt in a copy of Cosmopolitan, and the demon-hearing-lady, muttering on a corner bench, at my favorite nurse, lecturing the phlebotomist on the proper disposal of used syringes.

There was nothing there I wouldn't enjoy forgetting. Padding past the front desk, I saw Limone and Brady waiting for me in the entryway. Posters of Hep C all around.

"Darling!"

"Darling!"

I followed them out the entryway and into the hazy-bright metropolis and the
street.

Chapter 12
triggers

The night I was released, Limone and I sat in the Axum Café, watching the hand-painted lanterns against the copper walls. The plastic placemats had green maps of Ethiopia with a red dot for Addis Ababa.

I put my finger of the dot and said, "Huh. What do you think we get the vegetarian combination?"

Limone folded her parchment menu and said, "Sure. What is it?"

"It's good if you want to try a bunch of stuff. You get five things, the Alicha, the Hamli – that's spinach, it's really good, this mushroom dish that's called Kintishara, I think, and then lentils. And a salad with cilantro dressing."

"Sound's great. Since I've gone vegan – did I tell you about that?"

"I miss three days, I miss a lifetime. No, why did you go vegan?"

"I just wanted to be healthier, to cleanse my body of all of those nasty toxins. Check it out, I bought this book called – "

A waiter with grey at the temples came up to our table. He flicked a blue ballpoint between his fingers, tapping it against his notebook.

"And hello. Are you ready to order?" There was a burst of chatter as a group got up to hug, consecutively, the new arrival.

Turning away from the girl's lapis top, Limone said, "Okay. We'll have the vegetarian combination and…" Her eyes flashed to mine.

"A glass of honey wine."

"Make that two," said Limone. "Thank you."

The man nodded and walked towards the back, where an elderly woman was tending bar. A young couple, looking earnest in handmade sweaters, were frantically discussing something unheard.

Limone turned back to me.

"So, anyway, I bought this diet book called *Skinny Bitch*."

"*Skinny Bitch*? Limone! But you are a skinny bitch."

"Oh, I know, I know. But I'm trying to switch around, to get all healthy after that shit we used to do."

"Okay."

"So I walk into Borders, right, and this girl at the counter was totally overweight, this rockabilly type, and I go up to her and say, 'I ordered this book, it's called…um….*Skinny Bitch*?"

"Oh my god."

"Yeah. She was, like, 'Oh yeah, we were all laughing about that in the back.' I just about died."

"Wonderful. So, was it worth it?"

"Well, it has some really interesting advice. I won't bore you with all of the details, but there was a lot of stuff about the toxins in fast food, and meat, and how you should eat all organic and stuff."

"I wish I could afford organic."

The waiter set down our glasses.

"You cook budget steaks at five in the morning," said Limone.

"I have paid for them in change."

"Yikes."

"At this point, it's like, the cow or me. I knew when I was selling my import Idoru's singing Serge Gainsbourg CD and I couldn't even get enough for a twenty-bag, I was, like, fine, force me to eat. Amoeba bitch gave me four bucks. Said it was scratched. Guys give me much better deals."

She snorted.

"It's gotten better, though, really. That was when I wasn't working."

"Are you working now?"

"Kind of. Off and on. I was at Wells Fargo for awhile, then this investment banking place, and, well, luckily I was between assignments when this whole breakdown thing happened, but I missed my Wednesday job. I had all these messages from them that I had to deal with. I mean, they expect you to be at their beck and call, reachable at all times. I had to tell them I went camping."

"Camping?"

"Hard to picture, I know. I don't like getting my boots dirty. Dirt under the fingernails. Scratches. God."

"But, no, what really happened that night?" Limone said, as the waiter set down a platter of injera. The circular flatbread covered the metal plate, with dollops of orange, yellow, red and brown. He set down two plates with more bread.

"Okay, this is what you do." I said. "You take this crepe thing, rip off a piece, and scoop up the food. Then you eat it."

She reached for the plate. "And that night?"

I sighed. "I don't really want to talk about it. It's – well – I just lost it, I don't know, I've always been afraid that that would finally happen. I would just freak out and end up homeless."

"And I'm sure the drugs don't help."

I sighed. "No, they don't. Well, the prescriptions do. The 'dietary supplements'…" I shoved a scoop of pureed garbanzos into my mouth. "Yeah, well, they're not so great. In fact, I told myself I would stop, it's just that – well, being in this neighborhood, I…"

"You seriously want to go see Miles again…or Donny? Is he back?" She set down her glass.

"I just…god, I really have no self-control, do I."

"Well, it's true, Duchamp's is not that far away. Triggers."

"I don't know. Would you hate me?" I said quietly.

"I don't judge. Really, I mean that. Besides, I'd be doing it too. I just shouldn't any more...well...I though you'd be off that after being in the crazy house."

"Well – ah – no. That is to say, well, no, I guess."

"It's up to you." Limone took a long sip of her wine and set it back on the lacquer table. A whisper of laughter came from a table to their left, where a blonde woman was giggling into her glass. It was very loud, over the low drums. The kaleidoscopic windows showed triangulations of the street outside.

On the corner of Haight and Divisidaro, the wind buffeted us against the graffitied brick.

I scrolled through my phone. "Wait, shit, I forgot, Miles is a no. I think he might be in trouble."

"What?"

"I don't have total verification on this, but I think Jesse turned him in."

"What? What are you talking about? Is this something I would have had to deal with when I was dealing? The bastard!"

"Yeah. Narc. He doesn't know about your stuff last year..."

"Lena, anything anyone does gets around here in about 15 minutes."

"You were...comment dit-on...a minor player."

"That's the last time I'm sharing with that guy. Ew. Fuck. Do you know anyone else?"

"You know, I do. Huh..." The phone bleeped. "Okay, here we go. Jay. I don't know him at all, he's just this other number I got off Donny before he went to Thailand."

"Hmmm....Does it matter?"

"Not really." I dialed.

"Jay?"

"Yeah. Who's this?"

"Yeah, this is Lena, I'm a friend of Donny's. He told me I could call you about business."

"Oh, okay. We can do that. Where are you?"

"I'm in the lower Haight."

"Go to, let's see, what's a bar near there...?"

"We always go to Duchamp's."

"Okay, that works. See you in half an hour. Later."

I looked up and saw Limone peering down Divisadero. She stepped forwards, looked from side to side in the growing darkness, and lifted her arm. A cab pulled up under the streetlight by the EZ Wash 'N' Fold, and we tumbled in. The streetlight's halo streaked away from us, as we careened down the street in warm pleather darkness. The man in the front was twiddling the radio between Mariachi and Bollywood, and I leaned my head back, momentarily, at peace.

At Duchamp's, arias flowed from the piano. Long, cold hands held mojitos.

Limone looked around as we edged in, and said, "Lena, are you sure Miles wasn't gay?"

"He was always talking about girls. Seriously, always. Who knows, though. Maybe he's just metro. He really liked his pineapple martinis."

A few silver balloons drifted towards the ceiling.

"I miss the guy, seriously. Not exactly a deep relationship, I know, but he was always really cool to me. Really, really nice, and funny, we'd sit here and have a drink as we did the deal."

"That's sad. You know it could be any of us."

A slow breath. "That's the thing I'm trying not to think about. That's one of them."

A rumpled looking kid, about twenty, ambled in the door. He wore a "Party Naked" shirt with his crew-cut.

"Hmmm…. Strike one for conspicuous," Limone said.

"I think he's new at this." I caught his eye and waved. He nodded and came over, his puffy tennis shoes nudging the floor softly.

"Hey. You Lena?"

"Hey. Yeah. This is Limone."

"Cool. Okay, so what were you looking for?"

"Do you do forties?"

"Gram is sixty. I cut it up all at once, so that's all I got."

"That's cool. Okay…" I looked down at my lap, scuttling in my purse. I pulled three twenties from my wallet, and slid them under the table to him.

"Thank you!"

"Sure."

"Hey, I don't want to pry or anything, but have you seen Miles?" I pressed concern into my eyes, pushing goodwill across the table.

He blanched. "Miles. Shit, yeah. He's still in there, just in Eighth Street waiting for his trial."

"Oh God. So he *is* in jail. Do you know if he's getting bail or anything?"

"Yeah, I mean, it's there, but who's got that kind of money, you know? Sure, I'd love to help the guy, but what can you do?"

"I see what you mean. Yeah, I'm broke. I shouldn't be getting this."

"C'mon, enjoy your shit. Go to your bullshit clubs." He shrugged. "Ain't my problem, I just do this on the side."

"That's cool. Thanks for hooking us up."

We left him playing with a napkin. Cocktail square, with a picture of two olives on a silver toothpick. It was too sharp.

I looked around for Limone as we left the bar, and saw her running a hand along the handlebars of a mint green Vespa.

"Shhh…Not yours. Lay off it."

"Oh, but they're so cool, though. I want one!"

"Sell your car. At least they'd be easy to park."

"True that. Do you think we can get a cab from here?"

"I think so…yeah, over there." Cars streaked by the red-curbs. We were perched on an acute angle, a silver toothpick pressed into the street. Del'issio Café, all red and yellow awnings and French Provencal trim, loomed to the left, while the Crazy Eight's Liquor and Deli blared behind a record store crusted with colored vinyl. A broken 32 oz shimmered on the sidewalk. There was no one around.

I told too easily.
His laughing face.
I told too easily.
Hands around my throat.
Emotions dead from the drug, dead from fear. I could care only for myself.

Zed flicked his knife against the champagne cork, then passed it over to me. We were sitting on a grassy knoll in Dolores Park, crystal sky over Mission High School's sandstone tower. An old man pushed past on the grass, his whitewashed tin cart with decals of lime and mango fruit bars, drumsticks and ice cream sandwiches. A bell hung on the handrail, jingling as he walked, and he whistled a low, lilting tune.

"Ice cream?"

Zed looked up from the orange juice he was opening, and said, "Do you have any It's It's? The mint kind."

"No. You wanna popsicle?"

"No, s'alright."

He walked off, and I began to work the cork out with my fingers, padded by a towel. I pointed it at Zed.

"Hey now."

"Oh, me, what was I doing. Hey, I've almost got it." Streamers of kites hung purple in the sky. We were surrounded by other picnickers, the wide grassy slope of the park dotted with blankets, intrepid dogs, bicycle messengers, dykes on and off of bikes, the odd acoustic guitar, and a rising smell of veggie-burgers.

I watched a Siberian husky with a bandana around its neck lope by, turning to glare with its ice blue eyes.

I was watching the dog weave off when the cork finally freed, popping loudly and leaving a gush of fluid on my hands. Setting it down, propped against the Bi-Rite bag that held the food, I reached inside the bag and pulled out a carton of figs and some sesame thins.

"Do you like figs? I think they're kind of sexy." He said.

Picking one up, I examined the sloping, plum exterior, the curve of it. I bit into it. Small seeds caught in my teeth.

Smiling, Zed took one and started to chew.

I took the mimosa he had made and drank, letting the fresh plume fall down my throat. The sun was bright. I shaded my forehead with a hand, knowing I would burn.

I took another gulp and looked at him. Twig arms in a ripped T-shirt. Black jelly bracelets. White knuckles around his plastic cup. We had gotten the clear party ones, and I watched the grass curve gentle green around the cup. The shadows of hidden blades springing above the orange liquid.

"So," he said.

"Um...so."

I took another drink. Zed refilled his and began to twist a napkin between his fingers. I watched the condensation seep from his hands to the towel. Condensation on the edges of my glass. Tiny bubbles.

"How's Catastrophic?"

"Oh, it rules. Why don't you ever go?"

"I...I went that one time, remember?"

"One time."

"Well, I just get busy, I guess."

"Busy doing what?"

"I don't know, whatever it is that I do with my time. Sleeping, painting. I work sometimes and your thing is on a Monday, so it's kind of a hard night for me."

"Well, okay."

"Plus, I don't know, I mean, I just...feel kind of weird about seeing you there, I mean, after how we...how we hooked up and stuff."

"That was ages ago."

"I get awkward."

The bell tolled from Mission Dolores, and I started. Three o'clock. And I was getting drunk. Zed fiddled with his shoelaces, neon green on black converse, and poured himself another.

There was a long pause.

"So."

"So."

I took another sip, gravely. It was as if we were discussing something of great seriousness that didn't actually exist. The ephemeral nothingness of the sky. The grass verdant beneath our feet. There was, in the end, nothing to say. Nothing to say that hadn't been said before.

My drink was half empty. Three quarters. We refilled.

I watched his fingers edging closer to mine, and as I bent mine to meet his I thought, *didn't we come here to talk?* But I was falling against his slight shoulder, his mouth reaching around to grab mine, and I fell into the kiss as easily as sunshine. Upon a barren wall.

Our kiss became more frantic, and soon we had knocked over my drink and my foot was dangerously close to the fig basket.

"Hey, Zed said. "Do you want to, um, go back to my place? I live on Capp Street, it's not too far away."

I nodded. Dropping my cup into a trash can shaped like a turtle, I turned and followed him down the long path leading to the sidewalk.

I rattled the looping chain that rimmed the path. Soft, smooth metal, warmed by the sun. A boy with a knit cap and dreadlocks was passing out Falun Gong pamphlets, and I waved them away with irritation.

Capp Street wasn't far.

Lifting my head from his pillow, I saw that his clock read 10:45 pm. We had come back around four, finished the rest of the champagne, and gone out for vodka. His downy face was burrowed into the pillow. I watched him sleep, a certain tenderness mixed with mistrust. They were most honest when they slept. I could be honest never. Since I had gotten DSL, the addictive MSN relationship advice told me to lie and conceal, to preserve my desirability. I knew that the face I compulsively moisturized, and body I whittled with drugs, would eventually show someone different than the disco ingénue I wanted to be. I was twenty-nine, not twenty-three anymore.

Part of what lured me to Jesse what that he was unafraid to be flawed, found his dirty glamour in the mythos of cheap tricks. For a man, this was sexy. A certain cultural type. For a woman, the word was washed-up whore.

Sure, there was all sorts of feminist this-and-that to fight for, and I had tried. But since I had penned "female agency a go-go" on my college notebooks and tried to make fuckery a political act, I had still found skank to be my surname.

Now, stroking the thighs of my lover. I smile, knowing that after a certain point I drew my lines and did not care.

The N-Judah pulled to a whistling halt in the station, and I weaved between suits and student backpacks to the doors. Inside the car, a few seats were empty, the bright plastic scratched from endless wear. I slid down, tucking my purse onto my lap. Work had been long and tiring, and I slumped my head into my chin, closing my eyes, feeling the rhythm of the train as it pulled away from Montgomery station and headed down the unseen tracks to Powell. I opened my eyes when the doors scratched, and five teenagers jumped on. They wavered in the middle of the car, trying to sit together amid the sullen workers, shopping bags, and oldsters with walkers. When they finally sat down, I realized I didn't understand what they were saying.

"Look, I'm totes trigued with this, but could you, like text me when you wanna get dumb?" The slang fell like empty signifiers, an empty egg carton left forever on a rack.

Cold. The train was cold. I stared around the mute, tired faces, the ancient woman closing her eyes against the fluorescent light, the dim graffiti ricocheting past the windows like full sleeves on an old man in a bar. Weathered, obscured, flashes of pink and yellow flared against the dark.

The men and women with their briefcases and grocery sacks, Macy's bags and trashbag liners, were all shuffling their eyes from the floor, side to side, dodging eye contact as they checked each other out. Eye to eye, some less than a foot apart, they scraped through each other. The wheels rumbled against the tracks.

The train careened forward with its passive burden, stopping at Civic Center for another influx. On to Van Ness station, and then it came rising out from underground to the glorious spring sunshine and Castro Safeway. There was a faint smell of urine and sweat.

Church Street was rattling with street kids roaming around the rescue mission, its murals opening arms down the sidewalk. So many came to San Francisco with flowers in their hair, ended up fucked. Like a one-way Greyhound to Hollywood and a fluffer part at Vivid. I watched listlessly as the train trundled up Duboce, stopping at the playground and diving back into a flickering tunnel. I stared fixedly at the blonde opposite, fiddling anxiously in my purse for the keys, as the train pulled up to Carl and Cole.

The following is a story that Limone told me.

Limone stared at Iris, folding her hands together. They were seated on Iris' bed, the fluffy white duvet turned over and over in bunches. The room was sparsely furnished, white walls and a lone cubist painting. A deeply recessed window, with a Stila lipgloss palette resting on the sill like a command, looked out onto a deck and the verdant Marin hills. Limone watched as a crow emerged from the pines and cruised the deck, looking for the birdfeeder. It was overflowing with sunflower seeds. The bird fed rapaciously as Iris continued to talk. Her blonde hair fell around her face and her French-manicured fingers jabbed the air.

"I think we can really do this. This website, we'll travel around the world reviewing places, and then we'll put them all in this massive site. We'll get to go everywhere, see everything, it'll be fantastic. It'll be like Citysearch, with clubs and bars and obscure liqueurs."

She dropped her head and did a line off a framed picture of her parents. Settling the photo back on the bedside table, she looked expectantly at Limone.

"I don't know," she said. "I think we might want to, like, downscale it a little bit? We can't be everywhere at once. Where are we going to get the staff? Are we going to hire people for maintenance and set-up while we're off gallivanting around?"

"Come on, think big! Absinthe in Prague! Laptops in wi-fi cafes in Hong Kong!"

"Think reasonable," said Limone. "Restaurant reviews."

"Everyone does restaurant reviews."

"But they're useful."

"So are bar reviews. Especially in foreign countries."

"And how are we going to get to these foreign countries?"

"We'll get venture capitalists."

"To send us to Prague to drink?"

"Young, edgy capitalists."

"Right, sure. How about foreign correspondents, although then we'd have to get in touch somehow with qualified and literate people to do that. That's a Craigslist venture, though, that wouldn't be too hard."

"Yeah, see. We can totally do this."

"I've always wanted to start a business…my dad has been wanting me to do that for a long time. The last one didn't turn out so well."

"Tell me about it." Iris said. "I was getting worried about you. I mean, it was great to always be able to score, but, God, some of those people you were hanging around! That Lena chick was totally dragging you down."

"Hey, I like Lena. I've known her forever."

"I can't believe you slept with her, I mean, who knows how many places that cooch has been."

"Iris, please."

"Okay, whatevs. Point being, let's put together a business plan and get this together. We can make some money and start seriously being the jet-setters we've always wanted to be."

"I don't know, Iris."

I pulled the envelope from the mailbox and stared at it. Bank of America. Why someone would give me a credit card was beyond me, but I had filled out the application just the same, and thought I would try.

I ripped it open. The card tumbled into my hand. I would survive.

Iris, Limone and I giggled down the hallway, following Evran and Chris.

Iris had strictly warned me in the cab: "These are a certain type of people, and you must behave in a certain way." She chose her prospects carefully, and went in for the kill. Selling ads for the future website. Young, edgy, venture capitalists.

We left a party in Pacific Heights for Evran's place in SOMA. Past empty warehouses, storefronts gutted to galleries, the shafts of steel and concrete on the live-work spaces as they stabbed up.

Inside, we say around a three-legged table. Evran folded the tear-shaped segments out so they expanded and retreated.

"This is my first piece of really modern furniture, I'm so into it!" he said.

"Yeah, we've got to use coasters now." Chris flipped a few onto the table.

He dished out some coke from the saltshaker on the counter, next to some olive oil.

The hours from three until dawn passed; the warm brown blur of the leather panels on the doors, the light through the sweeping windows, the tingle through my body.

"Yeah, I feel like these walls need something, but I don't know what to put up. Nothing seems quite right."

"Oh, Lena paints, tell him about your stuff," Iris said.

"Oh, it's nothing, really."

"No, an artist, wow. I don't know any. What's your stuff like?"

"Well…" I looked around, cornered. But they seemed interested, like in a new form of sushi. I tried to entertain.

Chapter 13
when I go, I'm going like chelsea

I was paging through MySpace a few nights later, hiding from Brady's coughs in the kitchen, when the phone rang.

"Yeah?"

"It's Coco!"

"Coco? Langley-Porter? Hey!"

'Yeah, bet you thought I wouldn't call you. Well, I had to. When I meet someone I want to know, I have to call."

"Want, need, whatever"

"Right. You are coming to Bordello with me tonight, 'kay?"

"Oh, right on. Okay. I wasn't sure if I was going, I mean, I have some shit I need to do."

"What, alphabetize your CD's? No. I'll meet you at Bordello at midnight."

I slammed the phone into the mousepad.

"Now. I shall. Find some fun." I turned to my closet, thinking of *Cabaret*.

Oh Liza...I delved into sparkles and furs, leather and denim, the sequins looked out at me as if white heels and black lace scarves might be as right as asymmetrical zippers. It was all too early to tell.

I edged my way down the staircase with Limone, looking for Coco. The metal scaffolding was pocked with holes where a stray heel could fall. To go tumbling was not in the plan, so we held the railing, stepped carefully, edging down in the darkness.

I saw a red-brown shag veer out from the DJ booth, and I advanced through the main floor towards it. Coco. She was gesticulating madly at a guy with a polka-dot tie, who hugged her and then curved off into the crowd. She turned and began heading towards the bar. Framed by burlap banners with Japanese characters slashed in red, the bartenders ducked and whirled through the hands waving cash.

At the bottom of the stairs, Limone bumped into the coat check girl, who turned and sneered. "Oh, so that's what happened to you. Nice recovery." Pulling away with her head high, Limone took off into the crowd.

"Hey hey!" Coco grabbed me. "I got out! Finally! It took forever."

"That's awesome!"

"Hey. Do you want to go upstairs? It's impossible to talk down here, and I want to do a bump."

"Yeah." We pushed our way back through sharp elbows.

At the top of the stairs, we walked past the pool table, a smoking room overflowing with underage girls, and clattered down another set of metal stairs. A balcony spanning the width of the club spread around us, peppered with couches and mod plastic chairs.

"The couch, the couch!" Coco said.

"I can't believe we never saw you here, that was, seriously, our couch," I said.

"Well, I was at Langley-Porter for about five months."

"Damn."

Coco sighed. "Yeah. I am so glad to be out of there. And now I can get drugs again."

Limone's eyes flickered to mine. I turned away, knowing I functioned exactly the same way. Dear Limone, she was so often the mom now, the voice of reason. She was so often not heard.

But, did it matter? We plopped down. Dancers whirled and flailed downstairs, reduced to flecks of flesh and red. Coco flicked open her compact and pulled out a bag.

"Be careful, guys," said Limone.

"Oh, we will. Here, you go first," Coco said, holding the key out to me. I turned and faced the couch, my eyelids flickering against the black leather as I sniffed. Limone finished, and we settled back into the couch.

"So, where are you living, now?" I asked.

"I got this room with these kids in the Mission. It's pretty rad, I like it."

"Cool. I'm still living with Brady. He's great."

"Is he..." Limone said.

"I don't want to talk about it."

"Okay."

Coco furrowed her eyebrows.

"Are you working?" I said.

"Oh hell no. Trust fund. I'm on the last legs of it, though, so I kind of need to figure out what to do next."

"Uh oh, are you going to be okay?"

"I'll figure it out. For the moment, though, it's cool!"

I caught a glimpse of Jesse, sitting against the balcony rail with a young girl with drawn-on eyebrows.

"Oh shit, wait, that's Jesse."

"Well, you knew that he works here. Don't you run into him all the time?" said Limone.

"Yeah, and I know he has other girls on the side, too. He makes that clear. It's just that – well – I usually don't have to see it."

"Delusion is, I think, a big factor in your relationship with him."

"Thanks."

"Oh, is this that Jesse-fuck you told me about in there?" asked Coco.

"Um, yeah. With the chick."

"Is that Vanessa?" Limone took a sip of her beer, eyes narrowing.

"Well, yeah, I think so." The balcony railings, shadowed against the curtain's rouge, looked like the bars on my windows at home.

"Do you want to…" Limone said.

"Yeah. Let's go. Downstairs, at least, I mean, we don't have to leave altogether, but we should at least, like…" I squirmed. "I just don't want him to know that I'm here."

"Let's do another one, though, really quick." Coco crossed her legs, creamy skin emerging from her skirt. She reached into the green snakeskin of her purse. Pulling the silver compact through the darkness, it glistened in a sudden flash of light. I stiffened, then caught Coco laughing at me.

"We're okay. Now, come on. It's okay. Here." She lifted the bump to my nose, and as I sniffed, a flashlight's glare burst over us.

Caught. An huge security guard with a star on his blue shoulder flicked the flashlight back and forth over us, and said, "Out. Out out out. Couldn't you have waited for the bathroom?"

Blinded, I caught only Jesse's shadow as he stood to laugh, the young girl standing also. She was wearing a small hat with a veil. Trapped between the flashlight and the wall, the plush of the couch turned to burlap, I scrabbled in my lap, then rose as if a decision had been made.

"Let's go, come on, we have to just go. I don't want this to get even more embarrassing," I muttered, leading them down the stairs and away from the guard, who flicked his light after us like the harsh cold light of morning when you know just exactly who you are.

Trudging into the house, I slumped my way onto the couch, bending my tense neck to sore positions on the upholstery. Brady was bustling around the kitchen, wiping down countertops with a Clorox wipe. I watched him for a few minutes, digging the back of my head into the sagging gold afghan draped over the couch. I splayed my hands on my thighs, watching the jagged, dirty nails, last month's manicure chipped rough from too many nights digging apart my mirror for the last gasoline grains. White birds. Nothing at all at the end of the night. I dug a hand into my bare leg, scraping the razorburn, where my cheap bic had scraped the delicate skin. Nothing about me was delicate anymore. I was bare adrenalin and splinters.

Raising my eyes, I turned to where Brady was finishing up. He daubed the stained faucet with the wipe, then flicked it in the air and shoved it into the trash. His eyes dashed upwards, and his head fell again.

"Where have you been?"

"Oh, I was at Bordello."

"Again."

"Oh, and again. And this time I got caught with drugs, seriously, this Coco chick that I met in the hospital, she's great, sure, a little crazy, but it really wasn't her fault, I've done the same thing too a bunch of times, and this time I finally got caught with it."

He came over and sat next to me. His long white hands like white lizards on the couch. He shrugged, and the shadow of his head stretched out along the wall. Purple and red tatters down his arms, along the wall.

"Sounds like a pain."

"Embarrassing."

"Oh yes, and Jesse was there."

"Oh lord." He held out his hands. The red inside of the cuffs folded back velvet. I looked around, the shadows dashing over the TV, in the corner by the fridge.

We sat in silence for a moment.

"Listen, I'm really sorry about the other night," he said.

"No, no, I am. I was being ridiculous."

"You were being honest. I'm afraid of honesty." He looked at me, and the wolf blue of his eyes told me. "When I get too close to people, especially when I live with them, its like, this automatic distancing happens sometimes. Intimacy…it's hard."

"Used to know this girl, lived at the 13th and Failing house, and she had, 'When you have no one, no one can hurt you' tattooed above her breasts."

"Here." He got up, and went to the fridge, skidding a second on the wet tile. The refrigerator leaked constantly, and the landlord refused to fix it. There was nothing we could do. Brady skidded, righted himself, and opened the door, pulling out a half-eaten chocolate cake with a wax three lurching against a five. The candles were edged with mouse-eaten blue, the white wax caked with red from the plastic box. The five lurched against the plastic, then fell sideways.

"Do you want some cake?" He set it down on the coffee table, the ashtray filled with olive pits and coffee grounds spilling onto the burgundy cloth. I smiled despite myself, and reached out a hand to pick a stray slice from falling into a butt.

"Take that one," he said. "It was my birthday today. They gave me this at the food bank."

"Oh my god, you didn't tell me."

"I don't like telling people it's my birthday, it seems like I'm asking them to make a big thing over me, when I feel I can't really ask that of people. It's not my right." He shrugged again, and leaned over to take a slice.

I gripped mine in the hollow of my hand, and said, "I know what you mean… A couple years ago, I didn't tell anyone it was my birthday, and spent it with a bowl of ramen and some amaretto. Then my friend came over, shot up in my room – I didn't have any furniture, I'd just moved in to my old studio – and she just passed out, so I finished the bottle and did, too. Next day I went to work."

"You always just seem to get up and go to work. How do you do it?"

"Well, not always. There are always those days when I call in sick. It's mainly just that, with temping, I only work a few days a week, so I can balance out when I get fucked up and when I don't. I'm not really that good at it, though. I tend to get fucked up all the time, and then just show up shaking and sweating.

"Well, you do what you can."

"I guess you could say that. It's still not good, though. I seriously don't know how I'm going to keep this job."

"God. I don't know what to tell you. Clench your teeth. Go in and don't talk to anyone."

"Yeah, yeah, that's what I do, I go in and just don't talk to anyone, and they let me go at five. I just wait it out. I sit it out. When you temp, they don't really expect you to actually do anything."

"That's pretty nice."

"I suppose, except , after awhile, you forget how to do anything, until you can't do anything, you are just this useless wait-doll, and all you want to do is wait for eight hours to pass until you can go get fucked up and blast out the fact that you have to go back tomorrow and you don't know what you're doing and where you want to go."

"Oh, ideological discontent." Come on."

"I want to do something."

"What?"

"I don't know, that's the problem. I can't figure it out, I can't figure out what I want to do or how to get past my problems. If Jesse called right now I'd run to my room and pick out the perfect panties. All of this – gone. Thanks for the cake."

"Lena, Lena, listen, you'll figure it out. Everyone goes through this stuff. Just remember to breathe deeply and you'll work it out. Think, at least you're alive, at least you're out of the psych ward, at least you're not pregnant."

"Yes. At least I'm not pregnant."

"Be grateful for the small things. Chicken Soup for the crackhead soul."

I laughed. I rolled a bent fork between my hands, plucking it from the table and tucking it between my fingers. The moon outside was indistinguishable from the streetlights streaming through the window. Brady nodded his head slowly, and reached for more frosting

The door buzzer fuzzed, and I sat up halfway in bed. The room was dark, the red at the window backlit by dawn. My chair was a grasshopper shadow.

"Jesse. Shit." I got up, tripping as I fell out of bed, and limped over to the intercom.

"What?"

"Hey, let me in. I'm with Amos, so be decent."

I pressed the button, and stared around the cluttered room. Not quite a day to entertain. Looking down, I grumbled and went searching around for clothes. On the floor by my hair dryer was a dark huddle that, when lifted, became a black Jackie O dress.

I threw it on, fumbling with the broken zipper. Glancing in the mirror, I smeared on some lipstick and heard a scratching at the door.

Jesse pushed it open and shoved into the room.

"So, this my buddy Amos. You remember him." He gestured at the man who followed him in. Treading softly in snakeskin boots, he settled onto the bed. He was wearing one of Jesse's designs, a T-shirt with asymmetrical, erratic stitching and silk-screened gears.

He crossed his legs neatly and said, "Hey."

I smiled warmly. At least Jesse was unpredictable. He threw down his man-purse at the end of the bed, and darted out of the room. Right. I sat down on the pseudo-Eames chair and leaned forwards, crossing my legs. Amos. He was the guy from 24-Karat Gold.

I was about to speak when Jesse came falling back into the room, carrying the bottle of vanilla vodka I had stashed in the freezer. I had been saving it for myself, but... Oh well, I thought. Guests.

Jesse poured it into three glasses and passed them around. I sipped mine from a measuring cup. Ice cold. Delicious. I was going to pass out again.

"You got a mirror?" said Amos, fumbling around in his pocket.

"Oh, yeah, sure." I fetched it, and he began to shake coke onto the scratched surface.

"Here, you sit on the bed," said Jesse, motioning to me. I sat down at the head of the bed, leaning on a mascara-smudged pillow. I watched Jesse with calculated intensity as he settled sideways into my chair, tucking his arm over the back.

"Well, get to know one another," he said.

Amos passed me the mirror, his gold tooth-facings glinting.

"Right." I took it, staring into my own eyes as I swept up the line. I passed it to Jesse, who said, "No, no, him."

I passed it on. Amos was neat and quick. He handed it to Jesse.

As Jesse was bending his head, Amos turned to me and said, "Would you like a backrub?"

"Not right now, thanks."

"Lena – " Jesse started.

"Maybe later. I'll see how I feel."

He flicked the mouse with one hand, blasting music.

"Wait, come on, not so loud."

"I've got it." He lowered it an inch.

"Come on! Brady'll be pissed."

"This isn't loud."

"Jesse! It's six am! People have jobs. Bedazzle any thongs, lately?"

Amos shifted against the duvet.

"Come on, come on, please? Pretty please?"

"Okay, man, you heard her," Amos said.

"Fine."

"Backrub?" Amos asked.

"Fine. I mean, sure." He came around the side of the bed, and curled behind me, putting his legs on either side of mine. Oh God, this was going to be one of *those* backrubs. I widened my eyes. I still didn't know what I wanted to do with these guys. On one hand, I resented the assumption, but on the other hand, Amos was pretty foxy. I had always thought so. It might be easier to just go with it.

"Can I have another line?" I said.

"Of course. Take two." Amos passed me the mirror. I smirked inwardly and sniffed it up.

As his hands began working at my clavicles, Jesse stared listlessly at the ceiling. He snapped up and clapped his hands, saying, "Okay, Lena, time to take your clothes off."

"What? No." I pushed his hands off.

"Come on. That's what you're for. That's what you do."

"Look, you can't just boss me around like that." *At least not in front of other people. With a little pretty persuasion I would've gone with it.* I perched on the edge of the bed and clenched my hands. Watching them shake, I reached out and took my measuring cup. The vodka went down smooth.

"Here, why don't you give me a backrub?" said Amos.

"Oh…okay."

He lay down on the bed, and I stared at his body for a moment before straddling his back. I dug my hands into his shoulder muscles, cupped the grooves in his spine.

Jesse dished out three more lines and passed the mirror. I was feeling more comfortable with the idea. Not like I hadn't done it before. As I smoothed Amos' shoulders, I watched as Jesse fished two pills from his blazer pocket. "Xanax?" he said to me.

I took one.

Amos leaned to kiss me, setting the gold teeth on the floor, and with a glance at Jesse's greasy head I fell on top of him, kissing him, letting his hands move to my ass and neck. Jesse's hands came down around my shoulders, and I let his cock moved to its usual place.

Ambling through the Cala Foods with calculated nonchalance, I looked down at my basket. A pregnancy test and two bottles of André champagne. Whatever the result was, I knew I'd need them.

The fluorescent light above washed my features out as I peered at some oranges I had no intention of buying.

"Hmmm…" I picked up an avocado and squeezed it. "$2.99, Jesus. That's a no." Looping around the bouquets of blue-dyed carnations, I veered over to the sushi.

It was late afternoon and the supply had been plundered, leaving only some sad-looking tofu spring rolls and a couple of boxes of the $8.50 Shoreline Combo. The silken reds of the tuna seemed to taunt me.

"Ah, and that is also a no. Thanks, Pathways Personnel." The temp agency had been pretty sparing in the assignment department, and I was feeling the pinch. Even the pregnancy test felt like an extravagance.

I advanced to the check-out and set the test on the rubber, followed by the white-labeled bottles. The middle-aged woman grabbed the champagne, turned to the bagger, and began ranting in another language. I smiled. Either way, I thought to myself, either way.

Departing to their glares, I sighed and trudged past the security guard. The dispensers of butterfly stickers and Homies dolls stood mutely with gumballs as I turned towards home.

"I'm here..." I yelled, coming through the door. Soulwax remixes were blasting from Brady's room.

"Hello Dolly," he said.

"Look, I really need to take this pregnancy test, so if we could just take a moment, here?"

"Take your moment. Tell me how it turns out."

"Fine." I shuffled through the bag and darted into the bathroom.

Fifteen minutes later, I tip-toed to the leaking fridge and I pulled out the champagne.

"I'm not pregnant, I'm not pregnant!" I yelled, leaping across the tile.

I collapsed onto the bed and began scuttling with the bottle. A few hard twists and it popped. A light haze drifted up. I leaned over and turned on the space heater.

"I am not pregnant. I win!" I lifted the mug into the air, jumped to my feet, and yelled, "To not being pregnant!" *Hep C be dammed!*

I drank. As I was pouring a second glass, the buzzer rang.

"Shit." I got up and pressed the intercom button in my room.

"Yeah?"

"Hey, it's Limone. I've got news!" I buzzed the "door unlock" button, and moved towards the front door. The glass had been punched out a long time ago. I opened the door as she rounded the landing.

"So guess what, I just put down a deposit."

"You're moving back? God, it really has been awhile." We tromped through the kitchen to my room and went in.

"Well, I've been really busy with work...the site's going nuts."

"And I've been really busy with whatever the fuck I do with my time." I said. "Now where's the place?"

"It's two blocks down, on Oak Street. I'll be so close!"

"Yay! What made you decide to move?"

"Well, you know the parental situation. I had this whole drama with my dad about borrowing his digital camera to take pictures for MySpace."

"And?"

She took a deep breath. "So I tried to sweet-talk him into it, but then he wanted to take the pictures. He's of the 'line people up in straight rows with their arms around each other and make them say cheese' school of photography. I tried to explain that I would feel more comfortable taking them myself... and he was, like, "What sort of thing is this MySpace? Is this one of those - "

I smirked.

"Yeah. He was, like, 'I don't know, this sounds thoroughly odd. I don't really feel right about it. You say you want to take pictures of yourself, by yourself, that you don't feel comfortable taking with me, and then...put them on the internet?'"

"Oh God."

"Oh yes. And then I go off about how fantastic it is and how it's not full of sex perverts, and I wasn't going to be naked, and round it out by saying, 'I'm twenty-six years old, and if I did want to join a dating site it would be none of your business!'"

"That's just the living end."

"It was the last straw, really. I'm just so over it."

"Alrighty then. Welcome."

Taking tiny pecks at his beef Bolognese, Brady knitted his eyebrows together and sighed. It was dark outside the windows and a curdling wind tore at the frames. He was tucked into the loveseat, under the painting of the green, eyeless woman. I plunged my fork into the dish

He took a bite. "What else is up with you?"

"Well, I'm still not pregnant!"

"Keep that up. If you have one, we can call it Mimsy and keep it in the trash compacter."

"Right on. I can have an abortion shower to kick off the holiday season. Cupcakes with little death's heads, Dia de los Muertos stuff."

An apartment across the street blinked alight. Blooming.

"Oh check it out," I said. "It's Deirdre and Butch! Movie-time!"

"Oh, shit yeah!" Brady flung his meal to the table and grabbed the binoculars, jumping crosswise on the couch and peering at the window. Across the street, the peach-glow bay window was draped in white lace. Two silhouettes emerged, a woman and a big, muscular guy with a shaved head. He took off his shirt and took a long drag from a bottle.

"There he is! There he is!" Brady said. "The alpha-fuck."

The woman flitted about the room, arranging candles. The man took her shoulder and they embraced. Pulling apart, he took another sip and she lifted off a gauzy negligee.

I giggled. "It's cute, hon, but do you want to go to Catastrophic after this?"

"Sure....but check this out!"

I stared out the window at the peepshow, curious for all that I couldn't quite find, the minuscule acts, the monstrosities. The all-too-human lapses. Delightful in the shadows.

Brady sucked it in. the bodies colliding, the fluids exchanging, all that he wanted and couldn't quite hold. The language of flesh, of intimacy.

But the shadows at Catastrophic were mottled with guitar gods, glam metal projections on the walls as we walked in.

"Oh, get real," muttered Brady. Loping across the beer-splattered floor, his narrow frame seemed poised to fall.

I placed my hands on the bar and was about to order when I saw Zed Leopard spinning records.

"Oh shit," I muttered to Brady. "I totally forgot he does Thursdays here."

"Relax. Shot time." Brady leaned forwards and said, "Two Red Headed Sluts, please."

The bartender nodded and turned away.

"Red Headed what?" A guitar solo whirled to a halt.

"Red Headed Slut. It's Jagermeister with cranberry."

"Okay, sure. Why not."

"Good attitude." The bartender set down two shot glasses with a reddish-black mixture. Brady paid, and handed one to me.

"Now, ignore the fact that Zed is here, try to concentrate on the fact that we came here to have fun, and it will all be okay." We clinked glasses and drank. As I set the glass down, Zed poked me on the shoulder.

"Hey." I said.

He bounced up and hugged me. "Hey, I'm sorry I didn't call you, things were, ah..."

"Weird, yes, I know. But, whatever. You've got a ton of people here," I said as Brady edged away.

"Yeah. This night got pretty big. I try to MySpace it – "

"Three times a day under different headings, yes, I see it every week."

"Do you read them?" He smiled eagerly.

"Um...er...sure. Fascinating each time."

"Awesome! Well, hey, I gotta go change the record, but come see me before you guys go, 'kay?" He darted behind the bar. A bundle of Art Institute kids came squirming ahead of me, and I turned around to find Brady. He was talking animatedly to a guy in a sailor's jersey. Veering around the edge of the dance floor, I watched the bodies jerk through the projections. Shadows went dancing along the wall, obscuring Freddie Mercury's left leg.

I clenched my fingers, considered joining in, and then thought better of it. Across the room there was a 1950's trailer embedded in the wall. A hand-lettered sign offered tater tots and jello shots. *Well, aren't they so ingenious*, I thought, *a white trash bistro.* The face of my last one night stand drifted by. The look we didn't give each other was calculated. In the tumult, I wavered. I turned and fought my way past the too-young hipsters to Brady's side.

Chapter 14
powder to blood, proxy to body

Pacing in my room, I bent to the CD on my dresser and did another line. It was 5:45 am and I had been up all night, first with Brady at Catastrophic, and later by myself writing endless rants about my inertia, my angst, the lanky prettiness of the men I had seen, touched once, and forgotten. The relative merits of different vodkas and pharmacies and dealers and ways of avoiding commitment. After a thorough examination of my faults and manic tendencies, I had withdrawn to the mirror to talk, alone, waving a black lace fan. Wrapped in a green kimono, my intent completely sincere, I tried to channel Marlene Dietrich while fearing Mommy Dearest. Either way, the theatrics made me feel better. This was what I did at night, spent hours typing or smoothing on anti-aging creams and examining my grey roots. I smeared a daub of eye cream on a lid and sat down on a cushion, fanning myself and staring fixedly at my most recent painting, waiting for it to tell me something.

It was a picture of Mink, Lucas' roommate, with a ball gag in her mouth.

The phone rang, shrill.

"Hey, it's Jesse."

"Hey…" I toyed with the hem of my robe, picking at a thread.

"What are you doing?"

Laughing in a way I hoped was alluring, I murmured, "I'm just getting cracked out and talking to myself."

"Sound's delightful. You should come hang out with me and my friend."

"Where are you?"

"Come to Fulton and Baker. Come on now, get a cab, you need social interaction." Staring at my dilated pupils in the mirror, I took a deep breath. Leaving the room? For places unknown? I could do it.

"I'll be there." Setting the phone down with a giddy smile, I breathed in the release of my vigil. Somewhere to go. An adventure. Jesse, finally, coming out of his rabbit-hole and reaching out to me. All that had happened before this was melted, as always, into burnt caramel. I reached for my pomade.

The cab stopped at the corner, and I paid in change. Pulling myself out the door, I stepped up to the sidewalk. The Victorians were damp and mossy, the cedars breathing, the stillness overwhelming.

The phone slid into my purse beneath a wad of condoms. Advancing on chrome heels, I wandered across the street and peered anxiously down each corner. The streets were empty and the blue-white sky sang of morning. I saw Jesse as a shadow on my right, and turned to meet him, meekly waving. He was solid and welcoming beneath his old leather jacket and scarf.

Touching my shoulder lightly, he said, "Good. Be good. Okay, here's an old buddy of mine that you're gonna meet. C'mon." I followed him up a steep incline, bending under willows and suddenly shy. Pigeons warbled.

At the top of the hill, Jesse turned abruptly into an alcove. The door was polished wood, a beveled glass window amid blue tile. He opened the door and went in, pulling my sleeve with his hand. I followed eagerly. We descended a staircase and came into a cluttered studio with the wreckage of years piled inside. A bearded man with hollowed eyes sat pouring glasses of wine.

Leary acid-test books, a Masonic sword and stacks of records in milk crates. Jesse sat next to the man and said, "This is Walker. Now take off your coat and stay for awhile."

I obeyed. The wine he poured for me sat neatly in the lamp-lit circle, and as we drank and talked about conspiracy theories and lessons of the sixties, who owned which record store ten years ago and what was the virtue of Hooters, I fell deeper and deeper into intoxication. Soon we were doing lines off the coffee table, and I was snuggled next to Jesse with his arm around my shoulders.

"I hate acid," I said. "Make me crazy. I'm crazy enough."

"Oh, you just think you're crazy. Come on, Girl Interrupted," Jesse countered. "You should do acid with me. I have the best shit you've ever tried."

"Sound's fun, but...no."

"Hey, it's the original Timothy Leary shit they had in the sixties, seriously. They knew it was going to be illegal, so they made a huge bathtub-sized rock of it, 10,000-some hits, and I got ahold of some the other day. We'll do it sometime, we'll get a hotel room and..." Dancing hands around his cigarettes.

"Okay, you pay, I'll go," I sighed.

The TV was on to the fashion network, blaring plasticine faces and press-on eyes. Mid-morning light streamed through the shutters as I nestled in. Jesse stood up, slipping out from under my arm.

Walker stood up and gestured towards the door. "Here, do you want me to open up the guest room?"

"Sure."

I blinked, confused, as he took a key from the wall and led us upstairs. My ill-fitting shoes clattering on the hardwood floor, I followed them down a long hall to a door.

"Here you go. I'll bring up some stuff for you, and the bathroom is down the hall. The bed folds out, you know how." The man nodded and turned away, his bent frame retreating down the hall.

Jesse opened the door and we fell into sunshine. The TV was backlit by paper blinds, the light falling over a yellow couch and circular train tracks on the floor. He loomed over the couch and pulled it open like a sautéed mussel, setting the blue-striped mattress over the metal springs. He rummaged in the closet, pulling forth a gray duvet and some pillows. He threw them on the bed next to the couch cushions, lemon pale, and said, "Lie down."

I draped myself across the bare mattress, crossing legs and setting an arm over my knees. There would always be the poses, the urge to beguile, to win him when I was forcing myself into the meat grinder.

"Take off your clothes," he barked, above me. I twisted out of my shirt and threw it at the wall, unsnapped my skirt and pulled off my tights. The eggshell walls were pearl and untouched. I leaned back on the pillow, eyelids drooping.

"Ahh. Stay like that." And then he pounced, grabbing me by the leg and yanking me down the bed. My eyes flashed open.

He fell on top of me, naked, and stuck his thumb into the top of my underwear. "What is this for, take this off." I kicked the lacy bits into the TV as it roared with Saturday morning anime. Amid a volley of cartoon artillery, Jesse jumped on top of me, forcing my legs open with his knee. I yielded instantly, and as he pushed inside me it flashed into my head that there was no condom. After hours of wine and coke, my resolve was limp.

I fell back into the waxed burlap, my body convulsing. There was a grenade blast from the onscreen warfare, and I felt every pore of me being dissolve into this endless, brilliant motion.

The next few hours were a blur of ecstasy, scraping my knees to blisters on top of him, running to the bathroom to wash and then the pounce and yank.

Without the Trojan he was scalding inside me, so close, so deep, nothing separating us except the burden of skin. I wanted to own him. This was the only way I could. When he pulled out a second too late, I ran a hand across my thighs and left it there.

"Jesse, I think you weren't fast enough." I cuddled up to his bony shoulder, holding onto his chest. Pulling myself up, I felt myself dissolving into his body, exhausted, my knees raw.

"Baby Pigeon, you can just take the morning after pill again."

"I can't take it again, I just took it last month. I'll lose my mind. And kill myself, that shit fucks you up."

"Calm, calm." He smoothed my hair. "Just go to the pharmacy and sign up. But, really, I don't think it's anything to worry about." Pushing me gently to the side, he got up and pulled on his boxer briefs.

"Where are you going?"

"I'm having a cigarette."

I stretched out luxuriantly against the white and blue, feeling my body aching in unexpected ways. Crossing my legs, I watched the smoke drift through the golden light. It poured over Jesse as he leaned against the bed, lifting the cigarette to his lips with his eyes bent to the Food Network.

I pulled up the blanket and cocooned. After a few moments I crawled out and moved to the end of the bed. Irritation lined his face. Lifting the model locomotive from the tracks, he held it out to me.

"Look. Check out the detail on this, the inscription on the side. This is probably one of the oldest things you'll ever see." The toy was battered plastic, with the words, "Great Western 1886" in cursive on the conductor's compartment. The steel wheels spun useless. So many years. I thought of the Mayan artifacts I had seen in museums, with the skulls of prehistoric peoples draped under lit vitrines. They could tell the genders apart by the tilt of the pelvis. Tilt.

Jesse rose from the floor and climbed onto the bed, grabbing me by the shoulders and pulling me towards him.

"Spread your legs!"

"No, I can't, it hurts," I cried.

"You can, you want to. Come on, be my girlfriend." He pushed my legs apart.

"Be gentle. No!" I gasped. He pushed his cock in slowly. Wincing, I said, "Okay, that's okay, but slow, oh, ow, not there, stop!" He tried again, stopping before he was fully inside.

Staring into his eyes with my legs over his shoulders, I felt completely open as he thrust gently, slowly, delving in and out and I dug fingernails into his arm and whimpered. That he would stop for me when it hurt, would try and go slowly, this felt like love to me as I felt a wave of tenderness sweep over me. He was like a little boy. He knew not what he did.

"Ow!" I yelped. "Okay, okay, that's okay...darling."

"Yeah, see, all better. You wanted daddy all along. It'll all be okay." The cries of children thrummed through the open window. His arms were strong above me. I fell limp.

In the shower down the hall, the water hit my twat with a stab of pain. I ventured an exploratory finger to my clit and yelped. Something was wrong. The hot water was blasting against the emerald tile, and I switched it off quickly. Dripping, I emerged gingerly from the shower and swathed herself in Walker's best towel. As I fled back to the room, my knees rubbed bare flesh.

Limping into Jesse's line of sight, I dove under the covers. His big hand snaked out and he grabbed me by the arm, pulling me against him.

"I've been waiting. Now." He threw off the covers and pulled open my legs like a teenager's diary.

I whipped them closed, "No, it hurts!"

"Come on, you need it. You need me."

"I want to, but I can't," I whimpered, "It's really bad."

With a final tug, he got up and picked up the mirror on the dresser. There was a small pile of powder set out with two lines. A set of Readers Digest condensed books lay beneath.

"Here." A woman called for her child outside. He took a pinch of the cocaine and said, "Spread your legs."

"No."

"Lena, come on. This will numb it so it won't hurt anymore. You know, how they used to use coke as an anesthetic?"

"Okay, early Freud, dentistry, but…"

"Do it."

"Okay." He rubbed the powder on my labia and I cried out spasmodically, clenching inward and crying. "Fuck, no, oh god, oh god, it hurts, no, that wasn't a good idea at all." I tasted blood.

He clicked his tongue against his teeth. "Come on, be a trooper, now. The pain will stop. Calm down."

I stared meekly up at him, my body like a schizophrenic scribble. I licked my dry lips and tried to will the pain away, as it drove through to pure terror. He put a hand on my ankle.

"Come on, now." He lunged onto the bed, and I screamed as his cock stabbed into me. The toy locomotive teetered, the TV blasted knives through sirloin, the light was still golden, and I was fighting him, kicking, twisting, struggling.

"Stop, stop, I can't, it hurts!" I yelped.

"Sh, sh, he'll hear. Now, come on, I need to finish." He drove into me and I shoved him back fiercely, kicking. He fell back.

"Okay, okay, fine. You didn't have to go ballistic. But okay, right, I see. Fine. I need to take a shower." He threw me across the bed like an empty bottle and got up, pulling on his boxers. I fell limp across the mattress, whispering, "I'm sorry, I'm sorry I couldn't satisfy you, I just can't…please don't go."

"I'm taking a shower. A very cold, long one." He strode out the door.

"Hold me…" I whimpered to the empty hall. Falling water was the only answer.

The brocade marionette above my bed showed black hole eyes and a red scrawl for a mouth. I rolled over, throwing the blanket off, and felt my body seething. The ache would not stop. I had tried Advil, I had tried Aleve, I had ducked into a hot bath only to gasp, and finally I had returned to bed. Swathed in my yellow baby blanket I was content to wait it out, running the night through my mind and savoring each glorious detail. Even the pain. Especially the pain.

Treading carefully around the implications, around the fists and kicks and screams, I fell into a dream of what could have happened. What almost happened. How I felt so close to him, finally. I could smell his sweat on my arms, feel the sting in my rugburned knees. To at last not be separated by Vanessa, by the dawn, to go on.

My room was in twilight. Rain lapped against the half-open windows, where it drooled down to piles of magazines, warping leggy models and staining bee-stung lips with pools of grime.

The next night, the cabdriver sang survival hymns as he drove me through the rain. He bellowed out the window with wide gestures, waving grandiose to his audience of tenderloin cinderblocks. Past Turk and Ellis he took me, until the Thai restaurants gave way to peepshows and practice space tenements, warehouses blasted out and refilled with scrap carpet and scratches of electric violin. I must survive.

Coco came running at the door in faux-Chanel heels, indigo streaks on her arm. I was panting, four flights into a Stairmaster I hadn't expected. She grabbed my shoulder and pulled me inside.

"Hey, we have got to get some alcohol, do you want to go to FoodsCo?" she said.

I glanced down the stairwell.

"Sure."

Outside, the rain speared the headlights into tiny glowing drops. Pulling my angora scarf over my head, I shuddered and ran. Past the boarded-up windows of Adelita's Cake con Sabores, and the used car lot with its gleaming chrome, we ran towards the welcoming arms of the store. It glowed like a million birthday cakes when it wasn't really your birthday, a starburst that someone forgot.

Dashing under the overhang, I glanced back at the desolate parking lot. Puddles sprawled like dark spots under a corpse. Coco came up behind me.

"Did you see Jesse today?"

"The other night. It was a little too much of a good thing."

"Good thing?" the side of her mouth bent up.

The door blipped, and aisles of chorizo and beans opened wide. I bent over the aisle and scanned the rows of Popov and Malibu. The fluorescent lights scratched at my eyes. A thin trickle of water came spooling down my neck.

"Yeah," I said. "I just don't know how long I can do this, this whole "clawing at doors for love" routine. Everyone I want to date has a girlfriend. Or lives in fucking New York. Or Texas. Or is gay."

"Hey, Dallas isn't bad."

"Oh, right, the family oil fields."

"Not like that helps me now." She laid a hand on the Green Apple Smirnoff. "Tastycakes."

"How's the trust fund, anyway?" I looked sideways.

"Almost gone. But I figured it out, I'm selling my land, and that will get me rolling again. My mom doesn't want me to, she's furious, totally furious, but short of titty-dancing again, I don't know how I'm going to support myself."

A motorcycle revved sharp and screamed out of the parking lot. The fluorescence caught us in wax.

Coco sighed. "God, let's get out of this shithole."

As we slunk into the parking lot, I glanced back to see a shattered wine bottle drooling burgundy in the glare.

In her small orange room, in the amber glow of the lamp, Coco tucked her chin into her chest and flicked the lighter under the spoon.

I curled on the bed, tucking my feet under me with a neatness that approximated obsession.

The black lump hissed and dissolved, as she attacked the lighter. She shook the heat from her hand and swirled in the cotton.

"Hey," she said. "You don't have Hep C or anything, do you?"

"No, I really doubt it. I don't want to share needles, though, seriously."

My knees clenched together, my breath short. Headlights flickered on the blinds. Daubing spilled water with a Pucci scarf, Coco tossed it on a pile of laundry.

"No, no, here. This one's mine, and this one's yours." She held up two orange-capped syringes.

"'Do you go to the needle exchange for those?"

"No, I don't like other people getting all up in my shit about this stuff, so I just go to Walgreens and tell them I'm diabetic." Coco stuck the needle in the ball of fluff and pulled back the syringe.

"But...how are we going to tell them apart?"

She let out an exaggerated sigh. "Okay. You are such a child. I'll put this one," she waved the device she had just filled, "Over here, by the lamp." She set it on the bedside table. "And mine, I'll put this one here." She set it on the white cube we were using as a table. "Happy?"

I sighed. "Sure."

"Ready?"

"Sure."

Coco smiled broadly and leapt onto the bed, staggering to get her balance. She clasped my wrist and surveyed my arm.

"Alright, looks pretty good. I think...that one!" She tapped the blue beneath the skin. The vein twitched. Torpid.

Coco stuck in the needle.

"Okay, tell me if this hurts."

I waited for the pain that didn't come. I hadn't even felt the prick. As Coco pushed down the syringe and the point hit blood, I felt Brady's arms, the shattering warmth of being taken in, welcomed, loved. I fell back on the bed, my hands slack, staring at the bright dot of blood on my forearm, not seeing Coco stick the other syringe in her thigh. A sixty-watt exhilaration glowed through me as I felt, momentarily, whole. Finally, I slid the syringe out and set it limply on the floor next to hers. Hers and hers like towels. Soft pink and blue fluffy towels that my mother wrapped around me fresh from a hot bath, with dahlias and magnolias falling from our hair into an expanse of rabbit fur.

I ran a hand across her soft hair and smiled. In the end times.

The afternoon sun filtered through the windows onto the copper lamps and balsa chairs at Naan & Chutney. I kicked my legs back and forth, fidgeting, flipping through the Guardian as I waited for Jesse.

There were no customers. The steam trays hung hopeful in the open kitchen and the waiter stared idly at the swaying motion of the window blinds. A ceiling fan whirred white noise, palm fronds blurring indistinguishable from the sultry air. The smell of curry and warm bread wafted over my head.

I stared, unseeing, at the pages of sex shop ads, the massage parlors and escorts, lifting my head to glance at the menus taped to the window. An orchid sprung in delicate violet tones from a vase at my elbow.

I looked up again to see Jesse shoving his way through the door. He looked at me with a lost expression, shifting to arrogance when he realized I was looking back.

"You want the garlic naan," he said, thumping into the seat across from me.

"Alright, sure."

He looked at me appraisingly.

"You look better. You look like a woman, you don't look like death warmed over anymore."

"I can't imagine why that would be, believe me, I've been doing all sorts of bad things."

"Don't tell me you've been doing speed again."

"Worse. I tried heroin with Coco."

"Did you shoot it?"

"Yeah."

"That's it, you're off Team Mimosa." he said.

"Wait, what's that? I want to be on that!"

"I made it up just now. Vanessa's on."

"Come on."

"No buts. The White Horse is my territory."

"I liked it."

"Well, of course you liked it, dipshit. It's drugs. Drugs are fun. You just shouldn't stick them in your arm in less you know what you're doing. Abscesses hurt like fuck-all. Have you been tested lately?"

"I'd say it's a little too late to be worrying about that now. Have you?"

"Oh come on."

"Well, I haven't either."

"Well, you should," he said. "Really."

"I'd kind of rather not know. At this point I don't care what happens to me. It can't get worse than this."

"Are you ready to order?" said the waiter, looming suddenly by my elbow. His aquiline nose stood out on a long, lined face. "The palak paneer's really good today."

"We'll have the veggie korma. And a garlic naan," said Jesse, grabbing my menu and flipping it over.

I sighed. I had wanted the eggplant. A billow of hot air came through the door as it opened to let in a man in a Norway T-shirt and a fannypack.

I turned to face Jesse again.

"What were you saying?" My voice drifted off as he fixed me with a disgusted glare.

At Walker's, the wooden screen concealing his bed hid a paper bowl over a pile of coke and a rusty razor.

It was still barely morning. A large TV buzzed above us, radiating a Friskies commercial.

"So, I still haven't heard from that guy in Singapore." Jesse said, "I'm pissed."

"What guy in Singapore?" I said.

Walker nodded slowly, behind his beard.

"I told you, the guy that took my designs. You remember how when I was doing that clothing line with that guy?"

"The line I saw in your show?"

"That was the line resuscitated. Yeah, I mean, that guy just disappeared. I hate that. You can't trust anyone."

"I wouldn't trust anyone named Demi-Monsieur Gallant."

"That was just his stage name. Really, Lena."

"Okay, okay. But while we're on this trust thing, what the hell happened with Miles? I heard from this guy that he was in jail – I know that was you!"

Jesse lurched up in his chair.

"You weren't supposed to know that."

"How could I not? I mean, hello Captain Obvious!" I rubbed dry lips.

"Well, it was him or me."

"Oh."

Jesse thumped back into the yellow couch.

"Look. You liked it. I know how you like that stuff. Think of it this way. What do you owe him? He's your dealer. Don't mean shit. You actually helped me out, although it took me a fucking lot of effort to get it out of you, and so, well, you helped out a friend, good for you. Feel special, girl scout."

"He wasn't having the best of luck anyway," said Walker.

"Oh God. So will I have the Feds or his friends dropping in?"

"Well, maybe a little bit of both."

"Fantastic. What?"

"This is real life, honey. Deal with it." A copper lantern swayed from the ceiling, dawn through the blue and orange panes.

Walker reached up and batted it absentmindedly. He shuffled in his pocket and said, "Lena, if I give you twenty dollars, will you go get orange juice and champagne? I think it's time for a mimosa. You guys really need to let this go."

"Yes, that's a good idea..." Jesse said. "Lena, are we going to forget about this?"

"I... I don't know if I can. He was my friend."

"He was your dealer. Not friend. That's not your friend. You can always get another."

"I have. I have several."

"See? I'm impressed, I didn't think you'd be that fast."

"It's still not okay."

"He's disposable."

"Listen." I laid both hands on my thighs. "People are not disposable. Just because of his profession doesn't mean you can do this."

"Well, I just did. Now, are you going to get us some mimosas, or are you going to be a little bitch?"

"The coke's in the back. Go perk up." Walker said.

"Okay, okay." I pulled up from the couch, feeling the cold morning air. As I edged around the couch, bumping the sharp edges, I cursed myself for acquiescing, cursed myself for being weak, for telling him in the first place. As I bent to take my line, a brass lamp illuminating a circle around the razor, I felt again the shame of it. I had turned in Miles. Narc by proxy. Powder to blood, through my body as I replaced the paper bowl and turned away.

Limone shook me gently by the shoulders.

"Lena. Remember who you're dealing with. It's Jesse. He doesn't function rationally." I looked up at the pristine patterning sweeping up the walls to white molding and an antique chandelier. Limone's new place.

"But maybe I am disgusting."

"We all make our own choices. Maybe you can make other ones next time." She held my arm gently. Three bay windows folded around us, three floors up on Oak Street, white curtains drawn gauze across.

My fingers brushed the chenille pillows, burgundy on the blue couch. Soft as whiskers. Warm as whiskey. My head fell.

"Maybe you're right. I've got to just try to get it together. I've been thinking lately. Things keep getting worse and worse, and I don't know if I'm doing the right thing or not anymore. This was so fun in the beginning." A dark scrap of a cat drifted between our feet.

"Well, yeah." Light fell through the orange glass vase on the coffee table, a black IKEA block. Beads of air hung suspended in the glass, with a swath of liquid green shimmering around the rim. Flecks of golden light were falling on my hands, falling on worried hangnails and bone.

"I don't know if I can keep it up, really, honestly. It's going – well – I don't know. I don't know if I should just leave town, go away somewhere, or sort it out here myself."

"You can sort it out. I'm here for you," Limone said. A cantaloupe breeze wafted in from the kitchen.

I lifted my head and reached for her hand.

"Thank you."

The clatter of footsteps came from the hallway, and I quickly pulled away.

Opening the bathroom door at Bordello, the collaged Joss paper smooth against the stall wall, I saw Coco sitting on the toilet, Jesse's cock in her hand.

"What the fuck!"

Their eyes flashed panic, hands slamming the door closed. I threw myself against it. My own hands, fragile.

"Why didn't you tell me, I would gladly be the fucking bridesmaid. Coco, do you want a tissue? Do you want me to get you a drink? You'll need one, to get that stench off!"

"Call Security," Jesse said.

"Lena, really, I need to talk to you, this isn't – well, it – but, can I call you tomorrow?"

"You can call me never."

I stood against the window, pointing my finger at Brady.

"Why? Why not?"

"I just don't think I'm really that sick. I mean, sure, I get sick sometimes, but it's really not that big of a deal. I've been to the Haight-Ashbury Free Clinic, I've been using the inhaler, I mean, I think that's taking care of." He broke off in a ravaging cough, spitting mucous into the hollow of his hand.

"Yeah. What about that?"

"What about what?" He wiped his hand on the couch.

"Listen. You are not being reasonable."

"I don't want to go to the hospital."

"You're sick."

"I am not that sick. Besides, I can't afford it. Really."

"What about your Medi-Cal?"

"There's co-pays. Not to mention, General is not the nicest place to be."

"I know, I know, I've been."

"Ex-actly. And you want to send me there?"

"I just want you to be okay. You don't sound okay. And you haven't sounded okay for a month now."

"Well, I'm dealing with it."

"People die from bronchitis! People like you, especially."

"What the fuck, people like me? Look, I'm not going."

I slumped down on the couch, exhausted.

"Fine. Fine. And when I have to pick you up and throw you in Limone's car and take you there, don't say I didn't warn you." I grimaced, looking at the crumpled tinfoil ashtray on the table, wondering how much longer it would be.

Coco opened her door with a flourish and said, "Ta da! The fabulous disasters!"

"Er…right," I said. Edging my way past the half-circle of pennies and the broken mannequin leg in the landing, I peered momentarily down the four flights of stairs and shuddered.

"Are you alright?" I asked Coco. "That scene back there was a little much, even for you."

She grimaced. "Eh. Right as I'm ever gonna be. No, I'm packing. I'm out of here."

"Dallas?"

"Yeah. My mom's coming, and she is going to save me from this shit."

"Wow. I'm glad you called."

"Here, come inside. Better that way." Coco took my arm.

In the hall, between lime walls, we walked past beanbags and modular furniture to Coco's room. Small and orange.

We sat on the bed, sheets with russet squares on white, and I rested my hands on my thighs.

Coco slid onto the floor and began to stuff black clothing into a roller bag. Her arms were pocked with abscesses.

My eyes flashed to the syringe on the bedside table. It was half-hidden by the record player, where a Dolly Parton record played fitfully. Cars screeched by outside.

"Are you ever coming back?" I asked.

Coco looked up.

"Oh, yeah, I'm coming back to visit. I'll come back when I get out of rehab to celebrate. Sober celebrate. We'll have cake."

"Okay. Chocolate or coconut?"

"Coconut."

"Cool."

The moon glimmered silver through the window.

"Well, what are you doing with all of your stuff?"

"I'm taking my clothes and shit, but I'm selling the furniture. I gave Limone the orange cubes. She just has to come pick them up. Can you remind her when you see her? I'll be gone, I'm leaving tomorrow."

"Oh God, that's soon."

"I know. I just need to go, though, I can feel it. I've had it with this place."

"Yeah, I kind of know what you mean."

The room pressed tight around us as I dug my nails into my hand.

"Was it Jesse who hooked you up, back in Langley?"

She looked up. "Yeah. That started it. He had a better connection than me, and it just got so easy. I know he's your boyfriend, but you know how when you're all soft, and you want to touch something."

"Yeah... Or when you just want to talk to someone. He doesn't sleep, he was always awake when I was."

"He would always come over."

"I know....he hasn't been my boyfriend in a long, long time."

"I'm sorry, it was pretty fucked. It wasn't worth it. Hey, do you want this scarf?"

Pink and green swirls.

"Ok." I looked at her. "So, when are you coming back?"

"August. I'll see you.

"I'll miss you."

"Don't worry, don't worry, don't worry." Coco said rhythmically as she packed, sending me further and further down. The moon shone through the window like a silver dollar in a dirty saucer.

Chapter 15
blue roses

Brady fidgeted with the tubes between his IV and his wrist. The gurney was in
a cubicle in SF General. His throat ached with mucous, the bronchitis advancing.
I wish I'd brought something to read. Staring at the beige of the walls, the
blips of the machines, the drips of saline.
He heard rattling at the door.

Limone and I sat in my living room, beneath the faceless green lady the Brady
had loved and I had hated. I had never told him. Now was not the time. He had
called and asked us to come pick him up.
I balled a gum wrapper in my hand and pelted it at the kitchen trash. A puff
of gnats rose up. I took a deep breath. A flurry of air came through the windows.
"Thank god, thank god he's okay. Or stabilized, at least." My eyebrows
furrowed and I dropped my head.
"I'm parked on Fell Street, we should go," Limone said.
On the street, it was a damp four o'clock, the evening mist hazing in over bay
windows and fog. Boutiques and crêperies, lost and found. We walked down Clayton
past a pink and purple Victorian with a gold weathervane, past the iron gates and
crumbling charcoal of the burnt-out husk on the corner. An apartment building across
the street was being renovated, the entire bottom floor has been gutted and looked
like it was becoming a garage. Or a crêperie.
The jackhammers merged with the digeridoos and acoustic guitars from
Haight Street, and I closed my eyes, my hands rocking forwards as I walked.
It was quiet in the car. I watched the pastel buildings speed by, merging to 99
cent stores, used furniture stores, bars with happy hour crowds outside.
We drove down 24th Street and took a left on Potrero. Black mottled gates
were open to a brick building with "General Hospital: To the People of San
Francisco," carved in stone relief. Buildings with fantastical exterior staircases and
bars on the windows were assembled in squares. Circles of homeless people stood in
the courtyard, some limbless, some on crutches, some holding paper cups from the
Starbucks cart.
Limone winced. "He's here?"
"Medi-Cal."
"Shit."
"I've come here too. I'm on the SF Mental Health Plan. It's a party, let me tell
you."
"Let's throw a party for Brady. He deserves it."
"If he's up to it. That sounds exhausting."
"I thought you liked parties."
"I like parties that I have control over."

"Control?"

"Let's not talk about this. You know I hate talking about this. You're mom-ing me."

"Okay, sorry. I know. I won't."

Noticing the "Staff Only" parking lot sign, Limone turned the car around and parked in front of the bus stop.

"Nice job." I said.

"Yeah, maybe it's a good sign."

Tall, streaky windows and double glass doors lined the front of the building. People and pigeons were leaning against the windows, muttering.

I opened the door and stepped into a murky blue lobby. Dim tract lighting seeped from above.

"I'm here to see Brady Vosachek."

The woman spread her hands and tapped a button on the phone. "Okay, he'll be out shortly." She settled back into her seat and began readying a copy of InTouch. The plastic chairs were linked together by the armrest, burnt orange, like Coco's hair, like her walls, like her sheets.

I missed her so. But foremost I missed Brady, the ghost in the living room, the absence, the lack. The silence in the kitchen when all the dishes were put away. The avocado browning to rot, soft green edges fading away. The dark hole in my heart.

I looked up, and Brady was walking down the dim hall, his red cowboy boots slapping the institutional tile. Bloodstains. He had an expression of mute happiness on his face, widening to a smile when he saw me.

"God, I'm so happy you're back. You're okay, right?"

"I'm okay. So are we getting out of here? I really need to get out of here. Bye, Patrice," Brady waved to the receptionist. We formed a tight knot and charged through the crowd, ending, finally, at the old iron gates by the bus stop. A ragged man still wearing his hospital booties, clutching a pharmacy bag and a used bus transfer was hopping foot to foot. Brady looked away, turned back to us and began to speak, then shook his head and turned away. The sky above us was russet turned to pink dredged out to grey.

I came in the front door with a bouquet of daffodils and handed them to Brady.

"Whoa. Thanks?"

"Congratulations on your recovery. Are people here yet?" I looked around our apartment. Silver fabric was draped over the table with my devil-woman mannequin in the center. Her cold green eyes glared at the bottles of vodka and whiskey, the plastic cups, the wine blushing by the tonic. Hopefully people would bring their own, this stuff would go fast.

The Velvet Underground was dripping from the stereo, sending sonorous tones over the candles, the stacks of CDs by the stereo, the gleaming glass dishes of wasabi peas and candy hearts.

Gold candlelight on the rims of the plates, gold circles on the end table and on Brady's hands as he settled the flowers into a pint glass and said, "There, beautiful."

The room was a warm globe, a snow globe shook by a small child, and then the doorbell rang. I rocketed across the room to the console, buzzing them in sight unseen. Seconds later a volley of yells came from the door.

Peering through the broken glass, I saw Zed and Limone, and a bunch of people I didn't know. Hands shaking, I opened the door and let them flood in. Shoulders and necks and flashing arms. I took a step back and left the door partially ajar when they were done.

Zed fixed me with a sly glance and came up.

"Bet you thought you wouldn't see me," he said.

"I never know what to think." Gold circles on his arms, matchsticks, twigs. I watched his jelly bracelets tangle.

"When do the bands start?"

"Well, Lucas's solo project, Dardanella, is going on around 11:00."

"Cool, half an hour to go."

"Yeah, they're really good. It sucks that Brady can't play with him, the Dummies are amazing, but he's not feeling well."

"A cold?"

"Yeah, a cold." Tight lips. "Yeah."

"Okay," Zed flipped his hair. "Well, hey, I'm gonna go get a drink, I'll see you in a little bit, alright?"

I watched him bob away. Feeling a nudge at my shoulder, I turned and saw Brady. He handed me a drink.

"Cute, huh?" I said.

"Yeah, he is. I don't know, though, that's my type over there." He gestured at a tall, angular guy drinking a shot at the kitchen counter.

"Oooh, what's his name?"

"Raúl."

"Hot."

"Yes. Now, if you'll excuse me..." he looped off from my shoulder and ambled to his prey's vicinity. I watched as he flirted, noting his technique. I laughed, and took a long sip of my cocktail.

Brady watched Raúl as he took a deep drag of his American Spirit and blew it over his shoulder. The corners of his eyes were misting with drunkenness, the lights glowing incandescent in the corners of the room.

"So, do you like Mr. Dardanella?" Brady said.

"I like what I see. He's got that...that...tartness to him. So stubbly," said Raúl.

Brady ran a hand over the stubble he too had been nurturing with the fine acuity of an electric shaver. Raúl was electric-gaunt with fine cheekbones and an olive-amber tint to his skin. Too, too delicious. Would he? Brady always wondered, would-they, wouldn't-they, sometimes he didn't tell, sometimes they didn't ask. Sometimes he felt that he had to tell.

His eyes flitted around the room, settling finally on me. I looked away. He refocused on Raúl, who moistened his lips with his gin.

"So, you're a musician?"

"Yeah, I'm in this band called The Dummies."

"Oh, I've seen you around, yeah. You played the Eagle last month with Corpseparts Blush."

"Yeah, we play a lot of shows together."

"Adorable."

"What do you do?" Brady said.

"Me, I'm a filmmaker. I do a weekly film night at the Echo Lounge, Wednesdays."

"Oh, that's awesome. Did you go to school for it?"

Raúl winced, then smiled.

"Yeah, I went to the Art Institute. Got kicked out, though, because I made a film where I fingered a dog. My dog. They thought it was too wild, and threw me out."

"Oh God, that sucks."

"No, it's cool. I don't care, I do my own thing, now, and I don't have to get grades for it."

"As long as you're cool with it"

"I thought it was funny. The dog, she loved me afterwards, she used to follow me around for more. I just gave her little doggie treats and let her run around, cute doggie, my doggie."

A few hours later, the flat was packed, and I was weaving my way between jostling revelers, spilling my drink and smearing my lipstick. The pink Christmas lights glowed above the stove, and a dance party had started in the living room. Half of the candles had burned out and most of the alcohol was gone, but a fresh wave of people had come at midnight, bearing purse-sized pints of whiskey and forties.

Suddenly, I saw Jesse wedge himself through the door. He looked uncertain, weariness flitting across his face, followed by irritation. I hung back.

"Jesse?" I inched up and put a hand on his arm.

"Yeah, what?"

"Um...hi? Glad you came."

"Free booze."

"You're a doll. No, really, I'm glad you came."

He shrugged and looked off over the dance floor for a moment. A long, dark veil of hair flipped against a girl's dewy back. He looked at me again.

"Here, come do a bump with me."

"Okay." I followed him through to my room, and closed the door firmly. Flicking on a lamp, I settled onto my bed and pulled out the square mirror, scratched from use.

He slumped onto the chair across from me, his long legs parted slightly. Tapping the bag onto the mirror, he dished out two lines and handed me a bill. I took mine, and passed him the tray.

Looking up, he said, "I see that little fuck of yours is here. Leopard, is that his name?"

"Zed Leopard. So? It's a party. He can came. You can come too. See? Cooperation."

"What the fuck ever. You're in trouble, you know that. You belong to me, you know that now."

"Mmmm. What about Coco, does she belong to me, or to you?"

"Coco's a free agent. She's the variable."

A shiver of arousal went through me. Triangulation. Who's the hypotenuse? He rose abruptly from the chair and grabbed my leg, pulling me prostrate across the bed. Flat on my back, he pulled me to his hips, undoing his fly and reaching down to rip off my panties.

I was silent, knowing there were people everywhere, hearing the shrieks of laughter and words and drunken flurries through the walls. Praying no one would open the door, I let him pull up my skirt and shove his cock inside.

From above, on lifted arms, he said, "Now, who do you belong to."

I moaned, falling back against the sheets.

"You, only you."

"Who?"

"You."

Later, coming out of my room with my panties drenched and my hair in that unmistakable sex tangle, I wiped a crumb from my nose and looked back to watch him melt into the crowd.

From my seat at the coffeeshop, I could just see the park. Flush with street kids and dogs, selling glass pipes and hemp jewelry, yelling and fighting and playing the odd harmonica, I watched them as I sipped my coffee. Four stores down from Amoeba Records, across the street from Cha Cha Cha, Rockin' Java was a welcome calm. I opened my sketchbook to a blank page and began to draw.

A girl set down a latte with a yip and turned back to the espresso machine, singing along loudly. An old hippy fought the synths from an out-of-tune piano. Laptops hummed. Wood-topped tables were scarred with initials and water stains.

My phone rang.

"Lena? It's Coco! I'm in rehab."

"Really? How is it?"

"Not bad, could be worse. I'm eating, at least."

"God, I'm so glad you're okay. You cut out so quickly. Here, wait, I've got to go outside." Beats and thrums from the speakers, snipes of scales from the piano. I threw the sketchbook into my bag and looped it over a shoulder. Dodging dogs and chairs, I picked up a laminate flyer and left.

Between the door and the window I tucked a leg up and said, "Okay."

"Yeah. No, it's cool. I'm in this place in Dallas, it's a 30-day residential program, and I'm really getting a lot out of it."

"That's great. Better than Langley-Porter?"

"Langley-Porter didn't stick. Mainly because they threw me in there with all of the other crazies – like you."

I laughed.

"Yeah, like me. And that demon-hearing lady. She was a trip."

"Yeah. Anyway, this one is really focused and specialized, much more individual."

"Are you coming back when you get out?"

"No. Well, yes. To visit. But not to live."

"Wow."

"It has to be that way.'

"I guess."

"Well, it does. But don't worry. You'll see me again."

I looked up into the sun. Rare for San Francisco, it was filtering down through the clouds and warming me to the bone. I would wait.

I jolted through the door of the party and into a man with demon-sultry eyes. He reached out to grab me and pulled me up to dance. Brady's trick from the party.

"Raúl, Raúl. not you again, what do you want now?"

"I want to dance with you, my lovely one. My beautiful snob. You dirty thing."

"What do you mean by that?"

"You know what I mean." Girls in feather jackets and sequin masks waltzed around his arms. Red crystal lamps glared down.

"I'm a nice girl, really. Really."

He looped an arm around my waist and said, "Let's dance. Come on, my little one." We dipped and fell to the rhythm. His long arms felt like welcoming thighs. I fell back.

"Do you want to go to the porch? Have a cigarette?"

"Yeah, yeah, right on." We tapped down the hardwood floor to the ledge.

Staring back, I noticed a bleached blonde cleaning something off her hip in the kitchen sink. The girl was wearing a leaf-green beaded mini-dress with a spray paint heart and a fur jacket. She lifted her skirt to wash her pale stomach. Her pussy was shaved except for a mink stripe. The girl dropped her skirt and came up to us, reeling in the moonlight. Her head lolled back, and she took a swig from her pint of jack. She opened her mouth to speak, and her teeth were jagged and black, the front two missing.

Placing both hands on either side of the doorframe, she bent herself forwards and said to the crowd, "Pardon me, but could anyone give me some cocaine?"

There was a murmur but no reply.

"Hrmph. Whatever," the girl said. Grabbing Raúl's shoulder, she said, "Dance with me."

"I've got a girl, sorry."

We scuttled into the other room. In the corner, a boy glared at the wall. Rul grabbed my hands and began to dance. I turned to him, grabbed him by the shoulders in the dim blue light, and said, "Oh, come home with me!"

"I want to. Oh, I want to. You are just so sexy. But there's one complication."

"What?"

"My friend, Daniel, he's making a documentary about me, and he needs to follow me around for two weeks. If I go with you, he has to come."

I considered this. The stereo lulled higher with all those vodka crans. The Percoset and the half-gram lingered behind my eyes. "Okay. But nothing too heavy. I don't want to make a porn."

"Right on. Oh, you beautiful snob, before I thought you hated me and now I see you are with me. Great." Raúl darted away and came back with an iron-faced boy carrying a digital camcorder. "This is Dan. Be nice to him, he just wants to make his art. We are students, we make films, you see." The boy's Spock bangs clenched in steel eyes.

"Oh, I've heard about your art," I said as we wheeled through the hall. Pen and ink incised strippers on the walls, bills falling down. I looked away, my cheeks burning, as we trotted down the long stairs and into the street.

In my room, I turned on the blue Christmas lights and lit a candle. The two boys swam into view. They were frozen momentarily by the awkwardness of the task, Dan curling into a corner and training the camera on us, Raúl falling long-limbed onto a velvet pillow.

"So."

"So."

"So let's make out." Raúl rose and moved towards me, his lips pulled back over a Jon Waters moustache, his long hands reaching for my shoulders.

"Wait, shouldn't we, like..."

"What, you know why we came here. Not to knit. No crochet."

"Yes, yes." I reached out and took his arm, let him lead me to the mattress. I scuttled under the blankets. Dan crawled closer until the piercing eye of the camera was braced a foot from my head. I glowed with drink and glanced away.

"Now, all of this has to come off..." Raúl took hold of my top and swooped it off. The lens flickered.

We kissed, deeply, his tongue plunging inside my mouth in an invasion both honest and filmic. For screen or sorrow, I didn't care anymore, my lips undulating beneath his, my arms sweeping around his narrow torso to flick each rib urgently. To reach down to the cock beneath. I flipped her hand down his jeans and felt hot solid flesh.

Raúl was the point where Brady and I met. Could meet.
There was no going back.

Flicking an eye open, I caught the camcorder rapt against the edge of my bed, our reckless thighs all captured onscreen. Tumult and flashbulbs on a screen on Public Access. With a flicker of embarrassment I was over it. There was a certain thrill to the exhibitionism, to know someone was watching, to wonder what was rising inside Dan's pants at the sight of my tits, as Raúl sucked the nipples.

I curled inward as he forced his cock against my thigh. I moaned and saw the volume-meter on the cam flare red. I wanted him. I would be shown. For an instant I saw the shaved swell of my cunt onscreen, the crowd of bike messengers packed into Artist's Television Access, that murky storefront in the Mission, the accolades on Dan's stiff shoulders as the boys shared a PBR. Would I show up that night? The jolting squalor of the tiny room, the hot arms on my bare neck, my vanity leapt, and I felt Raúl plunge a finger into my pussy. And then another. And another. I fell into his chest as he thrust three fingers inside me and the dirty sheets squirmed under Jesus holograms and 3-D glasses. My foot flew off the mattress, and wandered across the floor until it hit cameraman.

Flitting upwards, I fondled his neck and drew my toes to his chest. Falling to his Kenny Rogers belt buckle, delving, I saw a hand jerking at Dan's exposed cock. Raúl. Taking both hands, I grabbed his shoulders and raked my claws to his waist.

"Take him, take him if it means that much to you. If you want him. I know what you boys want."

"You are so lovely. He is my friend, we have been making this film all month. You know, you know, he just has those...hands."

Dan jumped on the bed and grabbed my waist. Raúl dived to suck his cock. Moaning, he choked against me, as Raúl slid over and stroked his tongue through my pussy lips. I felt my heart expanding, and glanced up to see the rouged eye of the camera two feet from us as Raúl pressed Dan's cock into my cunt.

I pressed upwards to take him. The camera's tiny light flickered, and I heard Raúl spit on his cock and ease it into Dan's ass. Staring outward into the night, the static haze beneath my fairy lights and cellophane, the cock of this man I'd barely talked to fucked me harder than I'd ever thought before, and then a hand yanked it out and Raúl pushed his prick inside.

Dan, his camcorder abandoned, pressed his cock upwards to my mouth. Gasping, he pinching my nostrils and I sucked him deep. Loved it. Loved Raúl's prick as it plunged into my ass. Loved the moans from the two men as they thrust their tongues into each other's mouths and spider-wove fingers over ribs and nipples.

The boys lunged off me, and fell back against the sheets. Curling over, I fingered my self and watched them as Raúl dipped his nails into Dan's mouth. I crept off the bed and withdrew to the nightstand, where I lifted the camera and focused in on Raúl.

Their bodies undulated fiercely, drag queens glaring daguerrotypes over tawny backs and plunging lips. Suddenly, Raúl pulled out of Dan's mouth and began to cum in frantic, starlight tendrils across his hardened face. I dipped with the zoom lens, then tipped it to the nightstand and leapt up to fall between them. Dan flipped me over and wiped his semen-stained chin against my nape as he forced his cock up my ass.

"Aaah! Oh god…" I muttered as I submitted. As my ass opened to accept him, I rocketed forwards into Raúl waiting lap.

"Oh, my little." He fondled my shoulders, and lifted his penis until the purple head was thrusting against my mouth.

"Do you want to? Do you really want me to?"

"My god, Raúl, yes, do you even know?" My lips slid down his prick in a haze of pharmochemistry. Lavishing it, I jerked my head up and down in an effort to encase, to possess, to utterly own what I wanted so much…he had been with Brady…the hypotenuse.

"Raúl, will you, can you?"

"Baby." With a jet of precum falling sparklike across my cheek, he pulled out, slid down my breasts, and thrust his dick into my pussy. I gasped and rocked my pelvis into his cock. Jolting himself into her again and again, harder and harder, I looked up to see that Dan was daubing the head of his cock against my eyes, leaving damp droplets and reserving his hands for the camera as he focused in of our bodies.

"Please, Dan. Film it," I said as I lifted my hands to pull his cock into my warm, open mouth.

Alone in my room a week later, I scratched my twat. Burning. I had been laying in bed for days, watching the light fade in and out of the windows. I got up, unzipping my pants, pulling off my underwear, and sitting on the floor by the mirrored closet.

I parted my legs.

There was an angry boil the size of a quarter, glaring up from my stubbly labia. The pink rim was beginning to crust, orange and red pus, and the white inside was a fluid I couldn't name.

"Fuck-tastic."

I grabbed for my phone.

"Jesse?"

"What? Look, I'm busy, Vanessa is taking me out to lunch."

"You gave me herpes, cuntrag!"

"Oh, come on! You probably gave me herpes, you little shit-sucking whore."

"I need you to go to the clinic with me."

"And hold your fucking hand? Oh no, oh no. I am telling everyone that Lena had fucking herpes. You will never be able to…well, pretty much show your goddam whore-face in this town again. Have fun, bitch, I'm getting myself tested."

The phone went dead.

The flickering pain, the shimmer of it, like the shimmer of pleasure, but the opposite, like the flash of excitement from a spank, but like gangrene, gangrene like my foot had been, the flesh eating itself.

Jesse knocked on my door a few nights later. "It was open. Are you alright?"

"No."

"Lemme see it."

"No!"

He paced on the pink carpet, looking at the bed. "Are you going to get up and make me a drink?"

"No. I'm sick. I'm not in the mood."

"Bunny has a headache?"

"Can't you just leave me to my misery?" My head, emerging from the blankets.

"Fine. Well, then, look at this thing on my dick."

He opened his pants, leaning back against the chair. Pulling out his cock, he said, "Come over here and suck it, you owe me that. You got me into this. You all pretty at Audrey's house. I'm a sucker for a girl who wins at Scrabble. We could still get married, you know, and be herpes pals."

I looked at him, from the bed. Did it even matter, now? Might be my last chance at sex in awhile. I slid across the bed, and fell at his knees. I was nothing.

There were little bubbles along the shaft. He grabbed me by the hair and shoved my face down, and I took him in my mouth, knowing at this point there was no backwards and no forwards, no past and no future. He pulled his cock out and rubbed the sores all over my face, on my eyelids, across my lips.

I stopped leaving the house. I ate only government peanut butter.

The cans of it on the Dustbin counter, after a food bank run. The rumor that it was spiked with lithium.

Brady kept bringing it home.

The sores bloomed first across my cheeks, and spread to my eyes, foaming onto my hands. My cunt was a pus-factory. It hurt to piss, it hurt to stand.

Every night, Brady brought me half a gram from Donny, with cash he'd advanced from the credit card. My money was gone.

I was living only for coke, only for the pleasure it gave me, nothing else in the word was left.

I looked in the mirror, and I saw a face that had once been beautiful now leprous, scalding with sores. There were in the palms of my hands like stigmata. I didn't think I would fuck anyone ever again. I didn't think anyone would ever love me.

All I did was sit at the computer, do lines, and type, as my body became the vehicle for the virus, and everything else fell away.

My paintings hung around the bed, the umber eyes still there.

The phone rang, and I lifted up on one elbow, straining with the effort. Reaching out a hand, I put the phone to my ear.

"Coco?"

"Hey, I'm outside."

"You're here? You didn't tell me you left rehab!"

"I'm telling you now."

"Oh that's good, that's good." I lay on my back with the phone pressed limply to my head, excitement rising.

Coco barged through the front door with a suitcase rattling on wheels behind her.

"Baby doll, hey!" She spread her arms wide and caught me as I lurched into them. "Oh god, are you okay? What happened to your face?"

"I got herpes. And Jesse made sure I got the whole package."

"Oh damn! I'm so sorry. Listen I just got a room at the St. Regis, why don't you come for the night...god, I want to take you out of this." She nudged me towards the closet.

I fell back on one leg. "I'm kind of not, I mean, I'm not...I can't have anyone see me. And I don't know how contagious I am, like, if I touch anything."

"You'll make it. It might cheer you up a little to get out of here. Are you waiting to die?"

"Okay." Cowed, I winced my way into some clothes.

Coco waited, her face impassive, moving only to urge me on. She curved an arm around my elbow, and we inched down the hall. I looked back at the curtains fluttering in the afternoon breeze, the dour stare of the green woman painting, the peacock feathers on a chain link band affixed to Brady's doorknob. The showgirl drawing hanging spangles on my door, one corner taped up and the other three drooping. I wondered if I would ever see this place again, if I wouldn't just melt away into a puddle of lymph onto the hotel floor. Not even making a sound, just a slow dissolve on the black marble beside the wall of flame bisecting the doorman and the bar.

On Haight Street, She held up an arm.
"Taxi!"
Cabs and SUVs whizzed by. Passersby gave us a wide berth, more for my facial sores than Coco's glare. I caught a flicker of sunlight off of the Zona Rosa tacqueria façade across the street, and glanced, exhausted, at the pink plastic hands in the window of the salon. I looked down, the smell of donuts and pot and curry and Chanel Mademoiselle suddenly all too much. The garlic was blending with the jabber of shoppers, up for the weekend from Walnut Creek to load up on pointy boots and vintage blouses from Wasteland.

Coco hustled me into a cab, and I let myself be pulled. I leaned back, as the cab pulled out and began trundling its way downtown. Watching the fierce streams of sun around her, I said, "So…tell me, tell me…I mean…"
"Okay, I'll start here. I got clean."
"Awesome."
"Yeah, and then I sold my land, and now I'll never have to work ever again."
"Shit… You…I don't mean to ask how much, but, like how do you…"
"Sh…millions."
I exhaled slowly.
"Got all these staph-infected abcesses, though."
"Well, hey, I'm pretty much a pariah."
"Pustule-Posse rides again!"
"All fucking right!"
The cab pulled up at a glass skyscraper next to the MOMA, iridescent blue film over the shimmering lobby, sparkles on the sidewalk outside. "Is this it?"
"The St. Regis. Come on, honey." Coco led me out of the cab, pulling me past the doorman, his brass epaulets against navy girth. We strode across the black marble floor, past the bar with its wall of blue flame on river pebbles, past a bank of gold-trimmed elevators, the ceiling vaulted and a low hum of subdued talk echoing from the restaurant. Orchids hung from tiny shelves. A modernist slab of striated glass hung between the last two elevators, filled with rose petals suspended in a rising wave. I didn't have the energy to fuck Modernism.

At the front desk, a petite woman with a Teutonic clip to her voice took our names and handed Coco a leather folder. Her hair was swept back in a dark bun that looked ironed on.

Coco signed the receipt. The sculpture behind us, a gilt tracery of branches, was trickling streams of water that made a soothing sound.

I took a deep breath. Jesse seemed very far away. I had only the burden of my body, of what he had left behind. I lifted my eyes to the marble ceiling, black flecked with opalescence and iron.

"Buck up, Buttercup," said Coco, taking my elbow and propelling me into the elevator. Sucked away by the mirrors, I glanced around, the slick surfaces reflecting over and over as we rose.

At the door of room #607, Coco slid the keycard into the brass console. There was a beep, and she tried again, cursing. Her suitcase was propped against the mahogany wall, under orchids with lavender stamens.

The door beeped again, and I turned the handle. Inside, white silk panels lined the walls, with a flatscreen TV hung at one end. A marble bathtub divided the room, with a fluffy bathrobe draped next to the soap. There was another flatscreen suspended above the sink, where a vanity mirror encircled with lights zig-zagged steel from the wall. Light filled the room, flowing from the open windows, through which I could see the skyscrapers of the financial district. The Transamerica Pyramid loomed gracefully behind the tenth-story swimming pool of the Huntington Suites.

"My god."

"Oh yes. Well come in, come on. I've got this for three nights, and then I go back to Dallas, so I want to party a little."

I stepped back.

"Oh goodness, look at you. Now, lie down, here." Coco gestured at the low bed with the down duvet billowing white and cream pillows piled above. There was a single orchid on the turned back sheet. A bottle of San Pelligrino and two glasses stood on the end table. "Alright." Coco reached for the blue bottle and poured us each a glass. The sun glimmered around us, the water cold down my throat as I settled back into the sheets. I drank gratefully and sat it down on the bed, next to a console with a touch pad.

"Now, what does this do?" Coco pressed a button and the inner lining of the curtains began to descend, sending us into shadow for a moment. "No, no, no. Okay." She pressed another and the shades rose. Clocks, alarms, local sights, the butler, she flicked through the menus as I closed my eyes.

I was at peace. An ovoid sphere of warm nested comfort, of escape, of retreat from the world, hung inside of me. Jesse couldn't hurt me here. No one could find me here. No one could see me, in my abjection.

Coco tired of the touchscreen and landed on an ecru loveseat. She toyed with the pillow, then said, "Aha, room service. Lena, have you eaten? I want some food." She busied herself with the menus, the brown leather booklet draped across her lap, while I folded both hands onto my stomach and shut my eyes

I awoke to see Limone seated on the end of the bed. Her white fishnets were swathed with neon leg warmers, under a black dress. The wreckage of Coco's room service order lay in the corner of the room: a round, white-draped table with china coffee service for three, delicate saucers, spoons, lemons and sugarcubes. A monogrammed creamer. A rectangular black plate sat with streaks of caviar, next to latkes and the last remaining chunk of ahi tuna. A fork with "SR" embossed in entwining letters lay on the desk.

Limone was nursing a cup of coffee, the saucer cupped in one hand while she took tiny sips with the other.

"Someone's finally out of sleepy sleepykins," she said. "We've been waiting for you."

"Sorry, Brady gave me a codeine."

"Oh, so that's it," said Coco from the bathroom, where she was brushing quick dashes of rose and charcoal shadow across her eyes.

"No, all of that limping was authentic. I've been feeling pretty shitty, lately."

"That's okay, sugarplum," said Coco. She dropped the hairbrush and came back into the bedroom. "Do you want some coffee?"

"Urg, that's okay. Is there any tea?"

"We could order some."

"Oh no, don't do that. I'll just have water." Coco poured me a glass from a pitcher afloat with limes and cucumbers. I drank.

Mink's leonine shiver in Lucas's squat, the bob of her blue extensions as she squeaked, "I'm a whore." The bottle turning. The ripped tights turned to ropes to bind my wrists so long ago, turned to Jesse tossing me back on the mattress, ripping my legs apart like a teenager's diary. I loved what pained me, what destroyed me. Just as I loved the cocaine that thrummed through my nerves, I loved the rips and slaps and abuse that rent me, tore me, had brought me to this, bleeding on a silken bed I had never seen, herpes sores on my face, my niche infected, the fever humming. I looked up at the cream drapery of the curtains at half-mast, over the glittering panorama of the city.

"God, I have got to break it off with Jesse."

"Well, hello Captain Obvious," Coco jumped from the settee and poured herself a cup of coffee. A tall, thin sculpture made from overlapping circles of blonde wood stood in the hall like a flot of seaweed scrolling from the floor.

"Yes, as soon as I get back tomorrow." I rolled over and stared out the window, at the flickering dazzle of the city swathed in night, at the utter blackness of the bay. It seemed too difficult, and then with the shimmer of a cramp through my stomach it all fell into place like a spout of Horchata in a Styrofoam cup.

I hesitated in my room, hearing Jesse's feet down the hall. Clenching a nail-bitten hand, the turquoise polish in shreds, I watched the door as it swung open.

"Hey, you seem awfully alert. Do you have anything?"

"No, I'm on hiatus."

"I got a twenty if you want some." He strode to the edge of my bed and plunked down. A silkscreen of an eagle with a clipped wing marked his T-shirt, pulled tight across his narrow chest. He fiddled around in his shoe for the bag.

I paused, then forced myself to stand in front of him.

"Jesse."

"What, baby pigeon. Daddy's trying to find his blow."

"I think we should break up."

"We're not dating, Baby Herp. Where's your mirror?"

"No, I mean, I think we should stop fucking. I don't want to sleep with you ever again I don't want to see you ever again. I don't want to do this, whatever this is."

His face darkened. "Jesus, can't take a little outbreak? Come on! It's my gift to you! No one else will want you again, so you have to stay with me."

"Listen. I'm serious. It's over."

"Look," he said, rising. "I don't know who you've been listening to, maybe your dyke friends, but you belong to me. I think we've made that clear. You're not going anywhere. I'm not going anywhere. Our relationship is staying exactly the way it is. I like it the way it is. You. Are my precious little fuck-toy. And now that you're diseased, I've got some great new ideas about whoring you out."

"Fuck you, Jesse, this whole thing, these whole two years, have been traumatizing enough, I'm not going to go on with this."

"Well, aren't you the little screamer."

"I'm serious. You are an abusive, emotionally bankrupt asshole who can't even help with my herpes while he's got enough coke for every blushing sixteen year-old at Bordello. On a Friday night. With Kris Danger, who, by the way, is a much better DJ than you, you can't mix worth shit, and all of your clothes look like Forever 21 fucked Hot Topic."

"Cunt!" The slap came out of nowhere and knocked me back two feet. He grabbed me by the shoulders and shook me like an empty bottle, slamming me against the dresser and throwing me to the ground.

I yelped, the gauzy breath knocked out of me as terror took hold and I realized in a crimson flash that he could kill me. When he punched me I barely moved against the carpet. Swooping on long strands of mauve and gold, on holly and ivy clustered neatly in rows, folding over and over, so easy to get away.

I screamed. Louder. A high keen of terror, as he hit me again and again.

"Lena! What the fuck, what's going on in there, let me in!" Brady threw himself fiercely against the door.

"Bitch!"

"Let me in!" Brady fiddled with the lock and ripped it open, his sinewy arms poised to attack. Lizards in the black velvet jacket. His thighs were like keys. He jumped on Jesse and began pulling his hair, then punched him on the back of his neck.

Jesse let out a low, grunting noise and rolled over, catching Brady under the chin with his fist. He fell back. With ham-hands born of disconsolate fury, anger at the disorder of his perfectly ordered world, Jesse laid into Brady, slugging him in the middle of his chest, his face, rolling on top of his and overpowering him with his far greater weight. "Fuckin' faggot!" Jesse rammed his fist on the side of his face. Blood oozed from his nose.

I pulled myself up, fighting with the pain in my shoulder. I crawled towards the door of my room, trying to yell for help, warring with the twin impulses to call the police, or to keep it within our autonomous zone. If I could get Jesse busted for domestic violence, or asJayt, or possession, or all three, but this was all a blur to me as I warred against the fear that they would get me too, that they would find something I had left around, my coke mirror, an errant grain on the carpet, the licked-out baggies in my dresser drawer. It was a risk I would have to take.

"Help! Somebody! Help!" I yelled, hearing Brady's moans in the background with the low, sickening sounds of Jesse's fists on impact. I turned around and saw him holding Brady against the wall. Jesse's face was scarlet as he fumed, sweat and fury blazing from his eyes. Brady's nose was bleeding, running down his stubbly chin to the tiny flowers pocking his ruffled shirt.

I put a hand to my mouth. My lips were cold and shaking.

Jesse slammed his fist against the side of Brady's neck, snapping it sideways with a crack like all the love in the world beating an overturned trashcan on the corner of Ellis and Hyde. Beating the long nights of solace and endless cigarettes, of the tiny blond hairs at the back of his neck that were now soaked with blood. He fell to the floor.

Jesse staggered backwards, at once struck with the enormity of what he'd done. It was dawn and the first chirps of pigeons and legless sparrows were echoing, insurgent, from the lightwell. His face blanched out.

I began to cry. Before I could stop myself, tears fell like mildewed tinsel. Rushing to his side, I gripped his shoulder and said, "Brady, honey, are you okay, come on, talk to me."

"I...I don't know," he said slowly. "I should hurt....but I don't...." His face was grey, one pupil dilated and the other one small. I didn't know which one to believe.

His eyes closed. His mouth opened but no sound came out. I watched the arachnid shadows of his eyelashes, of the traces of eyeliner scattered around his eyes. Tracery of peacock feathers on his door, of brave keyboard scrolls piercing the club over transfixed heads and boys arched with ache. I thought of the emerald eyeless woman I had never told him that I loathed. I would never tell him. I would leave that painting up for as long as I lived on Haight St., leave the other painting of yellow and fuchsia blaring over spray paint.

I jerked out of my stupor and fell back to the counter, where a half-empty wine bottle was moldering with two oranges. Opalescence of rot on the rinds.

I was beyond words. I couldn't even think of what to say as we stood there, the both of us gazing at Brady's limp, bleeding body. Bruises, like blue roses.

Andrea Lambert is a Los Angeles-based writer and artist. She has lived in San Francisco, Portland, and San Diego. She holds an MFA in Critical Studies from CalArts, and a BA from Reed College. Her work can be seen at
www.andreaklambert.com.

Made in the USA
Las Vegas, NV
20 February 2024

86011603R00121